"追求卓越"学英语丛书（英汉对照）

经典的回声
——莎士比亚戏剧故事选

Echoes of Classics: Stories from Shakespeare

◎ 谢艳明　郑玉萍　译注

河南大学出版社
HENAN UNIVERSITY PRESS

图书在版编目（CIP）数据

经典的回声：莎士比亚戏剧故事选：英汉对照 / 谢艳明，郑玉萍译注． —开封：河南大学出版社，2008.4 (2014.1 重印)

（"追求卓越"学英语丛书）

ISBN 978-7-81091-777-3

Ⅰ.经… Ⅱ.①谢…②郑… Ⅲ.①英语—汉语—对照读物②戏剧文学—故事—英国—中世纪 Ⅳ.H319.4：I

中国版本图书馆 CIP 数据核字（2008）第 020635 号

责任编辑　卢志宇
封面设计　今日文教

出版发行	河南大学出版社			
	地址：河南省开封市明伦街 85 号	邮编：475001		
	电话：0378—2825001（营销部）	网址：www.hupress.com		
排　　版	河南第一新华印刷厂			
印　　刷	开封智圣印务有限公司			
版　　次	2008 年 4 月第 1 版	印　　次	2014 年 1 月第 3 次印刷	
开　　本	787mm×1092mm　1/16	印　　张	16.5	
字　　数	279 千字	定　　价	28.00 元	

（本书如有印装质量问题请与河南大学出版社营销部联系调换）

前　言

　　威廉·莎士比亚(William Shakespeare，1564～1616)是文艺复兴时期英国伟大的剧作家、诗人，也是人文主义的杰出代表。1564年4月23日，莎士比亚出生于英格兰沃里克郡埃文河畔的斯特拉特福镇(Stratford-upon-Avon，Warwickshire，England)，其父约翰·莎士比亚是经营羊毛、皮革制造及谷物生意的杂货商。莎士比亚幼年在当地文法学校读书，1582年同邻乡农家女安·哈瑟维(Anne Hathaway)结婚。1585年至1592年间，莎士比亚经历不详，传说他当过乡村教师、兵士、贵族家仆，并因偷猎乡绅托马斯·路希爵士(Sir Thomas Lucy)之鹿逃往伦敦。他先在剧院门前为人看马，后来进入剧团。他跑过龙套，也担任过导演，但主要是编写剧本。1597年，莎士比亚在斯特拉特福购置了房产，1599年，他成为环球剧场拥有1/10股份的股东。1610年莎士比亚卖出了他的股份，回乡隐居。1616年4月23日他在家乡病逝，葬于镇上的圣三一教堂。

　　莎士比亚的编剧工作是从改编旧剧开始的，二十余年间他共写了37部戏剧，另有长篇叙事诗2部、十四行诗一卷共154首。莎士比亚的主要成就是戏剧，他的创作通常被分为三个时期：

　　第一时期(1590～1600)以写作历史剧、喜剧为主，有9部历史剧、10部喜剧和2部悲剧。9部历史剧中除《约翰王》是写13世纪初英国历史外，其余8部是内容相衔接的两个四部曲：《亨利六世》(上、中、下)与《理查三世》；《理查二世》、《亨利四世》(上、下)与《亨利五世》。这些历史剧概括了英国历史上百余年间的动乱，塑造了一系列正、反面君主形象，反映了莎士比亚反对封建割据，拥护中央集权，谴责暴君暴政，要求开明君主进行自上而下的改革，建立和谐社会关系的人文主义政治与道德理想。10部喜剧《错误的喜剧》、《驯悍记》、《维洛那二绅士》、《爱的徒劳》、《仲夏夜之梦》、《威尼斯商人》、《温莎的风流娘儿们》、《无事生非》、《皆大欢喜》和《第十二夜》大都以爱情、友谊、婚姻为主题，主人公多是一些具有人文主义智慧与美德的青年男女，通过对他们争取自由、幸福的斗争的描写，歌颂进步、美好的新人新风，同时也温和地揭露和嘲讽旧事物的衰朽和丑恶，如禁欲主义者的虚矫、清教徒的伪善和高利贷者的贪鄙等。在这一时期，莎士比亚戏剧创作的基本情调是乐观、明朗的，充满着以人文主义理想解决社会矛盾的信心，以致写在这一时期的悲剧《罗密欧与朱丽叶》中也洋溢着喜剧的气氛。尽管

主人公殉情而死,但爱的理想战胜了死亡,换来了封建世仇的和解。然而,在这一时期较后的成熟喜剧《威尼斯商人》中,又带有忧郁色彩和悲剧因素,在鼓吹仁爱、友谊和真诚爱情的同时,反映了基督教社会中弱肉强食的阶级压迫和种族歧视问题,说明作者已逐渐意识到理想与现实之间存在着难以解决的矛盾。

第二时期(1601~1607)以写作悲剧为主,有3部罗马剧、5部悲剧和3部"阴暗的喜剧"或"问题剧"。罗马剧《尤利乌斯·凯撒》、《安东尼和克莉奥佩特拉》和《科里奥拉努斯》是取材于普卢塔克的《希腊罗马英雄传》的历史剧。四大悲剧《哈姆雷特》、《奥赛罗》、《李尔王》、《麦克白》和悲剧《雅典的泰门》标志着作者对时代、人生的深入思考,着力塑造了这样一些新时代的悲剧主人公:他们从中世纪的禁锢和蒙昧中醒来,在近代黎明的照耀下,雄心勃勃地想要发展或完善自己,但又不能克服时代和自身的局限,终于在同环境和内心敌对势力力量悬殊的斗争中遭到不可避免的失败和牺牲。哈姆雷特为报父仇而发现"整个时代脱榫"了,决定担起"重整乾坤"的责任,结果却是空怀大志、无力回天;奥赛罗正直淳朴、嫉恶如仇,却又轻信他人,在奸人的摆布下杀妻自戕,为追求至善至美反遭恶报;李尔王在权势带来的尊荣、自豪、自信中迷失本性,丧失理智,幻想以让权分国来证明自己不当国王而做一个普通人也能同样或更伟大,因而经受了一番痛苦的磨难;麦克白本是有功的英雄,性格中有着善和美的一面,只因王位的诱惑和野心的驱使,沦为"从血腥到血腥"、懊悔无及的罪人。这些人物的悲剧深刻地揭示了在资本原始积累时期已开始出现的种种社会罪恶和资产阶级的利己主义,表现了人文主义理想与残酷现实之间矛盾的不可调和性,具有高度的概括意义。在这一时期,莎士比亚剧作由于思想深度和现实主义深度的增强,使《特洛伊罗斯与克瑞西达》、《终成眷属》和《一报还一报》等喜剧也显露出阴暗的一面,笼罩着背信弃义、尔虞我诈的罪恶阴影,因而被称为"问题剧"或"阴暗的喜剧"。

第三时期(1608~1613)的主要作品是4部悲喜剧或传奇剧:《泰尔亲王配力克里斯》、《辛白林》、《冬天的故事》、《暴风雨》,这些作品多写失散、团聚、诬陷、昭雪。尽管仍然坚持人文主义理想,并对黑暗现实有所揭露,但矛盾的解决主要靠魔法、幻想、机缘巧合和偶然事件,并以宣扬宽恕、容忍、妥协、和解告终。

莎士比亚还与弗莱彻合作写了历史剧《亨利八世》和传奇剧《两位贵亲》,后者近年来被收入一些莎士比亚戏剧集。

莎士比亚的戏剧大都取材于旧有剧本、小说、编年史或民间传说，但在改写中注入了自己的思想，给旧题材赋予了新颖、丰富、深刻的内容。在艺术表现上，莎士比亚继承了古希腊古罗马、中世纪英国和文艺复兴时期欧洲戏剧的三大传统并加以发展，从内容到形式进行了创造性革新。他的戏剧不受束缚，突破悲剧和喜剧的界限，努力反映生活的本来面目，深入探索人物内心的奥秘，从而能够塑造众多性格复杂多样、形象真实生动的人物典型，描绘广阔的、五光十色的社会生活图景，并以其博大、深刻、富于诗意和哲理著称。

莎士比亚戏剧是英国文学史上的瑰宝，也颇得我国读者的喜爱。然而，经粗略调查，即使是英语专业的本科生，也很少有人在大学四年中将这 37 部戏剧读完。其原因是原著过于经典，有许多难懂的地方。于是，根据莎士比亚戏剧改编的、通俗易懂的故事集便应运而生。英国散文家查尔斯·兰姆(Charles Lamb, 1775~1834)和他的姐姐玛丽·兰姆(Mary Lamb, 1764~1847)从莎士比亚的 37 个剧本中精选出 20 个，改写成可读性很强的故事。本书根据英国作家伊迪斯·讷斯比特(Edith Nesbit, 1858~1924)改写的莎士比亚故事集编译而成。

编者
2008 年 1 月

目 录

1. All's Well That Ends Well ……………………………… (1)
   终成眷属 …………………………………………………… (9)
2. The Taming of the Shrew ……………………………… (15)
   驯悍记 ……………………………………………………… (23)
3. Two Gentlemen of Verona ……………………………… (28)
   维洛那二绅士 ……………………………………………… (38)
4. A Midsummer Night's Dream …………………………… (45)
   仲夏夜之梦 ………………………………………………… (52)
5. The Merchant of Venice ………………………………… (57)
   威尼斯商人 ………………………………………………… (63)
6. Much Ado about Nothing ……………………………… (67)
   无事生非 …………………………………………………… (79)
7. As You Like It …………………………………………… (87)
   皆大欢喜 …………………………………………………… (92)
8. Twelfth Night …………………………………………… (96)
   第十二夜 …………………………………………………… (103)
9. Romeo and Juliet ………………………………………… (108)
   罗密欧与朱丽叶 …………………………………………… (116)
10. Hamlet …………………………………………………… (121)
    哈姆雷特 …………………………………………………… (128)
11. Othello …………………………………………………… (133)
    奥赛罗 ……………………………………………………… (142)
12. King Lear ………………………………………………… (148)
    李尔王 ……………………………………………………… (152)
13. Macbeth …………………………………………………… (155)
    麦克白 ……………………………………………………… (163)
14. Timon of Athens ………………………………………… (169)
    雅典的泰门 ………………………………………………… (179)
15. The Comedy of Errors …………………………………… (186)
    错误的喜剧 ………………………………………………… (195)

16. Measure for Measure ……………………………………（201）
    一报还一报 …………………………………………（209）
17. Cymbeline ………………………………………………（215）
    辛白林 ………………………………………………（222）
18. Pericles ……………………………………………………（227）
    泰尔亲王配力克里斯 ………………………………（233）
19. The Tempest ……………………………………………（237）
    暴风雨 ………………………………………………（243）
20. Winter's Tale ……………………………………………（248）
    冬天的故事 …………………………………………（255）

1. All's Well That Ends Well

Bertram's Letter

In the year thirteen hundred and something, the Countess① of Rousillon② was unhappy in her palace near the Pyrenees③. She had lost her husband, and the King of France had summoned her son Bertram④ to Paris, hundreds of miles away.

Bertram was a pretty youth with curling hair, finely arched

---

① countess [ˈkauntis] n. 伯爵夫人,女伯爵
② Rousillon [rɔːˈsiɔn] n. 罗西昂
③ Pyrenees [ˌpirəˈniːz] n. 比利牛斯山脉(欧洲西南部的一条山脉,从比斯开湾沿着法国与西班牙边境延伸至地中海)
④ Bertram [ˈbəːtrəm] n. 勃特拉姆(男子名)

eyebrows, and eyes as keen as a hawk's. He was as proud as ignorance① could make him, and would lie with a face like truth itself to gain a selfish end. But a pretty youth is a pretty youth, and Helena was in love with him.

Helena was the daughter of a great doctor who had died in the service of the Count of Rousillon. Her sole fortune consisted in a few of her father's prescriptions.

When Bertram had gone, Helena's forlorn② look was noticed by the Countess, who told her that she was exactly the same to her as her own child. Tears then gathered in Helena's eyes, for she felt that the Countess made Bertram seem like a brother whom she could never marry. The Countess guessed her secret forthwith③, and Helena confessed④ that Bertram was to her as the sun is to the day.

She hoped, however, to win this sun by earning the gratitude⑤ of the King of France, who suffered from a lingering illness⑥, which made him lame. The great doctors attached to the Court despaired of curing him, but Helena had confidence in a prescription which her father had used with success.

Taking an affectionate⑦ leave of the Countess, she went to Paris, and was allowed to see the King.

He was very polite, but it was plain he thought her a quack. "It would not become me," he said, "to apply to a simple maiden for the relief which all the learned doctors cannot give me."

"Heaven uses weak instruments sometimes," said Helena, and she declared that she would forfeit⑧ her life if she failed to make him well.

---

① ignorance ['ignərəns] *n.* 无知,不知
② forlorn [fə'lɔ:n] *adj.* 被遗弃的
③ forthwith ['fɔ:θ'wiθ] *adv.* 立刻,不犹豫地
④ confess [kən'fes] *v.* 承认,坦白,忏悔
⑤ gratitude ['grætitju:d] *n.* 感谢的心情
⑥ lingering ['liŋgəriŋ] illness 慢性病
⑦ affectionate [ə'fekʃənit] *adj.* 亲爱的,挚爱的
⑧ forfeit ['fɔ:fit] *v.* 没收,丧失

"And if you succeed?" questioned the King.

"Then I will ask your Majesty to give me for a husband the man whom I choose!"

So earnest a young lady could not be resisted forever by a suffering king. Helena, therefore, became the King's doctor, and in two days the royal cripple could skip.

He summoned his courtiers, and they made a glittering throng in the throne room of his palace. Well might the country girl have been dazzled, and seen a dozen husbands worth dreaming of among the handsome young noblemen before her. But her eyes only wandered till they found Bertram. Then she went up to him, and said, "I dare not say I take you, but I am yours!" Raising her voice that the King might hear, she added, "This is the Man!"

"Bertram," said the King, "take her; she's your wife!"

"My wife, my liege①?" said Bertram. "I beg your Majesty to permit me to choose a wife."

"Do you know, Bertram, what she has done for your King?" asked the monarch②, who had treated Bertram like a son.

"Yes, your Majesty," replied Bertram, "but why should I marry a girl who owes her breeding to my father's charity?"

"You disdain③ her for lacking a title, but I can give her a title," said the King; and as he looked at the sulky④ youth a thought came to him, and he added, "strange that you think so much

~~~~~~~~~~~~~~~~

① liege [liːdʒ] n. 君主
② monarch ['mɔnək] n. 君主
③ disdain [dis'dein] v. 轻蔑,蔑视
④ sulky ['sʌlki] adj. 生气的,阴沉的

of blood when you could not distinguish① your own from a beggar's if you saw them mixed together in a bowl."

"I cannot love her," asserted Bertram; and Helena said gently, "Urge him not, your Majesty. I am glad to have cured my King for my country's sake."

"My honor requires that scornful② country's obedience," said the King. "Bertram, make up your mind to this. You marry this lady, of whom you are so unworthy, or you learn how a king can hate. Your answer?"

Bertram bowed low and said, "Your Majesty has ennobled the lady by your interest in her. I submit."

"Take her by the hand," said the King, "and tell her she is yours."

Bertram obeyed, and with little delay he was married to Helena.

Fear of the King, however, could not make him a lover. Ridicule helped to sour him. A base soldier named Parolles told him to his face that now he had a "kicky-wicky" and his business was not to fight but to stay at home. "Kicky-wicky" was only a silly epithet③ for a wife, but it made Bertram feel he could not bear having a wife, and that he must go to the war in Italy, though the King had forbidden him.

He ordered helena to take leave of the King and return to Rousillon, giving her letters for his mother and herself. He then rode off④, bidding her a cold good-bye.

She opened the letter addressed to herself, and read, "When you can get the ring from my finger you can call me husband, but against that 'when' I write 'never'."

① distinguish [dis'tiŋgwiʃ] v. 区别,辨别
② scornful ['skɔːnful] adj. 轻蔑的
③ epithet ['epiθet] n. 绰号,称号
④ ride off 骑马而去

经典的回声
Echoes of Classics:Stories from Shakespeare

Dry-eyed had Helena been when she entered the King's presence and said farewell, but he was uneasy on her account, and gave her a ring from his own finger, saying, "If you send this to me, I shall know you are in trouble, and help you."

She did not show him Bertram's letter to his wife; it would have made him wish to kill the truant Count; but she went back to Rousillon and handed her mother-in-law the second letter. It was short and bitter. "I have run away," it said. "If the world be broad enough, I will be always far away from her."

"Cheer up," said the noble widow to the deserted① wife. "I wash his name out of my blood, and you alone are my child."

The Dowager Countess, however, was still mother enough to Bertram to lay the blame of his conduct on Parolles, whom she called "a very tainted fellow②".

Helena did not stay long at Rousillon. She clad herself as a pilgrim③, and, leaving a letter for her mother-in-law, secretly set out for Florence.

On entering that city she inquired of a woman the way to the Pilgrims' House of Rest, but the woman begged "the holy pilgrim" to lodge with her.

Helena found that her hostess was a widow, who had a beautiful daughter named Diana.

When Diana heard that Helena came from France, she said, "A countryman of yours, Count Rousillon, has done worthy service for Florence." But after a time, Diana had something to tell which was not at all worthy of Helena's husband. Bertram was making love to Diana. He did not hide the fact that he was married, but Diana heard from Parolles that his wife was not worth caring for.

The widow was anxious for Diana's sake, and Helena decided to inform her that she was the Countess Rousillon.

---

① deserted [diˈzəːtid] adj. 荒芜的，为人所弃的
② tainted fellow 不道德的家伙
③ pilgrim [ˈpilgrim] n. 圣地朝拜者

"He keeps asking Diana for a lock of her hair," said the widow.

Helena smiled mournfully①, for her hair was as fine as Diana's and of the same color. Then an idea struck her, and she said, "Take this purse of gold for yourself. I will give Diana three thousand Crowns if she will help me to carry out this plan. Let her promise to give a lock of her hair to my husband if he will give her the ring which he wears on his finger. It is an ancestral② ring. Five Counts of Rousillon have worn it, yet he will yield it up for a lock of your daughter's hair. Let your daughter insist that he shall cut the lock of hair from her in a dark room, and agree in advance that she shall not speak a single word."

The widow listened attentively, with the purse of gold in her lap. She said at last, "I consent, if Diana is willing."

Diana was willing, and, strange to say, the prospect of cutting off a lock of hair from a silent girl in a dark room was so pleasing to Bertram that he handed Diana his ring, and was told when to follow her into the dark

room. At the time appointed he came with a sharp knife, and felt a sweet face touch his as he cut off the lock of hair, and he left the room satisfied, like a man who is filled with renown, and on his finger was a ring which the girl in the dark room had given him.

The war was nearly over, but one of its concluding chapters taught Bertram that the soldier who had been impudent③ enough to call Helena his "kicky-wicky" was far less courageous than a wife. Parolles was such a boaster, and so fond of trimmings to his clothes, that the French officers played him a trick to discover what he was made of. He had lost his drum, and had said that he would regain it unless he was killed in the attempt. His attempt was a very poor one, and he was inventing the story

---

① mournfully ['mɔːnfuli] adv. 悲哀地
② ancestral [æn'sestrəl] adj. 祖先的,祖传的
③ impudent ['impjudənt] adj. 放肆无礼的,厚颜无耻的

of a heroic failure, when he was surrounded and disarmed①.

"Portotartarossa," said a French lord.

"What horrible lingo② is this?" thought Parolles, who had been blindfolded③.

"He's calling for the tortures," said a French man, affecting to act as interpreter. "What will you say without 'em?"

"As much," replied Parolles, "as I could possibly say if you pinched④ me like a pasty." He was as good as his word. He told them how many there were in each regiment⑤ of the Florentine army, and he refreshed them with spicy anecdotes⑥ of the officers commanding it.

Bertram was present, and heard a letter read, in which Parolles told Diana that he was a fool.

"This is your devoted friend," said a French lord.

"He is a cat to me now," said Bertram, who detested our hearthrug pets.

Parolles was finally let go, but henceforth he felt like a sneak, and was not addicted to⑦ boasting.

We now return to France with Helena, who had spread a report of her death, which was conveyed to the Dowager Countess at Rousillon by Lafeu⑧, a lord who wished to marry his daughter Magdalen to Bertram.

The King mourned for Helena, but he approved of⑨ the marriage proposed for Bertram, and paid a visit to Rousillon in order to see it accomplished.

"His great offense is dead," he said. "Let Bertram approach me."

---

① disarm [dis'ɑːm] v. 解除武装
② lingo ['lɪŋɡəʊ] n. (尤指)方言,行话
③ blindfold ['blaɪndfəʊld] v. 将眼睛蒙起来
④ pinch [pɪntʃ] v. 挤压,捏
⑤ regiment ['redʒɪmənt] n. 团
⑥ anecdote ['ænɪkdəʊt] n. 轶事,奇闻
⑦ addicte to 沉迷于……
⑧ Lafeu [ləf'juː] n. 拉佛(男子名)
⑨ approve of 赞成,满意

Then Bertram, scarred in the cheek, knelt before his Sovereign, and said that if he had not loved Lafeu's daughter before he married Helena, he would have prized his wife, whom he now loved when it was too late.

"Love that is late offends the Great Sender," said the King. "Forget sweet Helena, and give a ring to Magdalen."

Bertram immediately gave a ring to Lafeu, who said indignantly, "It's Helena's!"

"It's not!" said Bertram.

Hereupon the King asked to look at the ring, and said, "This is the ring I gave to Helena, and bade her send to me if ever she needed help. So you had the cunning① to get from her what could help her most."

Bertram denied again that the ring was Helena's, but even his mother said it was.

"You lie!" exclaimed the King. "Seize him, guards!" but even while they were seizing him, Bertram wondered how the ring, which he thought Diana had given him, came to be so like Helena's. A gentleman now entered, craving permission to deliver a petition② to the King. It was a petition signed Diana Capilet, and it begged that the King would order Bertram to marry her whom he had deserted after winning her love.

"I'd sooner buy a son-in-law at a fair than take Bertram now," said Lafeu.

"Admit the petitioner," said the King.

Bertram found himself confronted by Diana and her mother. He denied that Diana had any claim on him, and spoke of her as though her life was spent in the gutter③. But she asked him what sort of gentlewoman it was to whom he gave, as to her he gave, the ring of his ancestors now

---

① cunning [ˈkʌniŋ] n. 狡猾,诡诈
② petition [piˈtiʃən] n. 请愿,请愿书,诉状
③ gutter [ˈgʌtə] n. 贫民区

missing from his finger.

Bertram was ready to sink into the earth, but fate had one crowning generosity① reserved for him. Helena entered.

"Do I see reality?" asked the King.

"O pardon! pardon!" cried Bertram.

She held up his ancestral ring. "Now that I have this," said she, "will you love me, Bertram?"

"To the end of my life," cried he.

"My eyes smell onions," said Lafeu. Tears for Helena were twinkling in them.

The King praised Diana when he was fully informed by that not very shy young lady of the meaning of her conduct. For Helena's sake she had wished to expose② Bertram's meanness, not only to the King, but to himself. His pride was now in shreds③, and it is believed that he made a husband of some sort after all.

终成眷属

公元13世纪左右，罗西昂伯爵夫人在比利牛斯附近的宫殿里闷闷不乐。这个可怜的女人刚刚失去了丈夫，而法国国王又要将她的儿子勃特拉姆召到数百里之外的巴黎王宫。

勃特拉姆是个美男子，头发卷曲，俊眉上弯，还有一双像雄鹰一样敏锐的眼睛。他妄自尊大、盲目无知，为达自私的目的，他撒起谎来面不改色，像真的一样。可是美男子毕竟是美男子，海丽娜深深地爱上了他。

海丽娜是名医之女，她的父亲在为罗西昂伯爵医治时死去，留给她的唯一的财产就是几剂药方。

勃特拉姆离开后，伯爵夫人注意到海丽娜落寞的神情，就对海丽娜说，她会像疼爱自己的孩子那样疼爱她。而海丽娜双眼含满泪水，因为她害怕伯爵夫人让她把勃特拉姆当作哥哥而不能嫁给他。伯爵夫人立刻猜出了这

---

① generosity [ˌdʒenəˈrɔsiti] n. 慷慨，宽大
② expose [iksˈpəuz] v. 使暴露，受到，使曝光
③ in shreds 一扫而尽

女孩的心思,海丽娜也承认说勃特拉姆对于她犹如太阳对于白天那样重要。

然而,她希望自己能够通过博取法国国王的恩德来赢得她的"太阳"。这位国王患了一种致使他跛脚的慢性病,连王宫里的名医们都束手无策,但海丽娜对她的一个偏方充满了信心,因为她父亲曾用这个偏方治好过这种病。

同伯爵夫人依依惜别后,她去了巴黎,国王接见了她。

国王彬彬有礼,但很显然他认为她只是个江湖郎中。他说:"让一位毫无经验的女子来医治连名医都无法治愈的疾病,这似乎不符合我的身份。"

"神仙也有打盹的时候。"海丽娜说,并声称如果治不好他的病,她就偿命。

"那如果你成功了呢?"国王问。

"那么请求陛下让我为自己挑选一位丈夫。"

备受病痛折磨的国王无法拒绝这位年轻女子的真诚,于是海丽娜成了国王的主治医生,两天后这位跛脚的国王竟然能跳了。

国王召见了朝臣,让他们群集在宫殿的御室中。看到眼前这么多年轻帅气的贵族,而其中会站着自己的梦寐以求的丈夫,这位乡下姑娘有点晕眩了。她的双眼一直在徘徊,直到找到了勃特拉姆。她径直走到他面前说:"我不敢说我选择了你,可是我属于你!"为了让国王听见,她提高了嗓门,又说:"就是他了。"

"勃特拉姆,"国王说,"牵着她,她是你妻子!"

"我的妻子,国王?"勃特拉姆说,"陛下,请允许我自己选择我的妻子。"

"勃特拉姆,你可曾知道她为你的国王做了什么?"国王问。他一直把勃特拉姆看做自己的儿子。

"我知道,陛下,"勃特拉姆回答,"可是你为什么让我娶一位靠我父亲的恩典长大的女子为妻?"

"如果你因她无头衔而瞧不起她,我可以赐给她一个。"国王说。看着这个闷闷不乐的年轻人,他想了想,接着说道:"把你的血和乞丐的血放在碗里混合在一起,既然你分辨不出哪是你自己的,为什么还这么在乎血统呢?"

"我无法爱她,"勃特拉姆坚持说。于是海丽娜柔声地说道:"陛下,不要强迫他了,我很高兴为了国家而治好了我王的病。"

"我的尊严要求这个妄自尊大的年轻人顺从我的旨意,"国王说道。"勃特拉姆,你自己决定吧,是要娶这位你根本配不上的女子呢,还是让一个国王来怨恨你呢?回答我!"

勃特拉姆深深地鞠了一躬,说道:"承蒙陛下隆恩,使这位女子位列贵族,我接受。"

"牵着她的手,"国王说道,"告诉她,她是你的妻子。"

勃特拉姆顺从了国王的旨意,毫不拖延地娶了海丽娜为妻。

然而,勃特拉姆仅仅是害怕国王而已,他无法爱上海丽娜。别人的嘲笑奚落更让他感到难为情。一位叫帕洛的卑鄙的士兵当面嘲笑勃特拉姆,说他现在有了个"河东狮",他现在的要务不是打仗而是赋闲在家。"河东狮"只是一个给妻子的绰号,但这使勃特拉姆无法容忍有妻子这一事实。尽管国王已经禁止他去意大利参战,他还是坚决要去。

他吩咐海丽娜向国王告别并返回罗西昂,让她带上他写给母亲和写给她的信,冷冰冰地对她说了声再见就骑马出发了。

海丽娜打开了写给她的那封信,信上写着:"只有到了你能从我手指上得到这枚戒指的那一天,你才能称我为丈夫,而'那一天'是'永远'也不会到来的。"

到国王那里告别的时候海丽娜已将眼泪擦干,而国王却为她担心,于是就从手指上取下了一枚戒指给她,并对她说:"如果你将这枚戒指送来,我就知道你身处危险,会立即去解救你。"

她没有让国王看勃特拉姆给她的那封信,因为那封信会让国王将这个逃婚的伯爵处死。回到罗西昂后她把第二封信交给了婆母,信的内容简短而苦涩:"我逃走了,世界有多大,我就躲多远。"

"振作起来,"伯爵夫人对她被遗弃的儿媳说,"我不再认他这个儿子了,你就是我的孩子。"

然而,这位伯爵夫人仍然深爱着自己的儿子勃特拉姆,把错都怪在了帕洛的头上,并称他是"不道德的家伙"。

海丽娜在罗西昂没待多久。她留了一封信给婆母,打扮成香客的模样,

悄悄地向佛罗伦萨出发了。

到了佛罗伦萨,她向一个女人打听香客休息的地方,而这位女人则恳请这位"虔诚的香客"和她住在一起。

海丽娜得知她的女房东是一位寡妇,有一个叫黛安娜的漂亮的女儿。

黛安娜听说海丽娜来自法国,就对她说:"你的一位同胞,也就是罗西昂伯爵,为佛罗伦萨立下了赫赫战功。"可是不久之后,黛安娜又把海丽娜的丈夫做的不光彩的事情讲给她听,勃特拉姆一直向黛安娜示爱。他并没有隐藏他已婚的事实,可黛安娜从帕洛那里得知他的妻子并不值得他爱。

这位寡妇很为女儿担心,海丽娜决定告诉她自己就是罗西昂伯爵夫人。

"他一直向黛安娜索要一缕头发。"这位寡妇说。

海丽娜悲哀地笑了笑,因为她的头发和黛安娜的一样美丽,而且是相同的颜色。她急中生智,说:"拿着这包金币,如果黛安娜帮我实施计划,我就给她三千克朗。如果我丈夫把他手指上的那枚戒指给她,就让她答应送给他一缕头发。那枚戒指是祖传的,罗西昂家族的五代伯爵都戴过它,然而他却为了你女儿的一缕头发而放弃它。一定让你女儿坚持让他在没有亮光的房间里剪下那缕头发,前提是她不能对他讲一句话。"

这位寡妇兜里揣着那包金币,认真地听着。最后,她说:"只要黛安娜愿意,我也愿意。"

黛安娜愿意帮这个忙,说来也怪,在没有亮光的房间里从一个不说话的女孩头上剪下一缕头发,这个想法让勃特拉姆喜出望外,他将戒指交给了黛安娜,并被告知跟她进入没有光亮的房间的时间。约定的时间到了,他带上一把锋利的刀,当他割下一缕头发时,他感觉一个甜蜜温柔的脸庞贴在了自己的脸上。手上戴着那枚在黑暗绣房里的姑娘送给他的戒指,像得到一堆荣誉的人一样,勃特拉姆心满意足地离开了。

战争渐进尾声,勃特拉姆终于看出那个厚颜无耻地称海丽娜为"河东狮"的士兵还不如一个婆娘勇敢。帕洛只会吹嘘,只喜欢衣服上的装饰品,于是法国军官就戏弄他,想看看他到底是怎样的一个人。他将战鼓弄丢了,他发誓除非他在冲锋中战死,否则他一定把战鼓夺回。然而,他的冲锋十分低劣,当被敌军包围缴获武器时,还自编了一个英雄式的失败的故事。

"炮桃保特塔塔罗萨。"一位法国贵族喊

着。

"他说的是什么恐怖的鬼话?"帕洛心想。他的眼睛已经被蒙上了。

"他在要求惩罚,"另一个法国人说,假装给他作解释,又问帕洛,"你有什么要说的?"

帕洛回答说:"如果他们像挤压馅饼一样折磨我,我就尽量多说些话。"他说到做到,告诉他们佛罗伦萨军队里每个团有多少人,并在法国军官的要求下,给他们讲轶闻趣事逗他们乐。

勃特拉姆走过来,听到有人在读一封信,信中帕洛告诉黛安娜勃特拉姆是个傻瓜。

"这就是你忠诚的朋友。"一位法国贵族说。

"他现在对我来说是只猫。"勃特拉姆说。他很讨厌蜷缩在壁炉前地毯上的宠物。

帕洛最终被放走,此后他感觉自己是一个小人,不再到处吹嘘了。

现在我们再回到法国海丽娜那里,有消息说她已经死了,其实是法国的一位贵族拉佛想把自己的女儿麦格达伦许配给勃特拉姆,因而向罗西昂伯爵夫人传达了这个消息。

国王为海丽娜感到难过,但他还是同意了拉佛提出的这桩婚事。于是,他去拜访了罗西昂伯爵夫人。

"他的绊脚石已经死了,"国王说,"让勃特拉姆来见我吧。"

于是,脸上带着伤疤,勃特拉姆跪在国王面前,说假若和海丽娜结婚之前不爱拉佛的女儿,他一定会善待妻子的,现在爱她却已经太晚了。

"迟来的爱会冒犯那位了不起的为爱付出的人,"国王说,"忘记温柔可人的海丽娜,把戒指给麦格达伦戴上吧。"

勃特拉姆立即把戒指递给了拉佛,拉佛愤愤地说:"这是海丽娜的戒指。"

"不是!"勃特拉姆反驳道。

于是国王要求看一下戒指,看了之后说:"这就是我赐给海丽娜的那枚戒指,叫她在需要帮助时送还给我,你却将这枚对她最有帮助的戒指骗到你的手中。"

勃特拉姆再三否认那枚戒指是海丽娜的,但是就连他的母亲都说那就是海丽娜的。

"你撒谎!"国王气愤地喊道,"来人,把他抓起来!"在侍卫抓他的时候,勃特拉姆还在纳闷,本是黛安娜送给他的戒指怎么会和海丽娜的那么相似

呢。就在这时一位绅士走了进来,急切地向国王呈上一封请愿书,这封请愿书的署名是黛安娜·凯普莱特,她向国王请求让勃特拉姆娶她为妻,因为勃特拉姆赢取她的芳心后就弃她而去。

"现在,我宁愿在集市上买个女婿也不愿意将女儿许配给他。"拉佛说。

"传请愿人。"国王说。

勃特拉姆发现黛安娜和她母亲就站在面前,他否认他和黛安娜之间有什么婚约,说起她的时候似乎她生活在贫民窟一样。黛安娜反问他那枚从祖先那儿留下来的戒指怎么从手上消失了,他把那枚戒指赠送给了一个怎样的淑女,是不是像她一样。

那一刻勃特拉姆真想钻进地缝里,然而命运却那么善待他,因为海丽娜走了进来。

"我不是在做梦吧?"国王问。

"哦,原谅我!原谅我!"勃特拉姆哭喊着。

海丽娜举着他那枚祖传戒指说:"现在它就在我手里,勃特拉姆,你会爱我吗?"

"我会爱你一生一世。"他哽咽着。

"我的眼睛酸了。"拉佛说。感动的泪水在他眼眶里打转。

得知这位年轻大方的小姐的所作所为的意义后,国王对黛安娜大为赞赏。为了海丽娜,她愿意向国王,更向勃特拉姆本人,揭露他的卑劣行为。现在他的傲慢被一扫而尽,相信他会成为一个称职的丈夫。

2. The Taming of the Shrew

Katharine Boxes the Servant's Ears

There lived in Padua① a gentleman named Baptista②, who had two fair daughters. The eldest, Katharine③, was so very cross and ill-tempered④, and unmannerly⑤, that no one ever dreamed of marrying

---

① Padua [ˈpædjʊə] n. 帕多瓦(意大利东北部的一个城市,位于威尼斯的西部,中世纪时是个重要的文化中心)
② Baptista [ˈbæptistə] n. 巴普提斯塔(男子名)
③ Katharine [ˈkæθərin] n. 凯瑟琳(女子名)
④ ill-tempered adj. 脾气暴躁的
⑤ unmannerly [ʌnˈmænəli] adj. 没礼貌的,粗野的

her, while her sister, Bianca①, was so sweet and pretty, and pleasant-spoken, that more than one suitor② asked her father for her hand. But Baptista said the elder daughter must marry first.

So Bianca's suitors decided among themselves to try and get some one to marry Katharine—and then the father could at least be got to listen to their suit for Bianca.

A gentleman from Verona③, named Petruchio④, was the one they thought of, and, half in jest, they asked him if he would marry Katharine, the disagreeable scold. Much to their surprise he said yes, that was just the sort of wife for him, and if Katharine were handsome and rich, he himself would undertake soon to make her good-tempered.

Petruchio began by asking Baptista's permission to pay court to his gentle daughter Katharine—and Baptista was obliged to own that she was anything but gentle. And just then her music master rushed in, complaining that the naughty girl had broken her lute over his head, because he told her she was not playing correctly.

"Never mind," said Petruchio, "I love her better than ever, and long to have some chat with her."

When Katharine came, he said, "Good-morrow, Kate—for that, I hear, is your name."

"You've only heard half," said Katharine, rudely.

"Oh, no," said Petruchio, "they call you plain Kate, and bonny⑤ Kate, and sometimes Kate the shrew, and so, hearing your mildness praised in every town, and your beauty too, I ask you for my wife."

"Your wife!" cried Kate. "Never!" She said some extremely disagreeable things to him, and, I am sorry to say, ended by boxing his ears.

① Bianca [ˈbjɑːŋkə] n. 比恩卡(女子名)
② suitor [ˈsjuːtə] n. 求婚者
③ Verona [viˈrəunə] n. 维洛纳(意大利北部的一个城市,位于威尼斯以西阿迪杰河畔)
④ Petruchio [piˈtruːkiəu] n. 皮特鲁乔(男子名)
⑤ bonny [ˈbəni] adj. 漂亮的,健美的

经典的回声
Echoes of Classics:Stories from Shakespeare

"If you do that again, I'll cuff you," he said quietly; and still protested, with many compliments①, that he would marry none but her.

When Baptista came back, he asked at once, "How speed you with my daughter?"

"How should I speed but well," replied Petruchio.

"How now, daughter Katharine?" the father went on.

"I don't think," said Katharine, angrily, "you are acting a father's part in wishing me to marry this mad-cap② ruffian③."

"Ah!" said Petruchio, "you and all the world would talk amiss of④ her. You should see how kind she is to me when we are alone. In short, I will go off to Venice to buy fine things for our wedding—for—kiss me, Kate! We will be married on Sunday."

With that, Katharine flounced⑤ out of the room by one door in a violent temper, and he, laughing, went out by the other. But whether she fell in love with Petruchio, or whether she was only glad to meet a man who was not afraid of her, or whether she was flattered⑥ that, in spite of her rough words and spiteful⑦ usage, he still desired her for his wife—she did indeed marry him on Sunday, as he had sworn she should.

To vex⑧ and humble⑨ Katharine's naughty, proud spirit, he was late at the wedding, and when he came, came wearing such shabby clothes that she was ashamed to be seen with him. His servant was dressed in the same shabby way, and the horses they rode were the sport of everyone they passed.

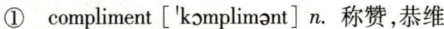

① compliment ['kɔmplimənt] n. 称赞,恭维
② mad-cap adj. 狂妄的
③ ruffian ['rʌfjən, -fiən] n. 流氓,恶棍
④ talk amiss of 讲错,说错
⑤ flounce [flauns] v. 突然离去
⑥ flatter ['flætə] v. 过分夸赞,奉承
⑦ spiteful ['spaitful] adj. 怀恨的,恶意的
⑧ vex [veks] v. 使烦恼,恼怒
⑨ humble ['hʌmbl] v. 使……卑下,贬抑; adj. 卑下的,谦逊的

And, after the marriage, when should have been the wedding breakfast, Petruchio carried his wife away, not allowing her to eat or drink—saying that she was his now, and he could do as he liked with her.

And his manner was so violent, and he behaved all through his wedding in so mad and dreadful a manner, that Katharine trembled and went with him. He mounted her on a stumbling①, lean, old horse, and they journeyed by rough muddy ways to Petruchio's house, he was scolding and snarling② all the way.

She was terribly tired when she reached her new home, but Petruchio was determined that she should neither eat nor sleep that night, for he had made up his mind to teach his bad-tempered wife a lesson she would never forget.

So he welcomed her kindly to his house, but when supper was served he found fault with everything—the meat was burnt, he said, and ill-served, and he loved her far too much to let her eat anything but the best. At last Katharine, tired out with her journey, went supperless to bed. Then her husband, still telling her how he loved her, and how anxious he was that she should sleep well, pulled her bed to pieces, throwing the pillows and bedclothes on the floor, so that she could not go to bed at all, and still kept growling and scolding at the servants so that Katharine might see how unbeautiful a thing ill-temper was.

The next day, too, Katharine's food was all found fault with, and caught away③ before she could touch a mouthful, and she was sick and giddy for want of sleep. Then she said to one of the servants, "I pray thee go and get

① stumbling [ˈstʌmblɪŋ] *adj.* 跌跌撞撞的
② snarl [snɑːl] *v.* 咆哮,吼叫,怒骂
③ catch away 拿走

me some repast. I care not what."

"What say you to a neat's foot?" said the servant.

Katharine said "Yes" eagerly; but the servant, who was in his master's secret, said he feared it was not good for hasty-tempered① people. Would she like tripe?

"Bring it me," said Katharine.

"I don't think that is good for hasty-tempered people," said the servant. "What do you say to a dish of beef and mustard②?"

"I love it," said Katharine.

"But mustard is too hot."

"Why, then, the beef, and let the mustard go," cried Katharine, who was getting hungrier and hungrier.

"No," said the servant, "you must have the mustard, or you get no beef from me."

"Then," cried Katharine, losing patience, "let it be both, or one, or anything thou wilt③."

"Why, then," said the servant, "the mustard without the beef!"

Then Katharine saw he was making fun of her, and boxed his ears.

Just then Petruchio brought her some food—but she had scarcely begun to satisfy her hunger, before he called for the tailor to bring her new clothes, and the table was cleared, leaving her still hungry. Katharine was pleased with the pretty new dress and cap that the tailor had made for her, but Petruchio found fault with everything, flung the cap and gown on the floor vowing his dear wife should not wear any such foolish things.

"I will have them," cried Katharine. "All gentlewomen wear such caps as these—"

"When you are gentle you shall have one too," he answered, "and not till then." When he had driven away the tailor with angry words—but

---

① hasty-tempered 急脾气的
② mustard ['mʌstəd] n. 芥菜,芥末
③ wilt [wilt] v. (古) will 的第二人称单数

privately asking his friend to see him paid—Petruchio said, "Come, Kate, let's go to your father's, shabby as we are, for as the sun breaks through the darkest clouds, so honor peereth in the meanest habit. It is about seven o'clock now. We shall easily get there by dinner-time."

"It's nearly two," said Katharine, but civilly① enough, for she had grown to see that she could not bully her husband, as she had done her father and her sister; "It's nearly two, and it will be supper-time before we get there."

"It shall be seven," said Petruchio, obstinately②, "before I start. Why, whatever I say or do, or think, you do nothing but contradict③. I won't go to-day, and before I do go, it shall be what o'clock I say it is."

At last they started for her father's house.

"Look at the moon," said he.

"It's the sun," said Katharine, and indeed it was.

"I say it is the moon. Contradicting again! It shall be sun or moon, or whatever I choose, or I won't take you to your father's."

Then Katharine gave in, once and for all. "What you will have it named," she said, "it is, and so it shall be so for Katharine." And so it was, for from that moment Katharine felt that she had met her master, and never again showed her naughty tempers to him, or anyone else.

So they journeyed on to Baptista's house, and arriving there, they found all folks keeping Bianca's wedding feast, and that of another newly married couple, Hortensio and his wife. They were made welcome, and sat down to the feast, and all was merry, save that Hortensio's wife, seeing Katharine subdued④ to her husband, thought she could safely say many disagreeable things, that in the old days, when Katharine was free

---

① civilly [ˈsivili] *adv.* 谦恭地
② obstinately [ˈɔbstinitli] *adv.* 倔强地,顽固地
③ contradict [ˌkɔntrəˈdikt] *v.* 驳斥,同……矛盾
④ subdue [sʌbˈdjuː] *v.* 征服

and froward①, she would not have dared to say. But Katharine answered with such spirit and such moderation②, that she turned the laugh against the new bride.

After dinner, when the ladies had retired, Baptista joined in a laugh against Petruchio, saying "Now in good sadness, son Petruchio, I fear you have got the veriest shrew of all."

"You are wrong," said Petruchio, "let me prove it to you. Each of us shall send a message to his wife, desiring her to come to him, and the one whose wife comes most readily shall win a wager which we will agree on③."

The others said yes readily enough, for each thought his own wife the most dutiful④, and each thought he was quite sure to win the wager⑤.

They proposed a wager of twenty crowns.

"Twenty crowns," said Petruchio, "I'll venture so much on my hawk or hound, but twenty times as much upon my wife."

"A hundred then," cried Lucentio, Bianca's husband.

"Content," cried the others.

Then Lucentio sent a message to the fair Bianca bidding her to come to him. And Baptista said he was certain his daughter would come. But the servant coming back, said, "Sir, my mistress is busy, and she cannot come."

"There's an answer for you," said Petruchio.

"You may think yourself fortunate if your wife does not send you a worse."

"I hope, better," Petruchio answered. Then Hortensio said, "Go and entreat⑥ my wife to come to me at once."

---

① froward [ˈfrəuəd] adj. 不易控制的，难驾驭的
② moderation [ˌmɔdəˈreiʃən] n. 适度
③ agree on 对……达成协议
④ dutiful [ˈdjuːtiful] adj. 忠实的，顺从的
⑤ wager [ˈweidʒə] n. 赌注；v. 下赌注，同……打赌
⑥ entreat [inˈtriːt] v. 恳求，乞求

"Oh—if you entreat her," said Petruchio.

"I am afraid," answered Hortensio, sharply, "do what you can, yours will not be entreated."

But now the servant came in, and said, "She says you are playing some jest①, she will not come."

"Better and better," cried Petruchio; "now go to your mistress and say I command her to come to me."

They all began to laugh, saying they knew what her answer would be, and that she would not come.

Then suddenly Baptista cried, "Here comes Katharine!" And sure enough—there she was.

"What do you wish, sir?" she asked her husband.

"Where are your sister and Hortensio's wife?"

"Talking by the parlor fire."

"Fetch them here."

When she was gone to fetch them, Lucentio said, "Here is a wonder!"

"I wonder what it means," said Hortensio.

"It means peace," said Petruchio, "and love, and quiet life."

"Well," said Baptista, "you have won the wager, and I will add another twenty thousand crowns to her dowry②—another dowry for another daughter—for she is as changed as if she were someone else."

So Petruchio won his wager, and had in Katharine always a loving wife and true, and now he had broken her proud and angry spirit he loved her well, and there was nothing ever but love between those two. And so they lived happy ever afterwards.

---

① jest [dʒest] v. 嘲笑
② dowry [ˈdauəri] n. 嫁妆,天资

驯悍记

帕多瓦住着一位绅士,名叫巴普提斯塔,他有两个美丽的女儿。大女儿凯瑟琳是一个性情暴戾乖张、很难管教的姑娘,没人想娶她为妻,而她的妹妹比恩卡则是一个温柔可人、美丽大方、嘴巴乖巧的姑娘,许多追求者都请求她的父亲同意他们向比恩卡求婚,而巴普提斯塔却坚持认为大女儿应该先出嫁。

于是比恩卡的追求者们决定他们之中必须有人娶了凯瑟琳,然后她父亲才会允许他们追求比恩卡。

有一位从维洛纳来的绅士名叫皮特鲁乔,他们半开玩笑地问他是否愿娶凯瑟琳。原以为会得到一顿臭骂,没想到,皮特鲁乔却说这种类型的女人正好适合他,并说如果凯瑟琳长得漂亮又富有,他就会立即应承下来,并使她的脾气好起来。

皮特鲁乔请求巴普提斯塔允许他向他那位"温柔的女儿凯瑟琳"求婚——而巴普提斯塔不得不承认自己的大女儿就缺温柔。就在这时她的音乐老师慌慌张张地闯了进来,抱怨说就因为他说她演奏得不对,那淘气的姑娘竟拿琴打他的头,把琴都打破了。

"没关系,"皮特鲁乔说,"我现在更爱她了,渴求跟她谈一谈。"

这时凯瑟琳进来了,他说:"早啊!凯特,我听说这是你的小名啊。"

"那你才听说了一半。"凯瑟琳粗鲁地说。

"噢,不,"皮特鲁乔说,"他们叫你直爽的凯特,也叫你漂亮的凯特,有时候人家也叫你'泼妇凯特'。听到人家称赞你温柔贤德、美貌出众,所以我想请你做我的妻子。"

"做你的妻子!"凯特大叫着,"不可能!"她对他说着相当刻薄的话,并且,我很遗憾地说,皮特鲁乔还被捆了几巴掌。

"如果你再这样做,我就铐上你。"他平静地说。然后仍一边赞美她,一边坚持说非她不娶。

巴普提斯塔回来后,马上问皮特鲁乔:"你和我女儿谈得怎么样了?"

"进展得不错。"皮特鲁乔回答说。

"怎么样,凯瑟琳,我的女儿?"这位父亲继续问凯瑟琳。

"我感觉不怎么样,"凯瑟琳生气地说,"你身为父亲,竟然希望我嫁给这个轻狂的流氓。"

"啊!"皮特鲁乔说,"您和世界上所有人都错看了她。您应该看到我们单独相处的时候她对我有多好。长话短说,我要去威尼斯置办上好的结婚用品了——来,吻我一下,凯特,咱们星期天就结婚。"

凯瑟琳转身离开房间,狠狠地关上了门,而皮特鲁乔呢,大笑着,从另一扇门出去了。或仅仅是爱上了皮特鲁乔,她是否很高兴看到这个对她一点儿也不发憷的人,尽管她以恶言恶语相待,他仍然希望她成为他的妻子——星期天她真的嫁给了他,他也应验了他发过的誓言。

为了杀杀凯瑟琳的傲慢之气,在婚礼上皮特鲁乔故意迟到。最后终于到了,却穿了一身破旧不堪的衣服,凯瑟琳羞于和他站在一起,他的仆人也穿得非常寒碜,连他们骑的马儿都被路人随意摆弄。

完婚后,本来该吃顿婚礼早餐,皮特鲁乔却把妻子带走,不许她吃喝,并且说她现在是他的了,他想怎么待她就怎么待她。

婚礼上他行为粗暴,举止疯癫可怕,凯瑟琳吓得战战兢兢地跟在他的后面。回家时,故意给她骑一匹走路不稳、瘦弱不堪的老马,他们走的路坑坑洼洼,处处都是泥泞,皮特鲁乔一路上还狂叫乱骂。

到了新家,凯瑟琳已是疲惫不堪了。可是那天晚上,皮特鲁乔既不让她吃饭也不让她睡觉,因为他下定决心要给他这个坏脾气的妻子一个永生难忘的教训。

他很和蔼地欢迎她回家,可是晚饭端上来时他总是找茬——要么是肉烧煳了,要么是做得不好,他说这样做是太爱她了,不愿让她吃不合口味的东西,只让她吃最好的。走了这么久的路,凯瑟琳累坏了,最后她连晚饭都没有吃就去睡觉了。她的丈夫仍然说他有多么爱她,多么希望她能睡个好觉,却把床铺上的东西弄得乱七八糟,又把枕头和铺盖扔到了地板上,这样一来她根本没法睡觉。接着呢,皮特鲁乔又不停地对仆人们责骂咆哮,这使凯瑟琳意识到脾气不好是一件多么丑陋的事情。

第二天,凯瑟琳的饭菜还是毛病一堆,还是没等她吃到一口就被端走了,她因为缺乏睡眠而头昏眼花。于是她对一个仆人说:"求你去给我弄点吃的,什么都可以。"

"你想吃牛蹄子吗?"这个仆人问。

凯瑟琳急切地说"是",而这位仆人知道主人心思,说吃这个怕对急脾气的人不好，问她要不要吃内脏。

"给我拿来吧。"凯瑟琳说。

"我认为吃这个对急脾气的人也没有什么好处，"仆人说，"牛肉芥末怎么样？"

"我喜欢。"凯瑟琳说。

"可是芥末太辣了。"

"好吧，我只要牛肉，不要芥末了。"凯瑟琳叫喊着说。她现在越来越饿了。

"不行，"仆人说，"你必须吃芥末，否则的话我就不给你牛肉吃。"

"那么，"失去耐心的凯瑟琳哭喊着说，"无论牛肉还是芥末牛肉，给我什么都行。"

"那么，"仆人说，"只有芥末，没有牛肉！"

凯瑟琳知道他是在拿她取乐，就掴了他耳光。

这时，皮特鲁乔给她拿来了一些饭菜。恰巧裁缝给她带来了新衣服，她还没吃饱饭菜就被撤走了，她依然是饥肠辘辘。凯瑟琳对裁缝给她做的衣帽非常满意，可是皮特鲁乔却对所有的东西倍加挑剔，把长袍和帽子扔在地板上，并发誓说他心爱的妻子不能穿这样愚蠢的东西。

"我要穿，"凯瑟琳哭着说，"所有的淑女都会戴这种帽子的。"

"等你变成淑女了，你才能戴这种帽子，"他回答说，"只有到了那时才行。"他恶言恶语地把裁缝赶走后，暗地里却让朋友帮忙把钱付了。皮特鲁乔说："来，凯特，我们去你父亲家，就穿旧衣服，因为太阳穿过最黑的云，荣耀来自最卑微的习惯。现在大约七点，我们正好可以在晚饭时间赶到那里。"

"快两点了。"凯瑟琳说。她的语气谦恭多了，因为她渐渐明白她不能再像对待父亲和妹妹那样粗暴地对待丈夫了。"现在将近两点了，我们吃晚饭的时候赶不到那里了。"

"我们七点出发，"皮特鲁乔毫不相让地说，"无论我说什么，做什么，或想什么，你总是跟我唱反调。好，我今天不走了。等走的时候，我说几点钟就是几点钟。"

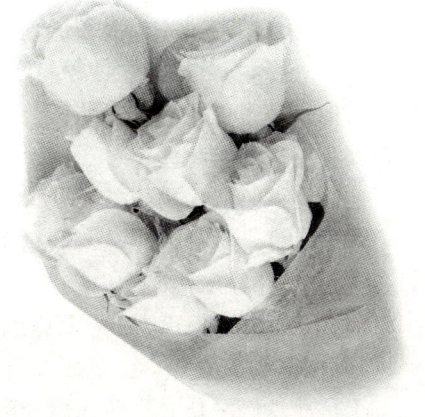

最后他们终于动身去她父亲家了。

"看那轮月亮。"他说。

"那是太阳啊。"凯瑟琳说,那确实是太阳。

"我说那是月亮,你又唱反调!我说它是月亮,它就是月亮;我说它是太阳,它就是太阳。你要是不同意,我就不带你去你父亲那里了。"

凯瑟琳这次是真的屈服了。"您高兴管它叫什么,"她说,"凯瑟琳也管它叫什么。"于是从那一刻起,凯瑟琳感到她真的遇见了她的主人,再也不对他及其他人发脾气了。

他们一路前行直到巴普提斯塔家中,到达之后,发现许多宾客正在参加比恩卡的结婚喜宴,举办喜宴的还有另外一对新婚夫妇,霍坦西奥和他的妻子。巴普提斯塔热情地欢迎了他们,于是二人就座参加喜宴。看到凯瑟琳对她丈夫服服帖帖,所有的人都为之高兴,唯独霍坦西奥的妻子闷闷不乐,原来她想起凯瑟琳过去许多令人不快的事情,那时候的凯瑟琳是一个自由放任、性情乖张的姑娘,她还不敢对凯瑟琳说不中听的话。可是现在凯瑟琳却用这样温柔平和的语气回答,使她不由得嘲笑起这个新娘子。

吃过晚饭,女宾客退场后,巴普提斯塔加入嘲笑皮特鲁乔的行列里了,说:"唉,皮特鲁乔贤婿,说句老实话,我担心你娶的是最泼悍的女人了。"

"您错了,"皮特鲁乔说,"为了证实我的话,咱们各自派人去叫自己的妻子过来,谁的妻子一叫就来,就算谁赢,那么我们协议的赌注就归谁所有。"

其他人都很乐意打这个赌,因为他们都认为自己的妻子是最顺从的,每个人都有把握赢取赌注。

他们提议赌注为20克朗。

"20克朗,"皮特鲁乔说,"我就是拿鹰犬打赌也要赌那么多,如今拿我的妻子打赌,赌注应当是20倍。"

"那么就100克朗吧。"卢森修说。他是比恩卡的丈夫。

"好。"其他人喊道。

于是卢森修派仆人去叫比恩卡到他身边来。同时巴普提斯塔也肯定他的小女儿会马上过来。仆人回来却说:"老爷,太太说她有事,不能来。"

"这就是你的答复了。"皮特鲁乔说。

"要是你的妻子不给你更糟糕的答复,你就算幸运了。"

"我希望最好是。"皮特鲁乔回答道。然后霍坦西奥对仆人说:"请我太太立即来这儿一趟。"

"哎呀,还要'请'她过来!"皮特鲁乔说。

"那么叫尊夫人过来吧,恐怕你请还请不来呢。"霍坦西奥尖刻地说。

这时仆人进来说:"太太说您大概要开什么玩笑,所以她不来了。"

"这回更糟了,更糟了,"皮特鲁乔叫仆人过来,说,"喂,你到太太那儿去,告诉她,我命令她到我这儿来。"

所有的人都哈哈大笑,说他们知道答复会是什么,她不会来的。

突然,巴普提斯塔嚷道:"呀,凯瑟琳来了!"是的,她真的过来了。

她温顺地问她丈夫:"您叫我来有什么吩咐吗?"

"你妹妹和霍坦西奥的妻子哪儿去啦?"皮特鲁乔问。

"她们在客厅里围着火炉谈天呢。"

"去,把她们找来!"

她去叫她们俩的时候,卢森修说:"真是怪事!"

"我想知道这意味着什么。"霍坦西奥说。

"意味着和睦,"皮特鲁乔说,"以及恩爱和宁静的生活。"

"好吧,"巴普提斯塔说,"你赌赢了,我要再额外加上两万克朗的陪嫁——就当是给我另外一个女儿的——因为她跟以前完全是判若两人了。"

于是皮特鲁乔赢取了赌注,他成功地制伏了他妄自尊大、性情暴戾的妻子,使凯瑟琳变得温顺而富有爱心,并对她呵护有加。此后,他们过着甜蜜快乐、恩爱幸福的生活。

3. Two Gentlemen of Verona

Valentine Writes A Letter for Silvia

Only one of them was really a gentleman, as you will discover later. Their names were Valentine① and Proteus②. They were friends, and lived at Verona, a town in northern Italy. Valentine was happy in his name because it was that of the patron saint of lovers; it is hard for a Valentine to be fickle③ or mean. Proteus was unhappy in his name, because it was that of a famous shape-changer, and therefore it encouraged him to be a lover at one time and a traitor at another.

One day, Valentine told his friend that he was going to Milan. "I'm

---

① Valentine ['vælǝntin] n. 瓦伦丁(男子名)
② Proteus ['prǝutjuːs] n. 普罗特斯(男子名)
③ fickle ['fikl] adj. (在感情等方面)变幻无常的

not in love like you," said he, "and therefore I don't want to stay at home."

Proteus was in love with a beautiful yellow-haired girl called Julia, who was rich, and had no one to order her about. He was, however, sorry to part from Valentine, and he said, "If ever you are in danger tell me, and I will pray for you." Valentine then went to Milan with a servant called Speed, and at Milan he fell in love with the Duke of Milan's daughter, Silvia.

When Proteus and Valentine parted Julia had not acknowledged① that she loved Proteus. Indeed, she had actually torn up one of his letters in the presence of her maid, Lucetta②. Lucetta, however, was no simpleton③, for when she saw the pieces she said to herself, "All she wants is to be annoyed by another letter." Indeed, no sooner had Lucetta left her alone than Julia repented of her tearing, and placed between her dress and her heart the torn pieces of paper on which Proteus had signed his name. So by tearing a letter written by Proteus she discovered that she loved him. Then, like a brave, sweet girl, she wrote to Proteus, "Be patient, and you shall marry me."

Delighted with these words Proteus walked about, flourishing Julia's letter and talking to himself.

"What have you got there?" asked his father, Antonio.

"A letter from Valentine," fibbed Proteus.

"Let me read it," said Antonio.

"There is no news," said deceitful④ Proteus; "he only says that he is very happy, and the Duke of Milan is kind to him, and that he wishes I were with him."

This fib had the effect of making Antonio think that his son should go to Milan and enjoy the favors in which Valentine basked. "You must

---

① acknowledge [əkˈnɔlidʒ] v. 承认
② Lucetta [luːˈsetə] n. 露西塔(女子名)
③ simpleton [ˈsimpltən] n. 笨蛋,傻子
④ deceitful [diˈsiːtful] adj. 欺诈的

go to-morrow," he decreed. Proteus was dismayed. "Give me time to get my outfit ready." He was met with the promise, "What you need shall be sent after you."

It grieved Julia to part from her lover before their engagement① was two days' old. She gave him a ring, and said, "Keep this for my sake," and he gave her a ring, and they kissed like two who intend to be true till death. Then Proteus departed for Milan.

Meanwhile Valentine was amusing Silvia, whose grey eyes, laughing at him under auburn② hair, had drowned him in love. One day she told him that she wanted to write a pretty letter to a gentleman whom she thought well of, but had no time; would he write it? Very much did Valentine dislike writing that letter, but he did write it, and gave it to her coldly. "Take it back," she said, "you did it unwillingly."

"Madam," he said, "it was difficult to write such a letter for you."

"Take it back," she commanded; "you did not write tenderly enough."

Valentine was left with the letter, and condemned to write another; but his servant Speed saw that, in effect, the Lady Silvia had allowed Valentine to write for her a love-letter to Valentine's own self. "The joke," he said, "is as invisible as a weather-cock③ on a steeple④." He meant that it was very plain; and he went on to say exactly what it was: "If master will write her love-letters, he must answer them."

On the arrival of Proteus, he was introduced by Valentine to Silvia and afterwards, when they were alone, Valentine asked Proteus how his love for Julia was prospering⑤.

"Why," said Proteus, "you used to get wearied when I spoke of her."

---

① engagement [in'geidʒmənt] n. 约会，婚约
② auburn ['ɔːbən] adj. 赤褐色的
③ weather-cock ['weðəkɔk] n. 风信标
④ steeple ['stiːpl] n. 尖塔
⑤ prosper ['prɔspə] v. 成功，兴隆，昌盛

"Aye," confessed Valentine, "but It's different now. I can eat and drink all day with nothing but love on my plate and love in my cup."

"You idolize① Silvia," said Proteus.

"She is divine②," said Valentine.

"Come, come!" remonstrated③ Proteus.

"Well, if she's not divine," said Valentine, "she is the queen of all women on earth."

"Except Julia," said Proteus.

"Dear boy," said Valentine, "Julia is not excepted; but I will grant that she alone is worthy to bear my lady's train."

"Your bragging astounds me," said Proteus.

But he had seen Silvia, and he felt suddenly that the yellow-haired Julia was black in comparison④. He became in thought a villain⑤ without delay, and said to himself what he had never said before—"I to myself am dearer than my friend."

It would have been convenient for Valentine if Proteus had changed, by the power of the god whose name he bore, the shape of his body at the evil moment when he despised Julia in admiring Silvia. But his body did not change; his smile was still affectionate⑥, and Valentine confided to him the great secret that Silvia had now promised to run away with him. "In the pocket of this cloak," said Valentine, "I have a silken rope ladder, with hooks which will clasp the window-bar of her room."

Proteus knew the reason why Silvia and her lover were bent on flight. The Duke intended her

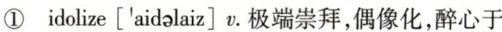

① idolize [ˈaidəlaiz] v. 极端崇拜,偶像化,醉心于
② divine [diˈvain] adj. 神的,神圣的
③ remonstrate [riˈmɔnstreit] v. 抗议
④ comparison [kəmˈpærisn] n. 比较,对照
⑤ villain [ˈvilən] n. 坏人,恶棍
⑥ affectionate [əˈfekʃənit] adj. 亲爱的,挚爱的

to wed Sir Thurio, a gentlemanly noodle for whom she did not care a straw.

Proteus thought that if he could get rid of Valentine he might make Silvia fond of him, especially if the Duke insisted on her enduring Sir Thurio's tiresome chatter①. He therefore went to the Duke, and said, "Duty before friendship! It grieves me to thwart② my friend Valentine, but your Grace should know that he intends to-night to elope with③ your Grace's daughter." He begged the Duke not to tell Valentine the giver of this information, and the Duke assured him that his name would not be divulged④.

Early that evening the Duke summoned Valentine, who came to him wearing a large cloak with a bulging pocket.

"You know," said the Duke, "my desire to marry my daughter to Sir Thurio?"

"I do," replied Valentine. "He is virtuous⑤ and generous⑥, as befits a man so honored in your Grace's thoughts."

"Nevertheless she dislikes him," said the Duke. "She is a peevish⑦, proud, disobedient⑧ girl, and I should be sorry to leave her a penny. I intend, therefore, to marry again."

Valentine bowed.

"I hardly know how the

---

① tiresome chatter 无聊的唠叨
② thwart [θwɔːt] v. 反对,阻碍,横过
③ elope [iˈləup] v. 私奔
④ divulge [daiˈvʌldʒ] v. 泄露,暴露
⑤ virtuous [ˈvəːtjuəs] adj. 善良的,有道德的,贞洁的
⑥ generous [ˈdʒenərəs] adj. 慷慨的,大方的
⑦ peevish [ˈpiːviʃ] adj. 易怒的,暴躁的
⑧ disobedient [ˌdisəˈbiːdjənt] adj. 不服从的

young people of today make love," continued the Duke, "and I thought that you would be just the man to teach me how to win the lady of my choice."

"Jewels have been known to plead① rather well," said Valentine.

"I have tried them," said the Duke.

"The habit of liking the giver may grow if your Grace gives her some more."

"The chief difficulty," pursued the Duke, "is this. The lady is promised to a young gentleman, and it is hard to have a word with her. She is, in fact, locked up."

"Then your Grace should propose② an elopement," said Valentine. "Try a rope ladder."

"But how should I carry it?" asked the Duke.

"A rope ladder is light," said Valentine. "You can carry it in a cloak."

"Like yours?"

"Yes, your Grace."

"Then yours will do. Kindly lend it to me."

Valentine had talked himself into a trap. He could not refuse to lend his cloak, and when the Duke had donned it, his Grace drew from the pocket a sealed missive③ addressed to Silvia. He coolly opened it, and read these words: "Silvia, you shall be free tonight."

"Indeed," he said, "and here's the rope ladder. Prettily contrived④, but not perfectly. I give you, sir, a day to leave my dominions⑤. If you are in Milan by this time tomorrow, you die."

Poor Valentine was saddened to the core. "Unless I look on Silvia in the day," he said, "there is no day for me to look upon."

---

① plead [pli:d] v. 辩护,恳求
② propose [prəˈpəuz] v. 计划,建议
③ missive [ˈmisiv] n. 信件
④ contrived [kənˈtraivd] adj. 人为的,做作的
⑤ dominion [dəˈminjən] n. 主权,领土

Before he went he took farewell of Proteus, who proved a hypocrite① of the first order. "Hope is a lover's staff," said Valentine's betrayer, "walk hence with that."

After leaving Milan, Valentine and his servant wandered into a forest near Mantua where the great poet Virgil② lived. In the forest, however, the poets (if any) were brigands③, who bade the travelers stand. They obeyed, and Valentine made so good an impression upon his captors that they offered him his life on condition that he became their captain.

"I accept," said Valentine, "provided you release my servant, and are not violent to women or the poor."

The reply was worthy of Virgil, and Valentine became a brigand chief.

We return now to Julia, who found Verona too dull to live in since Proteus had gone. She begged her maid Lucetta to devise a way by which she could see him. "Better wait for him to return," said Lucetta, and she talked so sensibly that Julia saw it was idle to hope that Lucetta would bear the blame of any rash④ and interesting adventure. Julia therefore said that she intended to go to Milan and dressed like a page.

"You must cut off your hair then," said Lucetta, who thought that at this announcement Julia would immediately abandon her scheme.

"I shall knot it up," was the disappointing rejoinder⑤.

Lucetta then tried to make the scheme seem foolish to Julia, but Julia had made up her mind and was not to be put off by ridicule⑥; and when her toilet was completed, she looked as comely⑦ a page as one could wish to see.

Julia assumed the male name Sebastian, and arrived in Milan in time

---

① hypocrite ['hipəkrit] *n.* 伪君子, 伪善者
② Virgil ['vəːdʒil] *n.* 维吉尔(公元前70年—公元前19年), 古罗马诗人
③ brigand ['brigənd] *n.* 土匪, 强盗
④ rash [ræʃ] *adj.* 轻率的, 匆忙的, 鲁莽的
⑤ rejoinder [ri'dʒɔində] *n.* 反驳
⑥ ridicule ['ridikjuːl] *n.* 嘲笑, 奚落
⑦ comely ['kʌmli] *adj.* 清秀的, 标致的

to hear music being performed outside the Duke's palace.

"They are serenading① the Lady Silvia," said a man to her.

Suddenly she heard a voice lifted in song, and she knew that voice. It was the voice of Proteus. But what was he singing?

"Who is Silvia? what is she,

That all our swains commend her?

Holy, fair, and wise is she;

The heaven such grace did lend her

That she might admired be."

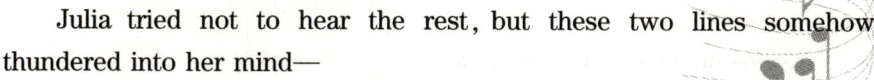

Julia tried not to hear the rest, but these two lines somehow thundered into her mind—

"Then to Silvia let us sing;

She excels each mortal thing."

Then Proteus thought Silvia excelled Julia; and, since he sang so beautifully for all the world to hear, it seemed that he was not only false to Julia, but had forgotten her. Yet Julia still loved him. She even went to him, and asked to be his page, and Proteus engaged her.

One day, he handed to her the ring which she had given him, and said, "Sebastian, take that to the Lady Silvia, and say that I should like the picture of her she promised me."

Silvia had promised the picture, but she disliked Proteus. She was obliged to talk to him because he was high in the favor of② her father, who thought he pleaded with her on behalf of Sir Thurio. Silvia had learned from Valentine that Proteus was pledged to a sweetheart in Verona; and when he said tender things to her, she felt that he was disloyal③ in friendship as well as love.

Julia bore the ring to Silvia, but Silvia said, "I will not wrong the woman who gave it him by wearing it."

"She thanks you," said Julia.

---

① serenade [ˌserɪ'neɪd] n. 小夜曲; v. 唱小夜曲

② in the favor of 支持, 赞成

③ disloyal [dɪs'lɔɪəl] adj. 不忠的, 背叛的

"You know her, then?" said Silvia, and Julia spoke so tenderly of herself that Silvia wished that Sebastian would marry Julia.

Silvia gave Julia her portrait for Proteus, who would have received it the worse for extra touches on the nose and eyes if Julia had not made up her mind that she was as pretty as Silvia.

Soon there was an uproar① in the palace. Silvia had fled.

The Duke was certain that her intention was to join the exiled Valentine, and he was not wrong.

Without delay he started in pursuit, with Sir Thurio, Proteus, and some servants.

The members of the pursuing party got separated, and Proteus and Julia (in her page's dress) were by themselves when they saw Silvia, who had been taken prisoner by outlaws② and was now being led to their captain. Proteus rescued her, and then said, "I have saved you from death; give me one kind look."

"O misery, to be helped by you!" cried Silvia. "I would rather be a lion's breakfast."

Julia was silent, but cheerful. Proteus was so much annoyed with Silvia that he threatened her, and seized her by the waist.

"O heaven!" cried Silvia.

At that instant there was a noise of crackling branches. Valentine came crashing through the Mantuan forest to the rescue③ of his beloved. Julia feared he would slay Proteus, and hurried to help her false lover. But he struck no blow, he only said, "Proteus, I am sorry I must never

---

① uproar [ˈʌprɔː] n. 喧嚣,骚动
② outlaw [ˈautlɔː] n. 歹徒,逃犯
③ rescue [ˈreskjuː] v. 援救,营救

trust you more."

Thereat Proteus felt his guilt, and fell on his knees, saying, "Forgive me! I grieve! I suffer!"

"Then you are my friend once more," said the generous Valentine. "If Silvia, that is lost to me, will look on you with favor, I promise that I will stand aside① and bless you both."

These words were terrible to Julia, and she swooned②. Valentine revived③ her, and said, "What was the matter, boy?"

"I remembered," fibbed Julia, "that I was charged to give a ring to the Lady Silvia, and that I did not."

"Well, give it to me," said Proteus.

She handed him a ring, but it was the ring that Proteus gave to Julia before he left Verona.

Proteus looked at her hand, and crimsoned④ to the roots of his hair.

"I changed my shape when you changed your mind," said she.

"But I love you again," said he.

Just then outlaws entered, bringing two prizes—the Duke and Sir Thurio.

"Forbear⑤!" cried Valentine, sternly. "The Duke is sacred."

Sir Thurio exclaimed, "There's Silvia; she's mine!"

"Touch her, and you die!" said Valentine.

"I should be a fool to risk anything for her," said Sir Thurio.

"Then you are base," said the Duke. "Valentine, you are a brave man. Your banishment⑥ is over. I recall you.

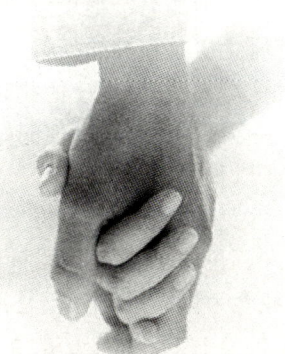

---

① stand aside v. 站开,躲开,不做事
② swoon [swuːn] v. 昏晕
③ revive [ri'vaiv] v. (使)苏醒
④ crimson ['krimzn] adj. 深红色的; n. 深红色
⑤ forbear [fɔː'bɛə] v. 忍耐,克制
⑥ banishment ['bæniʃmənt] n. 放逐,驱逐

You may marry Silvia. You deserve her."

"I thank your Grace," said Valentine, deeply moved, "and yet must ask you one more boon①."

"I grant it," said the Duke.

"Pardon these men, your Grace, and give them employment. They are better than their calling."

"I pardon them and you," said the Duke. "Their work henceforth shall be for wages."

"What think you of this page, your Grace?" asked Valentine, indicating Julia.

The Duke glanced at her, and said, "I think the boy has grace in him."

"More grace than boy, say I," laughed Valentine, and the only punishment which Proteus had to bear for his treacheries② against love and friendship was the recital in his presence of the adventures of Julia-Sebastian of Verona.

维洛那二绅士

正如你后来发现的那样,他们两人中只有一位是真正的绅士。他们一个叫瓦伦丁,一个叫普罗特斯,这对好朋友住在意大利北部的小镇维洛那。瓦伦丁对他的名字很满意,因为它的意思是恋人的守护神,想让他做出薄情或卑鄙之事是很难的。普罗特斯对自己的名字不满意,因为它源于一个著名的变形人,因而它让他此时是一个恋人,彼时却又背叛自己的感情。

一天,瓦伦丁告诉他的好友他要去米兰,并对他说:"我不像你那样在恋爱,所以我不想待在家里。"

普罗特斯恋上了金发美女茱莉娅,她很富有,还没有定下终身大事。然而,和瓦伦丁分别让普罗特斯感到难过,他说:"如果你有什么麻烦就告诉我,我会为你祈福的。"于是瓦伦丁就带着一个叫斯彼得的家仆去了米兰,在那里他爱上了米兰公爵的女儿——西尔维娅。

---

① boon [buːn] n. 恩惠
② treachery [ˈtretʃəri] n. 背叛,背信弃义

普罗特斯和瓦伦丁分别时,茱莉娅还并未承认自己爱上了普罗特斯,她甚至当着侍女露西塔的面将普罗特斯写给她的情书撕得粉碎。露西塔呢,也不是傻瓜,看着这些碎片她心想:"茱莉娅巴不得人家再送一封情书来呢。"的确,露西塔刚刚离开,茱莉娅就为自己的行为感到懊悔,把署着普罗特斯名字的情书碎片塞进衣服,紧贴在胸前。撕过普罗特斯的信后,茱莉娅发现自己已经爱上了他。于是,这位美丽的姑娘大胆地给普罗特斯回了信:"耐心点吧,我会嫁给你的。"

看到这些话,普罗特斯很兴奋,他来来回回地走着,一遍遍地读着茱莉娅的信,并自言自语着。

"你手里拿的是什么?"他父亲安东尼奥问道。

"瓦伦丁的信。"普罗特斯搪塞道。

"让我也瞧瞧。"安东尼奥说。

"没有什么新鲜事,"普罗特斯遮遮掩掩地说,"他只是说他过得很愉快,米兰公爵对他很好,他希望我能和他在一起。"

这番搪塞之词却让安东尼奥想到儿子应该去米兰,和瓦伦丁一起分享米兰公爵的宠爱。"你明天就去吧。"他命令道。普罗特斯感到不知所措。"我需要些时间准备行装。"安东尼奥答应了,说:"你要是缺什么,我随后就会给你送去。"

定情刚两天,情人就要离去,茱莉娅感到很伤心。她给了普罗特斯一枚戒指,说:"为了我好好保存着。"普罗特斯也回赠了她一枚戒指。两人拥吻很久,似乎他们的爱情真的会到地老天荒。然后普罗特斯就去了米兰。

在米兰,瓦伦丁正与西尔维娅愉快地嬉戏,她灰色的眼睛在一头褐发之下冲着他笑,让他深深地坠入了爱河。一天,西尔维娅告诉他,她想给一位她心仪已久的男士写封情深意切的信,可是没有时间,问他能否代笔。瓦伦丁非常不情愿写那样的信,可他还是写了,并冷冷地给了她。"拿回去吧,"她说,"你很不情愿写这封信。"

"小姐,"瓦伦丁说,"替你写这种信真的很难。"

"你拿回去吧,"她命令说,"你写得不够动人。"

西尔维娅把那封情书扔给瓦伦丁,责令他再写一封。仆人斯彼得则认为,实际上西尔维娅小姐想让瓦伦丁代她写一封给他自己的情书。"这个玩笑,"他说,"就像塔尖上的风信标那样让人看不见。"他的意思是这件事显而易见;他继续说出了事情的真相:"如果主人愿意代她写情书的话,她的情人也必须回信啊。"

　　普罗特斯来到米兰,瓦伦丁把他介绍给西尔维娅。之后,他们俩单独相处的时候,瓦伦丁向普罗特斯问起了他和茱莉娅的爱情进展的情况。

　　"怎么了?"普罗特斯说,"过去我一提她你就会厌烦。"

　　"啊,"他坦白地说,"可是现在不同了,我可以整天吃着盘中之爱,喝着杯中之情。"

　　"你迷上了西尔维娅。"普罗特斯说。

　　"她是神圣的。"瓦伦丁回答说。

　　"好啦,好啦!"普罗特斯抗议道。

　　"那么,即使她不是神圣的,"瓦伦丁说,"那她也是世界上所有女人中的女王!"

　　"除了茱莉娅。"普罗特斯说。

　　"好啦,兄弟,"瓦伦丁说,"茱莉娅也不例外;我可以这么说,她只配为我心爱的女人牵长裙。"

　　"你这么夸海口真让我吃惊。"普罗特斯说。

　　但他见过西尔维娅,而且突然感觉到相比之下金发的茱莉娅黯然失色。毫不迟疑地,他想做一次恶人,并且自言自语地说了他往日从没有说过的话:"我对自己应该要比对朋友好一些。"

　　普罗特斯的名字带有上帝之威,如果在这个邪恶时刻,在他轻视茱莉娅而欣赏西尔维娅之时,上帝的威力改变了他的姿态,瓦伦丁应该觉得那是自然而然的事;但是他表面上并没有改变,他仍然面带诚挚的笑容。瓦伦丁向他吐露了一个重大的秘密,就是西尔维娅已经答应和他私奔了。"在这个长袍的口袋里,"瓦伦丁说,"我有一个丝质的绳梯子,上面的钩子可以钩住她房间窗户的横木。"

　　普罗特斯知道西尔维娅和她的恋人为什么下决心私奔。公爵要把她嫁给修里奥爵士,他是一个假装正经的笨瓜,西尔维娅根本没有将他放在眼里。

　　普罗特斯认为如果将瓦伦丁除掉,他就可以让西尔维娅喜欢上他,尤其是当公爵强行要她去忍受修里奥爵士喋喋不休的唠叨时。于是他到公爵那儿告了密,他对公爵说:"责任重于情谊。阻碍了我的朋友瓦伦丁让我感到很痛心,但是,殿下,您应当知道今天晚上,他要和您的女儿一起私奔。"他请求公爵不要告诉瓦伦丁泄密者是谁,公爵答应了他不会将他的名字泄漏出去。

　　那天晚上早些时候,公爵将瓦伦丁叫了过来,瓦伦丁穿着长袍,口袋鼓鼓的。

"你知道，"公爵对他说，"我想把女儿嫁给修里奥爵士。"

"我知道，"瓦伦丁回答说，"他品德善良，慷慨大方，正合殿下的心意。"

"可是她不喜欢他，"公爵说，"她脾气倔强，性情高傲，目无尊长。我一个子儿也不想留给她。而且，我还想再续一房妻室。"

瓦伦丁鞠了一躬。

"我几乎不知道现在的年轻人是怎样求爱的，"公爵继续说着，"我想你正可以教我如何赢得意中人的芳心。"

"珠宝更能打动女人的心。"瓦伦丁回答。

"我已经试过了。"公爵说。

"如果殿下再多给她些，她可能会逐渐喜欢上给他珠宝的人。"

"主要的困难，"公爵继续说，"是这位姑娘已经与一个年轻的绅士有了婚约，我很难和她说上话。实际上，她被锁起来了。"

"那么，殿下，你应该提议私奔啊，"瓦伦丁说，"试一下绳梯。"

"可是，我怎么带绳梯呢？"公爵问道。

"绳梯很轻，"瓦伦丁说，"你可以把它放在长袍里。"

"像你这样的长袍？"

"是的，殿下。"

"就用你的好了，借给我吧。"

瓦伦丁已经把自己套了进去，他不得不把长袍借给公爵。穿上长袍后，公爵从口袋里掏出一封给西尔维娅的封好口的情书。他将情书打开，读道："西尔维娅，今晚你就自由了。"

"实际上，"他说，"这就是绳梯，设计得很好，但不完美。我给你一天的时间离开这里。明天此时，如果你还在米兰的话，你将会被处死。"

可怜的瓦伦丁伤心欲绝。"除非我今天能见到西尔维娅，"他说，"不然我再也见不到她了。"

走之前，瓦伦丁向普罗特斯道别。"希望是恋人的精神支柱，"这个背叛瓦伦丁的彻头彻尾的伪君子说，"带着希望离开吧。"

离开米兰后，瓦伦丁和他的仆人流浪到曼图亚附近的一个森林里，大诗人维吉尔曾在这里居住过。然而，在这个森林里，如果有诗人的话，他们也都是强盗，他们向来往的过路人索取钱财。瓦伦丁和他的仆人在强盗面前

没有一点儿反抗,并给他们留下了深刻的印象,于是强盗们就要求瓦伦丁做他们的头目,否则的话就没有活路。

"我答应,"瓦伦丁说,"只要你们放了我的仆人,并且不要欺侮妇女和穷人。"

这个回答颇有维吉尔的遗风,就这样他留下来做了强盗头子。

我们再来说说茱莉娅。普罗特斯离开后,她感到维罗纳的生活极度无聊,就央求她的侍女露西塔想个能见普罗特斯的计策。"最好是等他回来。"露西塔说。她的回答非常巧妙,茱莉娅明白希望露西塔为任何有趣但鲁莽的冒险承担责任都是白搭。于是茱莉娅说她想乔扮成侍从去米兰。

"那么你就必须把头发剪掉。"露西塔说。她认为就这一个条件就足以让茱莉娅放弃这一计划。

"我把头发盘起来就行了。"这就是令露西塔失望的反驳。

于是露西塔设法让这一计划看起来愚蠢可笑,可是茱莉娅已经下定决心,不会因为嘲笑而耽搁行程。梳妆完毕,她看起来就是一个美目清秀、让人想多看几眼的侍从。

茱莉娅化名为塞巴斯蒂安,当她到达米兰的时候,正好听见在宫廷外面演奏的音乐。

"他们正在为西尔维娅小姐演奏。"一个人告诉她。

突然她听到一个熟悉的声音在唱歌,她听出那是普罗特斯的声音。可是他在唱什么呢?

> 西尔维娅伊何人,
> 乃能颠倒众生心?
> 神圣姣丽且聪明;
> 天赋诸美萃一身,
> 博令举世诵其名。

茱莉娅不想再听下去了,可是下面两句令她惊诧不已。

> 请君为伊歌一曲,
> 伊人美好世无伦。

普罗特斯认为西尔维娅要比茱莉娅强;并且,他的歌声如此动听,全世界的人都听得见。看起来,他不但对茱莉娅不忠,并且早已将她忘记。然而,茱莉娅仍然深爱着他。她甚至去他那里,请求成为他的侍从,普罗特斯答应了她。

有一天,普罗特斯交给了她那个她曾经送给他的戒指,说:"塞巴斯蒂安,把这枚戒指交给希尔维娅小姐,告诉她说我会喜欢她答应送给我的那幅画。"

西尔维娅答应过送给他那幅画,可是她并不喜欢普罗特斯。她不得不同他说话,因为她父亲很器重他,公爵认为普罗特斯是为了修里奥爵士而博取他女儿的欢心。西尔维娅曾从瓦伦丁那里得知普罗特斯的心上人在维罗纳;听到普罗特斯向她说着甜言蜜语,便认为他不仅背叛了友谊而且还背叛了爱情。

茱莉娅把那枚戒指交给西尔维娅,西尔维娅却说:"我可不愿意戴上这枚戒指而伤害了送他这枚戒指的女人。"

"她会感激你的。"茱莉娅说。

"怎么,你认识她?"西尔维娅问。茱莉娅把自己描述成一个体贴温柔的女人,西尔维娅希望塞巴斯蒂安能娶茱莉娅。

西尔维娅让茱莉娅把她的画像交给普罗特斯。如果茱利娅不认为她与西尔维娅一样漂亮的话,普罗特斯就会收到一幅鼻子和眼睛上被添了几笔的难看的画像。

不久,宫中发生了一阵骚动,西尔维娅出走了。

公爵认为她是去追随流亡的瓦伦丁了,事实的确如此。

毫不迟疑地,他立即带着修里奥爵士、普罗特斯和家奴们追赶而去。

追赶的队伍走散了,普罗特斯和茱莉娅(她穿着侍从的衣服)他们看到西尔维娅正要被劫匪押送到他们的头领那里去。普罗特斯将她解救出来,对她说:"我把你从死亡的边缘救了回来,给我一个好脸色行吗?"

"噢,不幸啊,被你救出来!"西尔维娅哭着说,"我宁愿去做狮子的早餐。"

茱莉娅沉默不语,但是暗地里窃喜。普罗特斯被西尔维娅惹恼了,他抓住她的腰威胁着她。

"噢,天哪!"西尔维娅哭喊着。

正在这时,传来一阵折树枝的沙沙声。瓦伦丁正穿越曼图亚森林来解救他的心上人。茱莉娅怕他会杀掉普罗特斯,慌忙去帮助她背信弃义的情人。然而,瓦伦丁并没有动他一下,只是对他说:"普罗特斯,非常抱歉,我再也不会相信你了。"

这时普罗特斯才感到愧疚,跪在地上说:"请原谅我!我很悲伤!我在受苦!"

"那么我再次把你当朋友,"宽容的瓦伦丁说,"如果我失去的西尔维娅

喜欢上了你,我保证我会走开,并为你们祝福的。"

茱莉娅听到这些话吓得昏了过去。瓦伦丁把她救醒,问:"你怎么了,小子?"

"我记得,"茱莉娅撒谎道,"我本来要送给西尔维娅小姐一枚戒指,可是我并没有给她。"

"好了,把它给我吧。"普罗特斯说。

她递给他一枚戒指,可是这枚戒指却是普罗特斯离开维罗纳之前送给茱莉娅的。

普罗特斯看着她的手,脸红到耳根。

"你改变主意时,我就改变我的形象。"她说。

"可是我又重新爱上你了。"他说。

就在这时,劫匪们走进来,押着两名战利品——公爵和修里奥爵士。

"住手!"瓦伦丁严厉地喊道,"公爵是无辜的。"

修里奥爵士惊呼:"西尔维娅在这儿,她是我的!"

"敢动她一个手指头,就叫你死!"瓦伦丁说。

"我要是为她冒险才是傻子呢。"修里奥爵士说。

"你这个卑鄙无耻的小人,"公爵说,"瓦伦丁,你是个勇敢的青年,你的流放到此结束。我要召你回去,你可以娶西尔维娅,你配做她的丈夫。"

"谢谢殿下,"深受感动的瓦伦丁说,"可是殿下,我想请您恩准一件事。"

"我准予。"公爵说。

"殿下,请宽恕这些人,并赐予他们活计。实际上他们要比他们的名字好得多。"

"我赦免他们,也赦免你,"公爵说,"以后他们干活会有报酬的。"

"殿下,这个侍从怎么办?"瓦伦丁指着茱莉娅问道。

公爵看了茱莉娅一眼说:"他倒是眉清目秀的。"

"要我说,她不止是眉清目秀。"瓦伦丁笑道。普罗特斯背叛了爱情和友谊,他所受到的唯一惩罚,就是当着大家的面讲述维罗纳的茱莉娅—塞巴斯蒂安的冒险经历。

4. A Midsummer Night's Dream

Titania: The Queen of the Fairies

  Hermia① and Lysander② were lovers; but Hermia's father wished her to marry another man, named Demetrius③.
  Now, in Athens, where they lived, there was a wicked law, by which any girl who refused to marry according to her father's wishes, might be

---

 ① Hermia [ˈhəːmjə] n. 赫米娅（女子名）
 ② Lysander [laiˈsændə] n. 拉山德（男子名）
 ③ Demetrius [diˈmiːtriəs] n. 狄米特律斯（男子名）

put to death. Hermia's father was so angry with her for refusing to do as he wished, that he actually brought her before the Duke of Athens to ask that she might be killed, if she still refused to obey him. The Duke gave her four days to think about it, and, at the end of that time, if she still refused to marry Demetrius, she would have to die.

Lysander of course was nearly mad with grief①, and the best thing to do seemed to him for Hermia to run away to his aunt's house at a place beyond② the reach of that cruel law; and there he would come to her and marry her. But before she started, she told her friend, Helena, what she was going to do.

Helena had been Demetrius' sweetheart long before his marriage with Hermia had been thought of, and being very silly, like all jealous people, she could not see that it was not poor Hermia's fault that Demetrius wished to marry her instead of his own lady, Helena. She knew that if she told Demetrius that Hermia was going, as she was, to the wood outside Athens, he would follow her, "and I can follow him, and at least I shall see him," she said to herself. So she went to him, and betrayed her friend's secret.

Now this wood where Lysander was to meet Hermia, and where the other two had decided to follow them, was full of fairies, as most woods are, if one only had the eyes to see them, and in this wood on this night were the King and Queen of the fairies, Oberon③ and Titania④. Now fairies are very wise people, but now and then they can be quite as foolish as mortal folk. Oberon and Titania, who might have been as happy as the days were long, had thrown away all their joy in a foolish quarrel. They never met without saying disagreeable things to each other, and scolded each other so dreadfully that all their little fairy followers, for fear, would creep into acorn cups and hide them there.

① mad with grief 伤心欲绝
② beyond [bi'jɔnd] prep. 在(到)……较远的一边
③ Oberon ['əubərən] 奥布朗(男子名)
④ Titania [tai'teiniə] n. 提泰尼亚(女子名)

So, instead of keeping one happy Court and dancing all night through in the moonlight as is fairies' use, the King with his attendants wandered through one part of the wood, while the Queen with hers kept state in another. And the cause of all this trouble was a little Indian boy whom Titania had taken to be one of her followers. Oberon wanted the child to follow him and be one of his fairy knights; but the Queen would not give him up.

On this night, in a mossy① moonlit glade, the King and Queen of the fairies met.

"Ill met by moonlight, proud Titania," said the King.

"What! jealous, Oberon?" answered the Queen. "You spoil everything with your quarreling. Come, fairies, let us leave him. I am not friends with him now."

"It rests with you to make up the quarrel," said the King. "Give me that little Indian boy, and I will again be your humble servant and suitor."

"Set your mind at rest," said the Queen. "Your whole fairy kingdom buys not that boy from me. Come, fairies."

And she and her train rode off down the moonbeams②.

"Well, go your ways," said Oberon. "But I'll be even with you before you leave this wood."

Then Oberon called his favorite fairy, Puck. Puck was the spirit of mischief③. He used to slip into the dairies and take the cream away, and get into the churn so that the butter would not come, and turn the beer sour, and lead people out of their way on dark nights and then laugh at them, and tumble people's stools from under them when they were

---

① mossy ['mɔsi] *adj.* 生苔的，青苔状的
② moonbeam ['muːnbiːm] *n.* 月光
③ mischief ['mistʃif] *n.* 恶作剧，淘气

going to sit down, and upset their hot ale① over their chins when they were going to drink.

"Now," said Oberon to this little sprite, "fetch me the flower called Love-in-idleness. The juice of that little purple flower laid on the eyes of those who sleep will make them, when they wake, to love the first thing they see. I will put some of the juice of that flower on my Titania's eyes, and when she wakes she will love the first thing she sees, were it lion, bear, or wolf, or bull, or meddling monkey②, or a busy ape."

While Puck was gone, Demetrius passed through the glade followed by poor Helena, and still she told him how she loved him and reminded him of all his promises, and still he told her that he did not and could not love her, and that his promises were nothing. Oberon was sorry for poor Helena, and when Puck returned with the flower, he bade him follow Demetrius and put some of the juice on his eyes, so that he might love Helena when he woke and looked on her, as much as she loved him. So Puck set off, and wandering through the wood found, not Demetrius, but Lysander, on whose eyes he put the juice; but when Lysander woke, he saw not his own Hermia, but Helena, who was walking through the wood looking for the cruel Demetrius; and directly he saw her, he loved her and left his own lady, under the spell of the purple flower.

When Hermia woke she found Lysander gone, and wandered about the wood trying to find him. Puck went back and told Oberon what he had done, and Oberon soon found that he had made a mistake, and set about③ looking for Demetrius, and having found him, put some of the juice on his eyes. And the first thing Demetrius saw when he woke was also Helena. So now Demetrius and Lysander were both following her through the wood, and it was Hermia's turn to follow her lover as Helena

① ale [eil] *n.* 麦酒
② meddling monkey 捣乱的猴子
③ set about 开始

had done before. The end of it was that Helena and Hermia began to quarrel, and Demetrius and Lysander went off to fight. Oberon was very sorry to see his kind scheme to help these lovers turn out so badly. So he said to Puck—

"These two young men are going to fight. You must overhang the night with drooping fog, and lead them so astray①, that one will never find the other. When they are tired out, they will fall asleep. Then drop this other herb on Lysander's eyes. That will give him his old sight and his old love. Then each man will have the lady who loves him, and they will all think that this has been only a Midsummer Night's Dream. Then when this is done, all will be well with them."

So Puck went and did as he was told, and when the two had fallen asleep without meeting each other, Puck poured the juice on Lysander's eyes, and said:

"When thou wakest,
Thou takest
True delight
In the sight
Of thy former lady's eye:
Jack shall have Jill;
Nought shall go ill."

Meanwhile Oberon found Titania asleep on a bank where grew wild thyme, oxlips, and violets, and woodbine②, musk-roses③ and eglantine④. There Titania always slept a part of the night, wrapped in the enameled skin of a snake. Oberon stooped over her and laid the juice on her eyes, saying:

"What thou seest when thou wake,

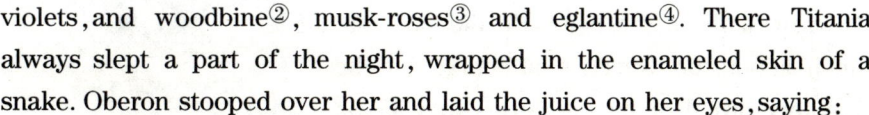

① astray [əs'trei] *adv.* 迷途地，入歧途地
② woodbine ['wudbain] *n.* 忍冬属植物；金银花
③ musk-rose *n.* 麝香蔷薇
④ eglantine ['egləntain] *n.* 野蔷薇

Do it for thy true love take."

Now, it happened that when Titania woke the first thing she saw was a stupid clown, one of a party of players who had come out into the wood to rehearse① their play. This clown had met with Puck, who had clapped an ass's head on his shoulders so that it looked as if it grew there. Directly Titania woke and saw this dreadful monster, she said, "What angel is this? Are you as wise as you are beautiful?"

"If I am wise enough to find my way out of this wood, that's enough for me," said the foolish clown.

"Do not desire to go out of the wood," said Titania. The spell of the love-juice was on her, and to her the clown seemed the most beautiful and delightful creature on all the earth. "I love you," she went on. "Come with me, and I will give you fairies to attend on you."

So she called four fairies, whose names were Peaseblossom, Cobweb, Moth, and Mustardseed.

"You must attend this gentleman," said the Queen. "Feed him with apricots② and dewberries, purple grapes, green figs, and mulberries. Steal honey-bags for him from the bumble-bees③, and with the wings of painted butterflies fan the moonbeams from his sleeping eyes."

"I will," said one of the fairies, and all the others said, "I will."

"Now, sit down with me," said the Queen to the clown, "and let me stroke your dear cheeks, and stick musk-roses in your smooth, sleek head, and kiss your fair large ears, my gentle joy."

"Where's Peaseblossom?" asked the clown with the ass's head. He did not care much about the Queen's affection, but he was very proud of having fairies to wait on him.

"Ready," said Peaseblossom.

---

① rehearse [riˈhəːs] v. 预演,排演
② apricot [ˈeiprikɔt] n. 杏,杏树
③ bumble-bee n. 大黄蜂

"Scratch my head, Peaseblossom," said the clown. "Where's Cobweb?"

"Ready," said Cobweb.

"Kill me," said the clown, "the red bumble-bee on the top of the thistle yonder①, and bring me the honey-bag. Where's Mustardseed?"

"Ready," said Mustardseed.

"Oh, I want nothing," said the clown. "Only just help Cobweb to scratch. I must go to the barber's, for methinks I am marvelous② hairy about the face."

"Would you like anything to eat?" said the fairy Queen.

"I should like some good dry oats," said the clown—for his donkey's head made him desire donkey's food—"and some hay to follow."

"Shall some of my fairies fetch you new nuts from the squirrel's house?" asked the Queen.

"I'd rather have a handful or two of good dried peas," said the clown. "But please don't let any of your people disturb me; I am going to sleep."

Then said the Queen, "And I will wind thee in my arms."

And so when Oberon came along he found his beautiful Queen lavishing③ kisses and endearments④ on a clown with a donkey's head.

And before he released her from the enchantment⑤, he persuaded her to give him the little Indian boy he so much desired to have. Then he took pity on her, and threw some juice of the disenchanting flower on her pretty eyes; and then in a moment she saw plainly the donkey-headed clown she had been loving, and knew how foolish she had been.

Oberon took off the ass's head from the clown, and left him to finish

① yonder ['jɔndə] adj. 更远的
② marvelous ['mɑːvələs] adj. 引起惊异的,不可思议的
③ lavish ['læviʃ] v. 浪费,滥用,慷慨给予
④ endearment [in'diəmənt] n. 亲爱,钟爱
⑤ enchantment [in'tʃɑːntmənt] n. 迷惑

his sleep with his own silly head lying on the thyme and violets.

Thus all was made plain and straight again. Oberon and Titania loved each other more than ever. Demetrius thought of no one but Helena, and Helena had never had any thought of anyone but Demetrius.

As for Hermia and Lysander, they were as loving a couple as you could meet in a day's march, even through a fairy wood.

So the four mortal lovers went back to Athens and were married; and the fairy King and Queen live happily together in that very wood at this very day.

仲夏夜之梦

赫米娅和拉山德是一对情侣,可赫米娅的父亲却要把她许给另外一个叫狄米特律斯的年轻人。

当时,在他们居住的雅典城有一项缺德的法律:要是女儿不按其父的意愿出嫁,可以将她处死。赫米娅违背了她父亲的意愿,她父亲非常生气,就将她带到雅典的公爵面前,说如果女儿仍然不服从他的意愿就要求将其处死。公爵给赫米娅四天的时间考虑,到了最后期限,如果她还是拒绝嫁给狄米特律斯,就将被处死。

拉山德当然伤心欲绝,对他和赫米亚来说最大的希望就是逃亡到他姑妈家。在那里,这个残酷的法律就失去了效力;在那里,他就可以同她走到一起并结为夫妻。可是在走之前,赫米娅将计划告诉了闺中密友海丽娜。

在赫米娅同狄米特律斯这桩被认为愚蠢的错配婚姻发生之前,海丽娜是狄米特律斯的心上人。狄米特律斯不娶她而要娶赫米娅,这并不是可怜的赫米娅的错,而像其他心怀妒忌的人一样,糊涂的海丽娜看不清这一点。她明明知道如果告诉狄米特律斯赫米娅要离开雅典的消息,他定会追她而去。她想:"我就可以跟着他,至少可以看到他了。"于是她把赫米娅要出走的秘密告诉了狄米特律斯。

现在,拉山德要去那个树林子会赫米娅,而另外两个人决定跟踪他们。那个树林子里到处是精灵,像大多树林子一样,在这里你一睁开眼睛就可以看见他们。而在当晚,仙王奥布朗和仙后提泰尼亚就在这个小树林中。精灵们虽然都很聪慧,然而偶尔也会像凡人一样愚蠢。奥布朗和提泰尼亚本可整天快快乐乐地在一起,却莫名其妙地吵了起来,把所有的快乐都抛到了九霄云外。这两个小人儿见面就吵得不可开交,直吵到小精灵们都吓得跑到橡果壳里躲了起来。

在月光皎洁的夜晚,他们没有像往常一样举行夜宴,通宵达旦地跳舞,相反,仙王带着他的随从在树林的一处散步,仙后带着她的随从在另一处散步。这次不快的争吵的原因就是提泰尼亚把一个印度小男孩当作了随从。奥布朗想让这个孩子跟随他成为他的一名精灵骑士;可是仙后就是不愿意将这个小男孩给他。

在这个月光明媚的夜晚,仙王和仙后在青苔空地上碰面了。

"真不巧又在月光下碰见了你,骄傲的提泰尼亚。"仙王说。

"怎么,妒忌鬼,是你吗?奥布朗?"仙后回答说,"你的争吵真的很扫兴,好了,我们走吧,精灵们,我再也不和他好啦。"

"是你先找茬的,"仙王说,"把那个印度小男孩给我,我会再次做你卑贱的仆人和追随者。"

"你还是省省心吧,"仙后说,"你拿整个仙国也别想从我这儿把那个孩子买走。我们走吧,精灵们。"

于是她和她的精灵们滑下月光。

"好,你走你的吧,"奥布朗说,"在你离开树林之前我就把你摆平。"

于是奥布朗把他的心腹小精灵帕克叫了过来。帕克是淘气精灵,他经常钻进奶酪里把奶油拿走,溜进搅乳器里让黄油出不来,让啤酒发酸,在漆黑的夜晚把人引到错路上,然后再嘲笑人家,看到有人要坐下的时候把凳子从那人的屁股下抽出来,看到有人要喝热麦酒时,把麦酒从那人的下巴洒落。

奥布朗对这个小精灵说:"现在去给我摘些叫做'爱懒花'的花。把那种紫色小花的花汁滴在正在睡觉的人的眼睛上,就能让他在醒来时第一眼看到什么就爱上什么。在我的提泰尼亚睡着的时候,我要把那种花的花汁滴在她的眼睛上去,她醒来后第一眼看见的东西,不管是狮子、熊、狼,还是牛、爱捣乱的猴子或忙手忙脚的猩猩,她都会爱上的。"

帕克离开的空儿,狄米特律斯穿过那片空地,可怜的海丽娜跟在后面,温柔地告诉他她有多爱他,让他回忆他往日所有的承诺,而他却说他不爱她并且不能爱她,他的承诺算不了什么。奥布朗很同情可怜的海丽娜,当帕克带着花回来后,奥布朗让他紧跟着狄米特律斯并把一点花汁滴在他眼睛上,这样,等他醒来后就会爱上他看到的海丽娜,正如她深爱着他一样。于是帕克开始在树林中晃荡,他没有找到狄米特律斯,却发现了拉山德,就把花汁

滴在了他的眼睛上;可是,拉山德醒来后看到的不是他的赫米娅,而是满林子寻找狠心的狄米特律斯的海丽娜。在这紫色小花的魔咒下,拉山德一看见海丽娜就爱上了她,并离开了自己的心上人。

赫米娅醒来后发现拉山德不见了,就在树林里四处寻找他。帕克回去对奥布朗讲述了他所做的一切,但奥布朗很快就发现帕克弄错了,就开始寻找狄米特律斯,找到之后就把花汁滴到了他的眼睛上。狄米特律斯醒来第一眼看到的也是海丽娜,于是他和拉山德都跟在海丽娜身后,正如海丽娜以前做的那样,赫米娅开始跟着她的心上人啦。结果海丽娜和赫米娅吵了起来,狄米特律斯和拉山德也要打起来了。看到自己越帮越忙,奥布朗感到很愧疚,于是他对帕克说——

"这两个年轻人要打起来了,你必须让树林起雾并使他们迷路,这样他们就不会找到彼此了。等筋疲力尽的时候他们就会睡着,你再把花汁滴到拉山德的眼睛上,他就会恢复原来的视力并找回旧爱。这样他们俩都会拥有爱着他们的女人,并且认为现在的这一切仅仅是仲夏夜的一个梦而已。等这些都做完了,一切就都会好起来了。"

于是帕克就执行命令去了,这两个年轻人没有找到彼此就睡着了,帕克把花汁滴在拉山德的眼睛上,说:

"等你醒来,
你会尝到
欢乐开怀,
旧爱眼睛
发出光彩:
各找所爱;
错不重来。"

就在这时奥布朗发现提泰尼娅正睡在河畔,周围长满了野麝香草、莲香花和芬芳的紫罗兰,还有金银花、麝香蔷薇和野蔷薇。提泰妮娅晚上总要在这儿睡一阵,她盖着上了釉的蛇皮。奥布朗弯下腰将花汁滴在了她的眼睛上并说道:

"一觉醒来眼睁开,
　所见之人是真爱。"

这时,提泰尼娅醒来了,她第一眼看到了一个傻乎乎的小丑,一个来树林彩排的乐队演员。帕克曾见过这个小丑,也在他的肩膀上放了一个驴头,看起来就像原来长在那儿似的。提泰尼娅醒来后看到这么一个怪物却说:"啊!我看到的是怎样一个天使啊?你的聪明和你的美貌一样超凡脱俗吗?"

"要是我聪明得能走出这个树林子,那我就很知足了。"这个傻乎乎的小丑说。

爱情花汁的魔力起了作用,在她眼里这个小丑就是世界上最帅最令她着迷的人了。"不要走出这个林子,"她温柔地对他说,"我爱你,跟我来,我派精灵伺候你。"

于是,她叫来了4个小精灵,他们的名字分别是:豆花、蛛网、飞蛾和芥籽。

"你们要好好伺候这位可爱的先生,"仙后说,"给他吃杏仁、野草莓、紫葡萄、无花果,还有桑葚。把大黄蜂的蜜囊偷来给他吃,他睡着的时候,要用花蝴蝶的翅膀为他的双眼遮挡月光。"

"是。"其中一个小精灵答道。其他的小精灵也都跟着说:"是。"

仙后对小丑说:"来,和我一起坐在这花床上。让我爱抚你可爱的脸颊,把麝香玫瑰贴在你光滑美丽的头上,再让我亲吻你美丽的大耳朵,我温柔的宝贝。"

"豆花在哪儿?"长着驴头的小丑问。他并不怎么在意仙后对他说的情话,可是对有精灵服侍他感到很骄傲。

"在这儿。"豆花说。

"替俺挠挠头,豆花,"小丑说,"蛛网在哪儿?"

"在这儿。"蛛网说。

小丑说:"给我把那边那棵蓟上红色的大黄蜂杀死,把蜜囊给我拿来。芥籽在哪儿?"

"在这儿。"芥籽说。

"噢,没什么,"小丑说,"你只要帮豆花替俺挠挠头就行啦。我想我该理发了,觉得脸上怪毛髭髭的。"

"你想吃点什么吗?"仙后问。

"我想吃些上好的干燕麦,"小丑说——他戴上了驴头就有了驴的胃口,"再来些干草吧。"

"让我的精灵们从松鼠窝里给你拿些干果来好吗?"仙后问。

"我真想吃上一两把干豌豆,"小丑说,"我想睡觉了,别让你手下的人打扰我。"

"那我就把你搂在怀里吧。"仙后接着说。

正在这时,奥布朗走了过来,看到他美丽的仙后正抱着一个长着驴头的小丑一阵猛亲。

在为仙后解除魔法之前,奥布朗劝说她把他期待已久的印度小男孩给他,然后就怜悯起仙后来,他把解除魔咒的汁液滴在她美丽的眼睛上;霎时间,仙后发现自己竟然爱上了一个驴头小丑,感到自己愚蠢至极。

奥布朗把驴头从小丑身上拿了下来,还原了他自己愚蠢的脑袋,让他继续躺在百里香和紫罗兰上睡觉。

于是一切又变得清晰明了,奥布朗和提泰尼亚言归于好,并且比往日更相亲相爱。狄米特律斯眼里只有海丽娜,而海丽娜除了他也没有爱上过其他人。

至于拉山德和赫米娅,无论你在行走中,还是在仙林里,你都会遇见他们,那一对恩爱甜蜜的情侣。

于是这两对情侣一起回到雅典并举行了婚礼;从那一天起,仙王和仙后也在小树林里生活得甜甜蜜蜜。

5. The Merchant of Venice

Antonio Signs the Bond

Antonio① was a rich and prosperous② merchant of Venice. His ships were on nearly every sea, and he traded with Portugal③, with Mexico, with England, and with India. Although proud of his riches, he was very generous④ with them, and delighted to use them in relieving⑤ the wants of his friends, among whom his relation, Bassanio⑥, held the first place.

Now Bassanio, like many other gay and gallant⑦ gentlemen, was

~~~~~~~~~~~~~~~~~~~~

① Antonio [æn'təuniəu] n. 安东尼奥(男子名)
② prosperous ['prɔspərəs] adj. 繁荣的,富裕的
③ Portugal ['pɔːtjugəl] n. 葡萄牙
④ generous ['dʒenərəs] adj. 慷慨的,大方的
⑤ relieve [ri'liːv] v. 减轻,解除,援救
⑥ Bassanio [bə'sɑːniəu] n. 巴萨尼奥(男子名)
⑦ gallant ['gælənt] adj. 英勇的,豪侠的

reckless and extravagant①, and finding that he had not only come to the end of his fortune, but was also unable to pay his creditors, he went to Antonio for further help.

"To you, Antonio," he said, "I owe the most in money and in love, and I have thought of a plan to pay everything I owe if you will but help me."

"Say what I can do, and it shall be done," answered his friend.

Then said Bassanio, "In Belmont is a lady richly left, and from all quarters of the globe renowned② suitors come to woo her, not only because she is rich, but because she is beautiful and good as well. She looked on me with such favor when last we met, that I feel sure that I should win her away from all rivals for her love had I but the means to go to Belmont, where she lives."

"All my fortunes," said Antonio, "are at sea, and so I have no ready money; but luckily my credit is good in Venice, and I will borrow for you what you need."

There was living in Venice at this time a rich money-lender, named Shylock③. Antonio despised and disliked this man very much, and treated him with the greatest harshness④ and scorn. He would thrust him, like a cur, over his threshold⑤, and would even spit on him. Shylock submitted to all these indignities⑥ with a patient shrug; but deep in his heart he cherished⑦ a desire for revenge on the rich, smug⑧ merchant. For Antonio both hurt

① extravagant [iks'trævəgənt] adj. 奢侈的，浪费的
② renowned [ri'naund] adj. 有名的，有声誉的
③ Shylock ['ʃailɔk] n. 夏洛克（男子名）
④ harshness [haːʃnis] n. 粗糙的事物
⑤ threshold ['θreʃhəuld] n. 门槛
⑥ indignity [in'digniti] n. 轻蔑，侮辱
⑦ cherish ['tʃeriʃ] v. 珍爱，怀抱
⑧ smug [smʌg] adj. 自鸣得意的

his pride and injured his business. "But for him," thought Shylock, "I should be richer by half a million ducats. On the market place, and wherever he can, he denounces① the rate of interest I charge, and—worse than that—he lends out money freely."

So when Bassanio came to him to ask for a loan of three thousand ducats to Antonio for three months, Shylock hid his hatred, and turning to Antonio, said: "Harshly as you have treated me, I would be friends with you and have your love. So I will lend you the money and charge you no interest. But, just for fun, you shall sign a bond in which it shall be agreed that if you do not repay me in three months' time, then I shall have the right to a pound of your flesh, to be cut from what part of your body I choose."

"No," cried Bassanio to his friend, "you shall run no such risk for me."

"Why, fear not," said Antonio, "my ships will be home a month before the time. I will sign the bond."

Thus Bassanio was furnished with the means to go to Belmont, there to woo② the lovely Portia③. The very night he started, the money-lender's pretty daughter, Jessica, ran away from her father's house with her lover, and she took with her from her father's hoards some bags of ducats and precious stones. Shylock's grief and anger were terrible to see. His love for her changed to hate. "I would she were dead at my feet and the jewels in her ear," he cried. His only comfort now was in hearing of the serious losses which had befallen Antonio, some of whose ships were wrecked. "Let him look to his bond," said Shylock, "let him look to his bond."

Meanwhile Bassanio had reached Belmont, and had visited the fair Portia. He found, as he had told Antonio, that the rumor of her wealth and beauty had drawn to her suitors from far and near. But to all of them

---

① denounce [di'nauns] v. 公开指责,公然抨击,谴责
② woo [wuː] v. 求爱,追求
③ Portia ['pɔːʃiə] n. 波西娅(女子名)

Portia had but one reply. She would only accept that suitor who would pledge himself to abide by① the terms of her father's will. These were conditions that frightened away many an ardent② wooer. For he who would win Portia's heart and hand, had to guess which of three caskets③ held her portrait. If he guessed aright④, then Portia would be his bride; if wrong, then he was bound by oath never to reveal which casket he chose, never to marry, and to go away at once.

The caskets were of gold, silver, and lead. The gold one bore this inscription⑤: "Who chooseth me shall gain what many men desire"; the silver one had this: "Who chooseth me shall get as much as he deserves"; while on the lead one were these words: "Who chooseth me must give and hazard all he hath." The Prince of Morocco, as brave as he was black, was among the first to submit to this test. He chose the gold casket, for he said neither base lead nor silver could contain her picture. So he chose the gold casket, and found inside the likeness of what many men desire—death.

After him came the haughty Prince of Aragon, and saying, "Let me have what I deserve—surely I deserve the lady," he chose the silver one, and found inside a fool's head. "Did I deserve no more than a fool's head?" he cried.

Then at last came Bassanio, and Portia would have delayed him from making his choice for very fear of his choosing wrong. For she loved him dearly, even as he loved her. "But," said Bassanio, "let me choose at once, for, as I am, I live upon the rack."

Then Portia bade her servants to bring music and play while her gallant lover made his choice. And Bassanio took the oath and walked up to the caskets—the musicians playing softly the while. "Mere outward

---

① abide by 坚持,遵守
② ardent [ˈɑːdənt] *adj.* 热心的,热情洋溢的
③ casket [ˈkɑːskit] *n.* 首饰盒,匣子
④ aright [əˈrait] *adv.* 正确地
⑤ inscription [inˈskripʃən] *n.* 题字,碑铭

show," he said, "is to be despised. The world is still deceived with ornament①, and so no gaudy② gold or shining silver for me. I choose the lead casket; joy be the consequence!" And opening it, he found fair Portia's portrait inside, and he turned to her and asked if it were true that she was his.

"Yes," said Portia, "I am yours, and this house is yours, and with them I give you this ring, from which you must never part."

And Bassanio, saying that he could hardly speak for joy, found words to swear that he would never part with the ring while he lived.

Then suddenly all his happiness was dashed with sorrow, for messengers came from Venice to tell him that Antonio was ruined, and that Shylock demanded from the Duke the fulfilment of the bond, under which he was entitled to a pound of the merchant's flesh. Portia was as grieved as Bassanio to hear of the danger which threatened his friend.

"First," she said, "take me to church and make me your wife, and then go to Venice at once to help your friend. You shall take with you money enough to pay his debt twenty times over."

But when her newly-made husband had gone, Portia went after him, and arrived in Venice disguised as a lawyer, and with an introduction from a celebrated lawyer Bellario, whom the Duke of Venice had called in to decide the legal questions raised by Shylock's claim to a pound of Antonio's flesh. When the Court met, Bassanio offered Shylock twice the money borrowed, if he would withdraw his claim. But the money-lender's only answer was—

"If every ducat in six thousand ducats, were in six parts, and every part a ducat, I would not draw them,—I would have my bond."

It was then that Portia arrived in her disguise, and not even her own husband knew her. The Duke gave her welcome on account of the great Bellario's introduction, and left the settlement of the case to her. Then in

---

① ornament ['ɔːnəmənt] n. 装饰物
② gaudy ['gɔːdi] adj. 绚丽的, 华而不实的

noble words she bade Shylock have mercy①. But he was deaf to her entreaties②. "I will have the pound of flesh," was his reply.

"What have you to say?" asked Portia of the merchant.

"But little," he answered;"I am armed and well prepared."

"The Court awards you a pound of Antonio's flesh," said Portia to the money-lender.

"Most righteous judge!" cried Shylock. "A sentence: come, prepare."

"Tarry a little. This bond gives you no right to Antonio's blood, only to his flesh. If, then, you spill a drop of his blood, all your property will be forfeited③ to the State. Such is the Law."

And Shylock, in his fear, said, "Then I will take Bassanio's offer."

"No," said Portia sternly④, "you shall have nothing but your bond. Take your pound of flesh, but remember, that if you take more or less, even by the weight of a hair, you will lose your property and your life."

Shylock now grew very much frightened. "Give me my three thousand ducats that I lent him, and let him go."

Bassanio would have paid it to him, but said Portia, "No! He shall have nothing but his bond."

"You, a foreigner," she added, "have sought to take the life of a Venetian citizen, and thus by the Venetian law, your life and goods are forfeited. Down, therefore, and beg mercy of the Duke."

Thus were the tables turned, and no mercy would have been shown to Shylock had it not been for Antonio. As it was, the money-lender forfeited half his fortune to the State, and he had

---

① mercy ['məːsi] n. 仁慈,宽恕
② entreaty [in'triːti] n. 恳求,乞求
③ forfeit ['fɔːfit] v. 没收,丧失
④ sternly ['stəːnli] adv. 严厉地,苛刻地

to settle the other half on his daughter's husband, and with this he had to be content.

Bassanio, in his gratitude① to the clever lawyer, was induced to part with the ring his wife had given him, and with which he had promised never to part, and when on his return to Belmont he confessed as much to Portia, she seemed very angry, and vowed she would not be friends with him until she had her ring again. But at last she told him that it was she who, in the disguise of the lawyer, had saved his friend's life, and got the ring from him. So Bassanio was forgiven, and made happier than ever, to know how rich a prize he had drawn in the lottery of the caskets.

威尼斯商人

安东尼奥是威尼斯一位很富有的商人,他的商船几乎遍布每个海域,同他有生意往来的国家有葡萄牙、墨西哥、英国,还有印度。尽管他以自己的财富而自豪,但是他并不吝于钱财,经常为需要救济的朋友慷慨解囊,接受他救济的人中首数他的好友巴萨尼奥了。

如其他豪爽而放纵的绅士一样,巴萨尼奥生性鲁莽,生活奢靡,他发现自己不仅把家产折腾光了,而且还无力偿还借款,于是他就向安东尼奥求助。

"安东尼奥,"他说,"我欠你的钱财和人情最多,如果你愿意帮助我的话,我已经想好了一个能够偿还你一切的计划。"

"说说我能做些什么,我会尽力做到。"他的朋友回答说。

巴萨尼奥接着说:"在贝尔蒙有一位小姐,她的父亲去世时留给她一大笔遗产。众多有名望的求婚者从四面八方涌来,不仅仅因为她富有,而且因为她美丽善良。我们上一次见面时,她含情脉脉地看着我,我想我应该能胜出其他竞争对手而博取她的芳心,可我却没有去贝尔蒙——她住的地方——的盘缠。"

"我所有的钱财,"安东尼奥说,"都在船上,所以我手上没有现钱,但幸运的是我在威尼斯的信誉很好,我会为你借些钱。"

那时,在威尼斯有个很有钱的放高利贷的人,叫夏洛克。安东尼奥不喜

---

① gratitude [ˈɡrætitjuːd] n. 感谢的心情

欢并且很鄙视这个人,对他很刻薄并经常嘲讽、挖苦他。他会把夏洛克像野狗一样扔出家门,甚至还会向他吐唾沫。对于这些侮辱,夏洛克只是耸耸肩忍受着;可是在他心里暗暗滋生了要报复这个财大气粗、自鸣得意的商人的念头。因为安东尼奥既伤害了他的自尊,又损害了他的生意。"对他来说,"夏洛克心想,"再有五十万达克特我就会更富有啦。在市场上,无论他走到哪儿都会谴责我索取利息,而且——更糟糕的是——他借钱给别人时竟然不收利息。"

当巴萨尼奥来要他向安东尼奥贷三千达克特,为时三个月时,夏洛克假惺惺地对安东尼奥说:"尽管往日你对我很刻薄,我还是愿意和你做朋友,获得你的友谊,所以我把钱借给你并不要你的利息。但是,为了好玩,让我们签一个契约,如果三个月后你不能把钱还给我,那么我就有权从你身上割下一磅肉,我选择哪块就割哪块。"

"不要,"巴萨尼奥对他朋友哭喊着说,"你不要为我冒险。"

"没什么,别害怕,"安东尼奥说,"我的商船会在这个期限之前一月抵达。我签约。"

于是,巴萨尼奥有了足够的盘缠去贝尔蒙,到那里向美丽的波西娅求婚。在他出发当晚,放贷人夏洛克美丽的女儿杰西卡和她的情人也从家里逃走,随身带走了她父亲秘藏的几袋钱和宝石。夏洛克悲愤到极点,对女儿的爱即刻变成了仇恨。"我宁愿她死在我的脚下,珠宝塞满她的耳朵。"他咆哮着说。现在他唯一的安慰就是听到安东尼奥的一些商船失事,遭受到惨重损失的消息。"让他遵守合约,"夏洛克说,"让他遵守合约。"

同时,巴萨尼奥已经抵达贝尔蒙,见到了美丽的波西娅。正如他告诉安东尼奥的那样,他发现有关她的财富和美貌的传言已经吸引了来自四面八方的求婚者。对他们所有的人波西娅只有一种回答,那就是,她只接受那位保证遵守她父亲遗言的追求者。这些条件吓跑了许多狂热的求爱者。因为条件是:追求者若想娶波西娅为妻,就必须猜中三个匣子中哪个里面有波西娅的画像。如果他猜对了,波西娅就成为他的新娘;如果错了,就依照他发过的誓言,永远不能说出他选中的是哪个匣子,不但要立即离开而且永远不能结婚。

这三个匣子分别是金匣子、银匣子和铅匣子。金匣子上刻着一句话:"谁选了我谁就会获得很多人期望得到的东西。"银匣子上写着:"谁选了我谁就会获得他应得到的东西。"铅匣子上写着:"谁选了我谁就将会失去他拥有的一切。"勇敢的摩洛哥亲王是第一个面对这个考验的人。他选择了金匣子,因为他说那个廉价的铅匣子和银匣子都不配盛放波西娅的画像。于是他选择了金匣子,结果,他发现里面有很多人期望的东西——死亡。

在他之后是傲慢的阿拉贡亲王,他说:"让我拥有我应该得到的——当然,我应该得到的正是这位美丽的小姐。"他选择了银匣子,发现里面有个白痴的头。"难道我应该得到的就是这个白痴的头吗?"他哭喊着。

然后轮到巴萨尼奥了,波西娅害怕她选错,想拖延一下时间。正如他爱着她一样,波西娅也深爱着巴萨尼奥。"可是,"巴萨尼奥说,"让我立即做出选择吧,现在对我来说,就像生活在肢刑架上。"

于是波西娅让仆人拿来乐器,在她勇敢的情人做选择的时候为他演奏。巴萨尼奥立下誓言,然后走到匣子面前——轻柔的音乐响了起来。"我轻视外表绚丽的东西,"他说,"世人仍被外表华丽的东西所迷惑,华而不实的金匣子还有闪闪发光的银匣子都不是为我准备的。所以我选择铅匣子,但愿结果令人高兴!"他打开匣子,看到波西娅的画像就在里面,然后转向她问她是否真的属于他了。

"是的,"波西娅说,"我是你的,这所房子也是你的,除了这些我还要把这枚戒指给你,你绝不能与它分开。"

巴萨尼奥高兴得几乎说不出话来了,发誓说只要他还活着,就不会把戒指取下来。

可是紧接着,他所有的快乐一下子被悲伤击碎了,因为就在那时从威尼斯传来消息说安东尼奥出事了,夏洛克向公爵要求安东尼奥履行合约,要从这个商人身上割下一磅肉。听说巴萨尼奥的朋友遇到了这样的危险,波西娅和巴萨尼奥一样伤心难过。

"首先,"她说,"带我去教堂举行婚礼,然后你马上回威尼斯去救你的朋友。你可以带上比这笔债务多20倍的钱。"

当新婚丈夫离开之后,波西娅随后追了过去。到了威尼斯,她假扮成一名律师,带着著名律师培拉里奥的一封介绍信,公爵曾向培拉里奥咨询过有关夏洛克向安东尼奥索取一磅肉的案子。开庭时,巴萨尼奥说假如夏洛克收回他的无理要求,他会偿还他两倍于贷款的钱。可这个放高利贷的人却说——

"即使这六千达克特里的每一达克特都可以分成六份,每一份又都可以变成一达克特,我也不要他们,我只要照约处罚。"

正在那时,乔扮成律师的波西娅赶到了,甚至连她自己的丈夫也没有认出她。由于大律师培拉里奥的介绍,公爵热情地欢迎了她,然后就将案子交

给她处理。波西娅好言好语地请求夏洛克仁慈一些。但是对于她的恳求,夏洛克置若罔闻。"我就想要一磅肉。"他回答说。

"你还有什么要说的?"波西娅向商人问道。

"没有,"安东尼奥回答说,"我已经准备好了。"

"法庭准许你割安东尼奥一磅肉。"波西娅对放贷人说。

"这是最公正的判决啊!"夏洛克呼喊到。"准备好,开始执刑。"

"等一下。这个合约只给你索取肉的权利,但是你没有权利要他的血。那么,如果你让他流了一滴血,你的财产就要被全部没收并上缴给政府。这是法律规定的。"

听到这句话,夏洛克感到害怕了,说:"那么我就接受巴萨尼奥给我的那些钱吧。"

"不行,"波西娅严厉地说,"除了履行合约,你别无选择。割你的那磅肉吧,记住,如果你割多或者是割少了,分量哪怕差了一丝一毫,也要没收你的财产,并处你死罪。"

这时夏洛克越来越害怕了:"还给我借给他的三千达克特,我放他走。"

巴萨尼奥正要把钱给夏洛克,可是波西娅却说:"不行!除了履行合约,他别无选择。"

"你这个异乡人,"她补充说,"谋设诡计,试图将一位威尼斯居民置于死地,按照威尼斯法律,你的小命和财产都要被没收掉。跪下,向公爵求情吧。"

局势就这样扭转了,要不是安东尼奥,就不会对夏洛克手下留情。事实上,这个放贷人把他的一半财产上交给了国家,另一半留给了他的女婿,事情发展到这个地步,他已经知足了。

巴萨尼奥,为了感谢这位聪明的律师,不得不将妻子送给他的戒指取下来给他,尽管他曾许诺不会把它取下。回到贝尔蒙后他将一切说给波西娅听,她看起来很生气的样子,并发誓说如果他不把戒指要回来,就永远不会对他好了。可是到了最后,她告诉丈夫说是她假扮了律师救了他朋友的性命,并从他那里拿到了戒指。因此,巴萨尼奥得到了原谅,当他意识到自己选择了那个小匣子却得到了这么大的奖励,感到更幸福了。

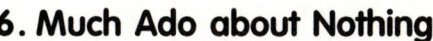

6. Much Ado about Nothing

Hero and Ursula

In Sicily is a town called Messina①, which is the scene of a curious storm that raged② several hundred years ago.

It began with sunshine. Don Pedro③, Prince of Aragon④, in Spain, had gained so complete a victory over his foes that the very land whence they came is forgotten. Feeling happy and playful after the fatigues⑤ of war, Don Pedro came for a holiday to Messina, and in his suite⑥ were his

---

① Messina [meˈsinə] n. 墨西拿(意大利西西里岛东北部的一个城市)
② rage [reidʒ] v. 大怒,狂吹
③ Don Pedro [dɔn ˈpeidrəu] n. 唐·彼德罗(男子名)
④ Aragon [ˈærəgɔn] n. 阿拉贡(古代西班牙东北部的一个地域和前王国)
⑤ fatigue [fəˈtiːg] n. 疲乏,疲劳
⑥ suite [swiːt] n. 随员

stepbrother Don John and two young Italian lords, Benedick① and Claudio②.

Benedick was a merry chatterbox③, who had determined to live a bachelor. Claudio, on the other hand, no sooner arrived at Messina than he fell in love with Hero, the daughter of Leonato, Governor of Messina.

One July day, a perfumer④ called Borachio was burning dried lavender⑤ in a musty⑥ room in Leonato's house, when the sound of conversation floated through the open window.

"Give me your candid opinion of Hero," Claudio, asked, and Borachio settled himself for comfortable listening.

"Too short and brown for praise," was Benedick's reply; "but alter her color or height, and you spoil her."

"In my eyes she is the sweetest of women," said Claudio.

"Not in mine," retorted Benedick, "and I have no need for glasses. She is like the last day of December compared with the first of May if you set her beside her cousin. Unfortunately, the Lady Beatrice is a fury⑦."

Beatrice was Leonato's niece. She amused herself by saying witty and severe things about Benedick, who called her Dear Lady Disdain. She was wont to⑧ say that she was born under a dancing star, and could not therefore be dull.

Claudio and Benedick were still talking when Don Pedro came up and said good-humoredly, "Well, gentlemen, what's the

① Benedick ['benidik] n. 培尼迪克(男子名)
② Claudio ['klɔːdiəu] n. 克劳迪奥(男子名)
③ chatterbox ['tʃætəbɔks] n. 喋喋不休者,唠叨的人
④ perfumer [pəːˈfjuːmə] n. 香料商
⑤ lavender ['lævində] n. 薰衣草花,淡紫色
⑥ musty ['mʌsti] adj. 发霉的,有霉味的
⑦ fury ['fjuəri] n. 狂怒,狂暴
⑧ be wont to 习惯

secret?"

"I am longing," answered Benedick, "for your Grace to command me to tell."

"I charge you, then, on your allegiance① to tell me," said Don Pedro, falling in with his humor.

"I can be as dumb as a mute," apologized Benedick to Claudio, "but his Grace commands my speech." To Don Pedro he said, "Claudio is in love with Hero, Leonato's short daughter."

Don Pedro was pleased, for he admired Hero and was fond of Claudio. When Benedick had departed, he said to Claudio, "Be steadfast in your love for Hero, and I will help you to win her. Tonight her father gives a masquerade②, and I will pretend I am Claudio, and tell her how Claudio loves her, and if she be pleased, I will go to her father and ask his consent to your union."

Most men like to do their own wooing, but if you fall in love with a Governor's only daughter, you are fortunate if you can trust a prince to plead③ for you.

Claudio then was fortunate, but he was unfortunate as well, for he had an enemy who was outwardly a friend. This enemy was Don Pedro's stepbrother Don John, who was jealous of Claudio because Don Pedro preferred him to Don John.

It was to Don John that Borachio came with the interesting conversation which he had overheard.

"I shall have some fun at that masquerade myself," said Don John when Borachio ceased speaking.

On the night of the masquerade, Don Pedro, masked and pretending he was Claudio, asked Hero if he might walk with her.

They moved away together, and Don John went up to Claudio and said, "Signor Benedick, I believe?" "The same," fibbed Claudio.

---

① allegiance [əˈliːdʒəns] n. 忠贞,效忠
② masquerade [ˌmæskəˈreid] n. 化装舞会
③ plead [pliːd] v. 辩护,恳求

"I should be much obliged then," said Don John, "if you would use your influence with my brother to cure him of① his love for Hero. She is beneath him in rank."

"How do you know he loves her?" inquired Claudio.

"I heard him swear his affection," was the reply, and Borachio chimed② in with, "So did I too."

Claudio was then left to himself, and his thought was that his Prince had betrayed him. "Farewell, Hero," he muttered; "I was a fool to trust to an agent."

Meanwhile Beatrice and Benedick (who was masked) were having a brisk exchange of opinions.

"Did Benedick ever make you laugh?" asked she.

"Who is Benedick?" he inquired.

"A Prince's jester," replied Beatrice, and she spoke so sharply that "I would not marry her," he declared afterwards, "if her estate were the Garden of Eden."

But the principal speaker at the masquerade was neither Beatrice nor Benedick. It was Don Pedro, who carried out his plan to the letter, and brought the light back to Claudio's face in a twinkling, by appearing before him with Leonato and Hero, and saying, "Claudio, when would you like to go to church?"

"Tomorrow," was the prompt③ answer. "Time goes on crutches till I marry Hero."

"Give her a week, my dear son," said Leonato, and Claudio's heart thumped with joy.

"And now," said the amiable Don Pedro, "we must find a wife for Signor Benedick. It is a task for Hercules."

---

① cure sb. of 把某人治愈
② chime [tʃaim] v. 鸣，打，和谐
③ prompt [prɔmpt] adj. 敏捷的，迅速的

"I will help you," said Leonato, "if I have to sit up ten nights."

Then Hero spoke. "I will do what I can, my lord, to find a good husband for Beatrice."

Thus, with happy laughter, ended the masquerade.

Borachio cheered up Don John by laying a plan before him with which he was confident he could persuade both Claudio and Don Pedro that Hero was a fickle① girl who had two strings to her bow. Don John agreed to this plan of hate.

Don Pedro, on the other hand, had devised a cunning plan of love. "If," he said to Leonato, "we pretend, when Beatrice is near enough to overhear us, that Benedick is pining for her love, she will pity him, see his good qualities, and love him. And if, when Benedick thinks we don't know he is listening, we say how sad it is that the beautiful Beatrice should be in love with a heartless scoffer② like Benedick, he will certainly be on his knees before her in a week or less."

So one day, when Benedick was reading in a summer-house③, Claudio sat down outside it with Leonato, and said, "Your daughter told me something about a letter she wrote."

"Letter!" exclaimed Leonato. "She will get up twenty times in the night and write goodness knows what. But once Hero peeped, and saw the words 'Benedick and Beatrice' on the sheet, and then Beatrice tore it up."

"Hero told me," said Claudio, "that she cried, 'O sweet Benedick!'"

Benedick was touched to the core by this improbable④ story, which he was vain enough to believe. "She is fair and good," he said to himself. "I must not seem proud. I feel that I love her. People will laugh, of course; but their paper bullets will do me no harm."

At this moment Beatrice came to the summer-house, and said,

---

① fickle [ˈfɪkl] adj. (在感情等方面)变幻无常的，浮躁的
② scoffer [ˈskɔfə] n. 嘲笑者
③ summer-house n. 凉亭
④ improbable [imˈprɔbəbl] adj. 不可能的

"Against my will, I have come to tell you that dinner is ready."

"Fair Beatrice, I thank you," said Benedick.

"I took no more pains to come than you take pains to thank me," was the rejoinder①, intended to freeze him.

But it did not freeze him. It warmed him. The meaning he squeezed out of her rude speech was that she was delighted to come to him.

Hero, who had undertaken the task of melting the heart of Beatrice, took no trouble to seek an occasion. She simply said to her maid Margaret one day, "Run into the parlor and whisper to Beatrice that Ursula and I are talking about her in the orchard."

Having said this, she felt as sure that Beatrice would overhear what was meant for her ears as if she had made an appointment with her cousin.

In the orchard was a bower, screened from the sun by honeysuckles②, and Beatrice entered it a few minutes after Margaret had gone on her errand③.

"But are you sure," asked Ursula, who was one of Hero's attendants, "that Benedick loves Beatrice so devotedly?"

"So say the Prince and my betrothed④," replied Hero, "and they wished me to tell her, but I said, 'No! Let Benedick get over it.'"

"Why did you say that?"

"Because Beatrice is unbearably proud. Her eyes sparkle⑤ with disdain and scorn. She is too conceited to love. I should not like to see her making game of poor

---

① rejoinder [ri'dʒɔində] *n.* 反驳
② honeysuckle ['hʌnisʌk(ə)l] *n.* 金银花
③ errand ['erənd] *n.* 差事,差使
④ betrothed [bi'trəuðd] *n.* 已订婚者; *adj.* 订婚了的
⑤ sparkle ['spɑːkl] *v.* 发火花,(使)闪耀

Benedick's love. I would rather see Benedick waste away like a covered fire."

"I don't agree with you," said Ursula. "I think your cousin is too clear-sighted① not to see the merits of Benedick."

"He is the one man in Italy, except Claudio." said Hero.

The talkers then left the orchard, and Beatrice, excited and tender, stepped out of the summer-house, saying to herself, "Poor dear Benedick, be true to me, and your love shall tame this wild heart of mine."

We now return to the plan of hate.

The night before the day fixed for Claudio's wedding, Don John entered a room in which Don Pedro and Claudio were conversing, and asked Claudio if he intended to be married tomorrow.

"You know he does!" said Don Pedro.

"He may know differently," said Don John, "when he has seen what I will show him if he will follow me."

They followed him into the garden; and they saw a lady leaning out of② Hero's window talking love to Borachio.

Claudio thought the lady was Hero, and said, "I will shame her for it tomorrow!" Don Pedro thought she was Hero, too; but she was not Hero; she was Margaret.

Don John chuckled noiselessly when Claudio and Don Pedro quitted the garden; he gave Borachio a purse containing a thousand ducats.

The money made Borachio feel very gay③, and when he was walking in the street with his friend Conrade, he boasted of his wealth and the

① clear-sighted [ˈkliəˈsaitid] adj. 目明的，聪明的，目光锐利的
② lean out 探身出去
③ gay [gei] adj. 快乐的

giver, and told what he had done.

A watchman overheard them, and thought that a man who had been paid a thousand ducats for villainy was worth taking in charge. He therefore arrested Borachio and Conrade, who spent the rest of the night in prison.

Before noon of the next day half the aristocrats in Messina were at church. Hero thought it was her wedding day, and she was there in her wedding dress, no cloud on her pretty face or in her frank and shining eyes.

The priest was Friar Francis.

Turning to Claudio, he said, "You come hither, my lord, to marry this lady?"

"No!" contradicted Claudio.

Leonato thought he was quibbling over① grammar. "You should have said, Friar," said he, "'You come to be married to her.'"

Friar Francis turned to Hero. "Lady," he said, "you come hither to be married to this Count?"

"I do," replied Hero.

"If either of you know any impediment② to this marriage, I charge you to utter it," said the Friar.

"Do you know of any, Hero?" asked Claudio.

"None," said she.

"Know you of any, Count?" demanded the Friar.

"I dare reply for him, 'None'," said Leonato.

Claudio exclaimed bitterly, "O! what will not men dare say!

① quibble over 诡辩，争论
② impediment [imˈpedimənt] n. 妨碍，阻碍，障碍物

Father," he continued, "will you give me your daughter?"

"As freely," replied Leonato, "as God gave her to me."

"And what can I give you," asked Claudio, "which is worthy of this gift?"

"Nothing," said Don Pedro, "unless you give the gift back to the giver."

"Sweet Prince, you teach me," said Claudio. "There, Leonato, take her back."

These brutal① words were followed by others which flew from Claudio, Don Pedro and Don John.

The church seemed no longer sacred. Hero took her own part as long as she could, then she swooned②. All her persecutors left the church, except her father, who was befooled by the accusations③ against her, and cried, "Hence from her! Let her die!"

But Friar Francis saw Hero blameless with his clear eyes that probed the soul. "She is innocent," he said, "a thousand signs have told me so."

Hero revived under his kind gaze④. Her father, flurried and angry, knew not what to think, and the Friar said, "They have left her as one dead with shame. Let us pretend that she is dead until the truth is declared, and slander⑤ turns to remorse⑥."

"The Friar advises well," said Benedick. Then Hero was led away into a retreat, and Beatrice and Benedick remained alone in the church.

Benedick knew she had been weeping bitterly and long. "Surely I do believe your fair cousin is wronged," he said. She still wept.

"Is it not strange," asked Benedick, gently, "that I love nothing in the world as well as you?"

---

① brutal ['bru:tl] *adj.* 残忍的，兽性的
② swoon [swu:n] *v.* 昏晕，惊讶
③ accusation [ækju(:)'zeiʃən] *n.* 谴责，指控
④ gaze [geiz] *v.* 盯，凝视
⑤ slander ['slɑ:ndə] *n.* 诽谤
⑥ remorse [ri'mɔ:s] *n.* 懊悔，自责

"It were as possible for me to say I loved nothing as well as you," said Beatrice, "but I do not say it. I am sorry for my cousin."

"Tell me what to do for her," said Benedick.

"Kill Claudio."

"Ha! not for the wide world," said Benedick.

"Your refusal kills me," said Beatrice. "Farewell."

"Enough! I will challenge him," cried Benedick.

During this scene Borachio and Conrade were in prison. There they were examined by a constable① called Dogberry.

The watchman gave evidence to the effect that Borachio had said that he had received a thousand ducats for conspiring against Hero.

Leonato was not present at this examination, but he was nevertheless now thoroughly convinced of Hero's innocence. He played the part of bereaved father very well, and when Don Pedro and Claudio called on him in a friendly way, he said to the Italian, "You have slandered my child to death, and I challenge you to combat."

"I cannot fight an old man," said Claudio.

"You could kill a girl," sneered Leonato, and Claudio crimsoned.

Hot words grew from hot words, and both Don Pedro and Claudio were feeling scorched② when Leonato left the room and Benedick entered.

"The old man," said Claudio, "was like to have snapped my nose off."

"You are a villain!" said Benedick, shortly. "Fight me when and with what weapon you please, or I call you a coward."

Claudio was astounded③, but said, "I'll meet you. Nobody shall say I can't carve a calf's head."

Benedick smiled, and as it was time for Don Pedro to receive officials, the Prince sat down in a chair of state and prepared his mind for

---

① constable ['kʌnstəbl] n. 治安官
② scorch [skɔːtʃ] v. 烧焦,枯萎
③ astound [əs'taund] v. 使惊骇,使大吃一惊

justice.

The door soon opened to admit Dogberry and his prisoners.

"What offence," said Don Pedro, "are these men charged with?"

Borachio thought the moment a happy one for making a clean breast of it. He laid the whole blame on Don John, who had disappeared. "The lady Hero being dead," he said, "I desire nothing but the reward of a murderer."

Claudio heard with anguish① and deep repentance②.

Upon the re-entrance of Leonato he said to him, "This slave makes clear your daughter's innocence. Choose your revenge."

"Leonato," said Don Pedro, humbly, "I am ready for any penance③ you may impose."

"I ask you both, then," said Leonato, "to proclaim④ my daughter's innocence, and to honor her tomb by singing her praise before it. As for you, Claudio, I have this to say: my brother has a daughter so like Hero that she might be a copy of her. Marry her, and my vengeful⑤ feelings die."

"Noble sir," said Claudio, "I am yours." Claudio then went to his room and composed a solemn⑥ song. Going to the church with Don Pedro and his attendants, he sang it before the monument of Leonato's family. When he had ended he said, "Good night, Hero. Yearly will I do this."

He then gravely, as became a gentleman whose heart was Hero's, made ready to marry a girl whom he did not love. He was told to meet her in Leonato's house, and was faithful to his appointment.

He was shown into a room where Antonio (Leonato's brother) and several masked ladies entered after him. Friar Francis, Leonato, and

---

① anguish ['æŋgwiʃ] n. 痛苦，苦恼
② repentance [ri'pentəns] n. 后悔，悔改
③ penance ['penəns] n. 忏悔
④ proclaim [prə'kleim] v. 宣布，声明
⑤ vengeful ['vendʒful] adj. 复仇心重的，报复的
⑥ solemn ['sɔləm] adj. 庄严的，隆重的，严肃的

Benedick were present.

Antonio led one of the ladies towards Claudio.

"Sweet," said the young man, "let me see your face."

"Swear first to marry her," said Leonato.

"Give me your hand," said Claudio to the lady, "before this holy friar I swear to marry you if you will be my wife."

"Alive I was your wife," said the lady, as she drew off her mask.

"Another Hero!" exclaimed Claudio.

"Hero died," explained Leonato, "only while slander lived."

The Friar was then going to marry the reconciled① pair, but Benedick interrupted② him with, "Softly, Friar; which of these ladies is Beatrice?"

Hereat Beatrice unmasked, and Benedick said, "You love me, don't you?"

"Only moderately," was the reply. "Do you love me?"

"Moderately," answered Benedick.

"I was told you were well-nigh dead for me," remarked Beatrice.

"Of you I was told the same," said Benedick.

"Here's your own hand in evidence of your love," said Claudio, producing a feeble③ sonnet which Benedick had written to his sweetheart. "And here," said Hero, "is a tribute④ to Benedick, which I picked out of the pocket of Beatrice."

"A miracle!" exclaimed Benedick. "Our hands are against our hearts! Come, I will marry you, Beatrice."

① reconcile ['rekənsail] v. 使和解，使和谐，使顺从
② interrupt [ˌintə'rʌpt] v. 打断，中断
③ feeble ['fiːbl] adj. 虚弱的，衰弱的
④ tribute ['tribjuːt] n. 贡品，礼物

"You shall be my husband to save your life," was the rejoinder.

Benedick kissed her on the mouth; and the Friar married them after he had married Claudio and Hero.

"How is Benedick the married man?" asked Don Pedro.

"Too happy to be made unhappy," replied Benedick. "Crack what jokes you will. As for you, Claudio, I had hoped to run you through the body, but as you are now my kinsman①, live whole and love my cousin."

"My cudgel② was in love with you, Benedick, until today," said Claudio; but, "Come, come, let's dance," said Benedick.

And dance they did. Not even the news of the capture of Don John was able to stop the flying feet of the happy lovers, for revenge is not sweet against an evil man who has failed to do harm.

无 事 生 非

在西西里岛有个叫墨西拿的小镇,几百年前,那里曾发生过一场奇怪的暴风雨。

故事要从阳光说起。唐·彼德罗是西班牙阿拉贡的亲王,他带领军队大胜敌军后却忘记了他们来时的方向。艰苦的战事过后,唐·彼德罗感到轻松快乐,于是就去墨西拿度假,随行的有他同父异母的弟弟唐·约翰和两位年轻的意大利贵族培尼迪克和克劳迪奥。

培尼迪克是个快乐的话匣子,他决定要过独身生活。与其相反,克劳迪奥刚到墨西拿就爱上了墨西拿总督里奥那托的女儿希罗。

在七月的一天,一个名叫波拉契奥的香料商正在里奥那托的一个发霉的房间里燃烧干燥的薰衣草时,听见了从开着的窗子外传来的说话声。

"坦率地说你觉得希罗怎么样啊?"克劳迪奥问。波拉契奥打算好好听听他们的谈话。

"她太矮,太黑,没法称赞,"培尼迪克回答道,"可是如果改变她的肤色和身高,就不再是她了。"

"在我眼里,她是最甜美的女人。"克劳迪奥说。

---

① kinsman ['kinzmən] n. 男性亲戚,同族者
② cudgel ['kʌdʒəl] n. 棍棒

"在我眼里可不是这样,"培尼迪克反驳说,"我的眼光正常。与她堂妹相比,就如同12月的最后一天和5月的第一天。不幸的是,贝特丽丝脾气太暴躁。"

贝特丽丝是里奥那托的侄女,她经常说些有关培尼迪克的或可笑或严肃的逸事来自娱自乐,培尼迪克称她是"亲爱的傲慢小姐"。她常说自己出生在一个舞动的星星下,因此注定不会呆滞愚笨。

克劳迪奥和培尼迪克谈得正起劲,唐·彼德罗进来诙谐地说:"哦,先生们,在说什么秘密啊?"

培尼迪克说:"我正想让殿下命令我说出来呢!"

"那么,我就命令你对我讲实话。"唐·彼德罗也幽默地说。

"我本来像哑巴一样沉默,"培尼迪克充满歉意地对克劳迪奥说,"可是殿下他非要命令我说。"他对唐·彼德罗说:"克劳迪奥爱上了里奥那托的矮女儿了。"

唐·彼德罗感到很高兴,因为他也欣赏希罗并喜欢克劳迪奥。培尼迪克走了之后,他对克劳迪奥说:"坚定地爱希罗吧,我会助你一臂之力来博取她的芳心。今晚她父亲会举办一场化装舞会,我会假扮成克劳迪奥,告诉希罗克劳迪奥多么爱她,如果她很高兴,我就去她父亲那里请求他同意你们结婚。"

许多人都会自己求婚,但如果你爱上了总督唯一的女儿,而亲王又愿意代你求婚,那你可真是幸运。

克劳迪奥是幸运的,同时也是不幸的,因为他有一个表面上是朋友的对手。这个对手就是唐·彼德罗的弟弟唐·约翰,他非常嫉妒克劳迪奥,因为他哥哥更喜欢克劳迪奥。

波拉契奥把他偷听到的谈话内容告诉了唐·约翰。

波拉契奥说完后,唐·约翰说:"在化装舞会上我自己也会很开心的。"

在化装舞会的那天晚上,唐·彼德罗戴上面具假装是克劳迪奥,问希罗是否愿意和他一起走走。

他们一起离开后,唐·约翰走到克劳迪奥面前说:"我想,那是培尼迪克先生吧?""我也这么想。"克劳迪奥搪塞说。

"那么,我应该请求你,"唐·约翰说,"如果你愿意请求我哥哥为他治愈他对希罗的相思之苦,她的门第不如他高。"

"你怎么知道他爱她呢?"克劳迪奥问。

"我听见了他的爱情誓言。"约翰回答。"我也听见了。"波拉契奥也随

声附和说。

克劳迪奥独自走开了,心想他的殿下背叛了他。"再见了,希罗,"他小声嘀咕着;"让别人替我求爱,我真是个傻瓜。"

与此同时,贝特丽丝和培尼迪克(培尼迪克戴着面罩)正在愉快地聊天。

"你有没有觉得培尼迪克很好笑?"她问。

"培尼迪克是谁?"他问。

"亲王的一个小丑。"贝特丽丝回答。她说话如此刻薄,以致培尼迪克后来断言说:"就算她的家产是伊甸园,我也不会娶她。"

然而化装舞会上的中心人物既不是贝特丽丝也不是培尼迪克,而是唐·彼德罗,他正在实施他的计划,他带着里奥那托和希罗一起出现在克劳迪奥的面前,说:"克劳迪奥,你想什么时候去教堂呢?"这使克劳迪奥立即重新容光焕发。

"明天吧,"克劳迪奥立即回答说,"在我娶希罗之前,时间是拄着拐棍前进的。"

"我亲爱的孩子,给她一星期的时间准备吧。"里奥那托说。克劳迪奥的心里充满了喜悦。

"现在呢,"和蔼的唐·彼德罗说,"我们必须帮培尼迪克先生找一位妻子。这可是一个重要任务噢。"

"我会助你一臂之力的,"里奥那托说,"那我必须在这里熬上十个晚上。"

接着希罗开口了:"殿下,我会尽力帮贝特丽丝找一位好丈夫的。"

化装舞会就这样欢乐收场。

波拉契奥想出了一条诡计,能让克劳迪奥和唐·彼德罗都相信希罗是个脚踏两只船的轻浮女人。这让唐·约翰振奋起来,他同意了这个仇恨诡计。

而在另一边,唐·彼德罗想出了一条恋爱妙计。他对里奥那托说:"如果贝特丽丝能在无意之中听到我们的谈话,我们就假装培尼迪克渴望得到她的爱,她就会怜悯他,看到他的优点并爱上他。也让培尼迪克在无意中听到我们说美丽的贝特丽丝爱上了培尼迪克这样无心的嘲弄者是一件多么令人难过的事,不出一个星期,保证他会跪在她面前求爱。"

于是有一天,当培尼迪克正在一个凉亭里看书的时候,克劳迪奥和里奥

那托坐在外面,克劳迪奥说:"您的女儿告诉我她写了一封信。"

"信!"里奥那托惊呼。"她一晚上要爬起来20次,天知道她写了什么。有一次希罗偷看了一下,看到纸上写着'培尼迪克和贝特丽丝',后来贝特丽丝就把它撕掉了。"

克劳迪奥说:"希罗告诉我她边哭边说'哦,心爱的培尼迪克!'"

培尼迪克傻乎乎地相信了这个虚构的故事,并且被深深地感动了。他自言自语地说:"她美丽善良,我不能再这么妄自尊大了,我觉得自己爱上她了。当然,有人会嘲笑我,可是那些流言飞语伤害不了我。"

这时候贝特丽丝也来到了凉亭,说:"他们硬叫我来请你进去吃饭,可不是我愿意过来的。"

"谢谢你,美丽的贝特丽丝。"培尼迪克说。

"叫你吃饭只是举手之劳,没有必要这么费事地谢我。"贝特丽丝反驳说,故意想惹他生气。

可是这话非但没有令他生气,他心里还热乎乎的呢。培尼迪克从她那些不客气的话里隐隐可以感觉出她很高兴来找他。

希罗也担负着一项任务呢,就是打动贝特丽丝的心,她不费吹灰之力就找到了一个机会。一天她对她的侍女玛格莱特说:"你跑到客厅里悄悄地告诉贝特丽丝,说我和欧苏拉正在果园里谈关于她的事情。"

说完,她确信贝特丽丝会跑过来偷听那些对她意味深长的话,感觉好像和堂妹约会一样。

果园里有一个凉亭,凉亭周围厚厚的一层金银花遮住了阳光。玛格莱特刚刚按她的吩咐离去,贝特丽丝就迫不及待地走进了凉亭。

希罗的侍女欧苏拉问:"你确定吗?培尼迪克真的是一心一意地爱着贝特丽丝吗?"

希罗回答说:"亲王和我的未婚夫都这么说,他们一定要我把这件事告诉她。可是我说,'不,让培尼迪克自己解决吧。'"

"你为什么那么说呢?"

"因为贝特丽丝高傲得令人无法容忍。她的眼睛里全是轻蔑和嘲笑的目光。她太自负了,不值得别人去爱。我宁愿看着可怜的培尼迪克的爱情像被覆盖的火焰一样消退下去,也不愿意看到她戏弄他的爱。"

"我不赞同你的说法,"欧苏拉说,"我觉得你的堂姐眼光很好,她不会看不到培尼迪克的优点的。"

"除了克劳迪奥外,在意大利他也算个人物呢。"希罗说。

聊天的人离开了果园后,贝特丽丝特别兴奋,心底升起了一股柔情,走出凉亭时她自言自语地说:"可怜的培尼迪克,真心对我吧,你的爱会驯服我这颗狂野的心的。"

我们现在再回到那个仇恨诡计。

就在克劳迪奥定下的婚期的前夜,唐·彼德罗和克劳迪奥正在房间里聊天,唐·约翰走了进来,问克劳迪奥是否于第二天举行婚礼。

"你明明知道的!"唐·彼德罗说。

唐·约翰说:"如果他跟我来看看我指给他看的情景后,就不会这么想了。"

他们跟他进了花园;看到一个女子正从希罗的窗子里探出身向波拉契奥示爱。

克劳迪奥以为那个女子就是希罗,说:"明天我再羞辱她!"唐·彼德罗也误认为那个人就是希罗;可她并不是希罗,而是玛格莱特。

克劳迪奥和唐·彼德罗离开花园后,唐·约翰不露声息地笑了;他给了波拉契奥一个钱包,里面装有1000达克特。

这些钱令波拉契奥喜形于色,他和他的朋友康拉德一起在街上走的时候,吹嘘着自己的财富及那个馈赠者,还把自己做的那些事情抖搂了出来。

一个看守无意间听到了他们的谈话,认为这个因做坏事却得到了1000达克特的人应该受到惩罚。于是,他逮捕了波拉契奥和康拉德,让他们在监狱中度过了下半夜。

第二天接近中午的时候,墨西拿一半的贵族都聚集在了教堂里。在希罗看来这是她大喜的日子,她穿着婚纱去教堂,美丽的脸庞上和率直明亮的眼睛里没有一丝阴云。

主持婚礼的牧师是弗兰西斯修士。

他转向克劳迪奥说:"大人,您来迎娶这位小姐吗?"

"不!"克劳迪奥否认道。

里奥那托以为他故意咬文嚼字,就对牧师说:"修士,你应该说'你来和这位小姐完婚'。"

弗兰西斯修士转向希罗说:"小姐,你来和这位伯爵完婚吗?"

"是的。"希罗回答说。

"假若你们任何一方对这个婚姻有不满之处,我希望你们能说出来。"修士说。

"希罗,你听说了什么吗?"克劳迪奥问。

"没有。"希罗说。

"你听说了什么吗,伯爵?"修士问。

"我能替他回答,'没有'。"里奥那托说。

克劳迪奥痛苦地说:"哦!我还有什么不敢说的呢!前辈,"他继续说,"您愿意把您的女儿托付给我吗?"

"愿意,"里奥那托回答说,"正如上帝将她馈赠于我一样。"

"我能给你什么呢,"克劳迪奥问,"什么才受得起这份厚礼呢?"

"没有,"唐·彼德罗说,"除非你再把这份礼物归还给馈赠者。"

"我的亲王,你教教我该怎么办吧。"克劳迪奥说。"那么,里奥那托,把她拿回去吧。"

接二连三的粗鲁语言从克劳迪奥、唐·彼德罗和唐·约翰嘴里飞出。

教堂看起来不再是神圣的地方了。希罗努力控制着自己,她晕了过去。那些迫害她的人都离开了教堂,除了她的父亲。她父亲被这些谴责蒙住了,他喊道:"别管她!让她去死!"

但是弗兰西斯修士用他那双能够洞察心灵的眼睛看到了希罗的清白。"她是清白的,"他说,"许多迹象告诉我是这样的。"

希罗在他和蔼的注视下苏醒了,她那心烦意乱的父亲也不知道该怎么办。修士说:"他们离去的时候她已经因羞耻而死,我们就假装她死了,直到真相大白、诽谤变成懊悔的那一刻。"

培尼迪克说:"修士的建议不错。"于是希罗就被带到一个地方暂时隐居起来,贝特丽丝和培尼迪克两人留在了教堂。

培尼迪克知道她已经痛哭了很久,对她说:"我确信你美丽的堂姐是被冤枉的。"可她仍哭个不停。

培尼迪克温柔地说:"这世界上除你以外我谁也不爱了,这不是很奇怪吗?"

"我也可以说世界上除你以外我谁也不爱了,"贝特丽丝说,"但是我不说。我很替我的堂姐难过。"

"告诉我能为她做些什么?"培尼迪克说。

"杀了克劳迪奥。"

"哈哈!世界这么宽广,我怎能杀他?"培尼迪克说。

"你拒绝就是要杀了我,"贝特丽丝说,"再见。"

"好了！我去向他挑战。"培尼迪克喊道。

此时，波拉契奥和康拉德在监狱里正接受一位叫道勃雷的狱吏的审问。看守提供证词说波拉契奥说过他为了1000达克特而陷害了希罗。

审问的时候，里奥那托不在场，可他此时完全相信希罗是无辜的。他仍然表现出丧失爱女的悲恸，当克劳迪奥和唐·彼德罗友好地去拜访他时，他对这个意大利人说："你已经将我的孩子诽谤致死，我要和你决一死战。"

"我不会和一位老人决斗的。"克劳迪奥说。

"那你却可以杀死一个姑娘。"里奥那托讥讽地说。克劳迪奥脸红了。

言辞越来越激烈，里奥那托离开、培尼迪克进来的时候，唐·彼德罗和克劳迪奥的情绪都异常激动。

克劳迪奥说："这个老家伙，快要把我的鼻子拧下来了。"

"你这个无耻的小人！"培尼迪克开口就说。"你乐意用什么武器就用什么武器，我要和你决斗，否则你就是个懦夫。"

克劳迪奥大吃一惊，说："好，我接受挑战。人们都知道我能劈开牛的脑袋。"

培尼迪克微笑了一下，该唐·彼德罗坐下来处理他下属的事情了，亲王坐在首席上正准备主持公道呢。

门开了，道勃雷把他的犯人带了进来。

"这些人被控诉犯了什么罪？"唐·彼德罗问。

波拉契奥马上向亲王招了一切，并把罪责都推给了已经逃走的唐·约翰。"希罗小姐已经死了，"他说，"除了杀人偿命，我别无他求。"

克劳迪奥听后悲恸万分，并陷入深深的自责中。

看到里奥那托走了进来，他说："这个奴才已经为您的女儿洗清了冤屈。你复仇吧。"

"里奥那托，"唐·彼德罗也谦恭地说，"我愿意接受你对我的任何惩罚。"

"那么，我就要求你们两个，"里奥那托说，"宣布我女儿是清白无辜的，并在她的墓前唱赞歌。至于你，克劳迪奥，我还要说，我弟弟有个女儿和希罗长得特别像，简直一模一样。娶她为妻，我的怨气就会消了。"

"高尚的爵士，"克劳迪奥说，"我是您的。"克劳迪奥于是走进房间，写了一首庄严的赞歌。然后和唐·彼德罗及随从们去了教堂，在里奥那托家族的纪念碑前唱了这首歌。唱完后他说："晚安，希罗，每年我都会这样做的。"

当时他的心已经属于希罗，毅然做好准备娶一位他不爱的姑娘。里奥

那托叫他到家中与这位女子见面,他遵守了与里奥那托的约定。

他被带进了一个房间,里奥那托的弟弟安东尼奥和几位戴面罩的女子跟着走了进来。弗兰西斯修士、里奥那托,还有培尼迪克也在场。

安东尼奥把其中的一位女子带到克劳迪奥的面前。

"亲爱的,"这个年轻人说,"让我看看你的脸。"

"先发誓娶她为妻。"里奥那托说。

"把你的手给我,"克劳迪奥对这位女子说,"在神圣的修士面前,如果你愿意做我的妻子,我发誓会娶你。"

"我活着的时候曾是你的妻子。"这位女子说着把面罩揭开了。

"另一个希罗!"克劳迪奥惊叹说。

里奥那托解释说:"只有当诽谤存在的时候,希罗才是死的呢。"

修士于是给这对复合的人儿主持了婚礼。培尼迪克却打断了他,说:"修士,等等,这些女子当中哪位是贝特丽丝?"

于是,贝特丽丝也揭开了面罩,培尼迪克问道:"你爱我,是吗?"

"一点点,"她回答说,"你爱我吗?"

"一点点。"培尼迪克回答说。

"听说你为我憔悴得快死了。"贝特丽丝说。

"我也听说你害相思病快死了。"培尼迪克说。

"这就是你表达你对贝特丽丝爱慕的证据。"克劳迪奥说着,拿出了培尼迪克为他的心上人写的一首十四行诗。希罗说:"这是我从贝特丽丝口袋里翻出来的送给培尼迪克的礼物。"

"真是奇迹!"培尼迪克惊呼。"我们的手背叛了我们的心!来吧,贝特丽丝,我要娶你为妻。"

"为了拯救你的生命,我就嫁给你吧。"贝特丽丝反驳道。

培尼迪克亲吻了她的柔唇;修士为克劳迪奥和希罗主持完婚礼后又接着为他们二人主持了婚礼。

"结了婚的男人感觉如何?"唐·彼德罗问培尼迪克。

"幸福极了,"培尼迪克回答说,"你们这高明的玩笑。至于你,克劳迪奥,我本来想刺死你的,可现在你成了我的亲戚,那就好好活着爱我的堂姐吧。"

"培尼迪克,我的棍子现在还很喜欢你呢。"克劳迪奥说。可培尼迪克却说:"来吧,来吧,我们来跳舞吧。"

然后他们就跳起舞来,甚至唐·约翰被抓获的消息也没有让这些幸福的人们停下脚步,因为报复邪恶的人并不是最佳选择,他会自食其果。

7. As You Like It

Rosalind and Celia

There was once a wicked Duke named Frederick, who took the dukedom that should have belonged to his brother, sending him into exile①. His brother went into the Forest of Arden, where he lived the life of a bold forester, as Robin Hood② did in Sherwood Forest in merry England.

~~~~~~~~~~~~~~~~~~~~~~~~

① exile [ˈeksail] n. 放逐，充军，流放
② Robin Hood n. 罗宾汉(12 世纪英国民间传说中以勇敢、具有骑士品质和劫富济贫而闻名的绿林好汉)

The banished①Duke's daughter, Rosalind②, remained with Celia③, Frederick's daughter, and the two loved each other more than most sisters. One day there was a wrestling match at Court, and Rosalind and Celia went to see it. Charles, a celebrated wrestler④, was there, who had killed many men in contests of this kind. Orlando⑤, the young man he was to wrestle with, was so slender and youthful, that Rosalind and Celia thought he would surely be killed, as others had been; so they spoke to him, and asked him not to attempt so dangerous an adventure; but the only effect of their words was to make him wish more to come off well⑥ in the encounter, so as to win praise from such sweet ladies.

Orlando, like Rosalind's father, was being kept out of his inheritance⑦ by his brother, and was so sad at his brother's unkindness that, until he saw Rosalind, he did not care much whether he lived or died. But now the sight of the fair Rosalind gave him strength and courage, so that he did marvelously⑧, and at last, threw Charles to such a tune, that the wrestler had to be carried off the ground. Duke Frederick was pleased with his courage, and asked his name.

"My name is Orlando, and I am the youngest son of Sir Rowland de Boys⑨," said the young man.

Now Sir Rowland de Boys, when he was alive, had been a good friend to the banished Duke, so that Frederick heard with regret whose son Orlando was, and

---

① banish [ˈbæniʃ] v. 流放，驱逐
② Rosalind [ˈrɔzəlind] n. 罗瑟琳（女子名）
③ Celia [ˈsiːljə] n. 赛利娅（女子名）
④ celebrated wrestler 著名的摔跤手
⑤ Orlando [ɔːˈlændəu] n. 奥兰多（男子名）
⑥ come off well 运气好，走运，（事情）有满意的结果
⑦ inheritance [inˈheritəns] n. 遗传，遗产
⑧ marvelously [ˈmɑːviləsli] adv. 不可思议地，非凡地
⑨ Rowland de Boys [ˈrəulənd də bɔiz] n. 罗兰·德·博尔斯（男子名）

would not befriend him. But Rosalind was delighted to hear that this handsome young stranger was the son of her father's old friend, and as they were going away, she turned back more than once to say another kind word to the brave young man.

"Gentleman," she said, giving him a chain from her neck, "wear this for me. I could give more, but that my hand lacks means."

Rosalind and Celia, when they were alone, began to talk about the handsome wrestler, and Rosalind confessed that she loved him at first sight.

"Come, come," said Celia, "wrestle with thy affections."

"Oh," answered Rosalind, "they take the part of a better wrestler than myself. Look, here comes the Duke."

"With his eyes full of anger," said Celia.

"You must leave the Court at once," he said to Rosalind. "Why?" she asked.

"Never mind why," answered the Duke, "you are banished. If within ten days you are found within twenty miles of my Court, you die."

So Rosalind set out to seek her father, the banished Duke, in the Forest of Arden. Celia loved her too much to let her go alone, and as it was rather a dangerous journey, Rosalind, being the taller, dressed up as a young countryman, and her cousin as a country girl, and Rosalind said that she would be called Ganymede①, and Celia, Aliena. They were very tired when at last they came to the Forest of Arden, and as they were sitting on the grass a countryman passed that way, and Ganymede asked him if he could get them food. He did so, and told them that a shepherd's flocks and house were to be sold. They bought these and settled down② as shepherd and shepherdess in the forest.

In the meantime, Oliver having sought to take his brother Orlando's life, Orlando also wandered into the forest, and there met with the rightful Duke, and being kindly received, stayed with him. Now, Orlando could

---

① Ganymede ['gænimiːd] n. 甘尼米德(男子名)
② settle down 定居

think of nothing but Rosalind, and he went about the forest carving her name on trees, and writing love sonnets and hanging them on the bushes, and there Rosalind and Celia found them. One day Orlando met them, but he did not know Rosalind in her country's clothes, though he liked the pretty shepherd youth, because he fancied a likeness in him to her he loved.

"There is a foolish lover," said Rosalind, "who haunts these woods and hangs sonnets on the trees. If I could find him, I would soon cure him of his folly."

Orlando confessed that he was the foolish lover, and Rosalind said—"If you will come and see me every day, I will pretend to be Rosalind, and I will take her part, and be wayward① and contrary②, as is the way of women, till I make you ashamed of your folly in loving her."

And so every day he went to her house, and took a pleasure in saying to her all the pretty things he would have said to Rosalind; and she had the fine and secret joy of knowing that all his love-words came to the right ears. Thus many days passed pleasantly away.

One morning, as Orlando was going to visit Ganymede, he saw a man asleep on the ground, and that there was a lioness crouching near, waiting for the man who was asleep to wake; for they say that lions will not prey on anything that is dead or sleeping. Then Orlando looked at the man, and saw that it was his wicked③ brother, Oliver, who had tried to take his life. He fought with the lioness and killed her, and saved his brother's life.

While Orlando was fighting the lioness, Oliver woke to see his brother, whom he had treated so badly, saving him from a wild beast at the risk of his own life. This made him repent of④ his

① wayward ['weiwəd] *adj.* 任性的
② contrary ['kɔntrəri] *adj.* 执拗的
③ wicked ['wikid] *adj.* 邪恶的，缺德的，
④ repent of 后悔

wickedness, and he begged Orlando's pardon, and from thenceforth they were dear brothers. The lioness had wounded Orlando's arm so much, that he could not go on to see the shepherd, so he sent his brother to ask Ganymede to come to him.

Oliver went and told the whole story to Ganymede and Aliena, and Aliena was so charmed with his manly way of confessing his faults, that she fell in love with him at once. But when Ganymede heard of the danger Orlando had been in she fainted; and when she came to herself, said truly enough, "I should have been a woman by right."

Oliver went back to his brother and told him all this, saying, "I love Aliena so well that I will give up my estates to you and marry her, and live here as a shepherd."

"Let your wedding be tomorrow," said Orlando, "and I will ask the Duke and his friends."

When Orlando told Ganymede how his brother was to be married on the morrow, he added: "Oh, how bitter a thing it is to look into happiness through another man's eyes."

Then answered Rosalind, still in Ganymede's dress and speaking with his voice—"If you do love Rosalind so near the heart, then when your brother marries Aliena, shall you marry her?"

Now the next day the Duke and his followers, and Orlando, and Oliver, and Aliena, were all gathered together for the wedding.

Then Ganymede came in and said to the Duke, "If I bring in your daughter Rosalind, will you give her to Orlando here?" "That I would," said the Duke, "if I had all kingdoms to give with her."

"And you say you will have her when I bring her?" she said to Orlando. "That would I," he answered, "were I king of all kingdoms."

Then Rosalind and Celia went out, and Rosalind put on her pretty woman's clothes again, and after a while came back.

She turned to her father—"I give myself to you, for I am yours." "If there be truth in sight," he said, "you are my daughter."

Then she said to Orlando, "I give myself to you, for I am yours." "If there be truth in sight," he said, "you are my Rosalind."

"I will have no father if you be not he," she said to the Duke, and to Orlando, "I will have no husband if you be not he."

So Orlando and Rosalind were married, and Oliver and Celia, and they lived happy ever after, returning with the Duke to the kingdom. For Frederick had been shown by a holy hermit① the wickedness of his ways, and so gave back the dukedom of his brother, and himself went into a monastery② to pray for forgiveness.

The wedding was a merry one, in the mossy glades of the forest. A shepherd and shepherdess who had been friends with Rosalind, when she was herself disguised as a shepherd, were married on the same day, and all with such pretty feastings and merrymakings as could be nowhere within four walls, but only in the beautiful green wood.

皆 大 欢 喜

从前有一个邪恶的公爵名叫弗雷德瑞克，他抢走了本该属于他哥哥的爵位后，又将他哥哥流放。他哥哥走进了阿登森林，就像英格兰舍伍德快活林的罗宾汉一样，他在森林里过着勇敢的守林人的生活。

这位被流放的公爵的女儿叫罗瑟琳，和弗雷德瑞克的女儿赛利娅生活在一起，她们二人感情笃深，犹胜于其他姐妹。有一天，宫廷里举行摔跤比赛，罗瑟琳和赛利娅跑去观看。一位颇有名气的摔跤手——查尔斯——也在那里，此人曾在诸多此类比赛中获胜。而他的对手奥兰多却年轻而瘦弱，这两姐妹认为他一定会像其他人一样被查尔斯杀死。于是她们俩劝说奥兰多不要去冒险，结果她们的话却使奥兰多更想与对手较量一番，以胜利来博取这两位甜美女士的称赞。

同罗瑟琳的父亲一样，奥兰多也被他的哥哥剥夺了继承遗产的权力。他为哥哥的不善之举感到难过，在遇到罗瑟琳之前，他早已不在乎自己是死是活。如今，美丽的罗瑟琳给了他勇气和力量，他表现得相当出色，结果不费吹灰之力，他就把查尔斯摔倒在地。弗雷德瑞克公爵对他所表现出的勇气特别满意，就询问了他的姓名。

---

① hermit [ˈhəːmit] *n.* 隐士，隐居者
② monastery [ˈmɔnəstri] *n.* 修道院，僧侣

这位年轻人答道:"我叫奥兰多,是罗兰·德·博尔斯爵士的小儿子。"

罗兰·德·博尔斯爵士在世的时候是那位被放逐的公爵的好友,因此,弗雷德瑞克得知奥兰多的身世后,对他冷淡了许多。然而,罗瑟琳得知这位年轻俊俏的陌生人是她父亲好友之子后特别兴奋。当他们要离开时,她再三回头称赞这位勇敢的年轻人。

她从脖子上摘下一串项链递给奥兰多,说:"先生,为了我,请你戴上它吧。我本可以给予更多,可我手头也不宽裕。"

罗瑟琳和赛利娅单独在一起时就会谈论起这位英俊的摔跤手,罗瑟琳坦白地说她对奥兰多是一见钟情。

"好啦,好啦,"赛利娅说,"控制一下你的感情吧。"

"噢,"罗瑟琳回答,"我的心思可全在那个摔跤手身上了,瞧,公爵来了。"

"他满脸怒气。"赛利娅说。

"你必须马上离开王宫。"他对罗瑟琳说。"为什么?"她问。

"没有原因,"公爵回答,"你被流放了,10天内离开这里,如果在离我的王宫20英里内发现你的话,你就死定了。"

于是罗瑟琳踏上了寻父的旅程,她的父亲,那位被放逐的公爵,还住在阿登森林。赛利娅太爱她的堂妹了,不忍心让她独自踏上这么艰险的旅途,就随她一起离开了。罗瑟琳个子高一些,装扮成一位乡下青年,赛利娅则装扮成村姑的模样,罗瑟琳又把名字改为甘尼米德,赛利娅则改名为爱丽娜。最后,当她们到达阿登森林时已是疲惫不堪。她们坐在草地上休息,这时一个乡下青年经过,甘尼米德就问他能否给她们些吃的。他给了她们食物,并告诉她们有个牧羊人正打算把羊群和房子卖掉。于是她们俩就买下了羊群和房子,并在森林里居住下来,一个是牧羊人,一个是牧羊女。

同时,奥利弗一直想要杀了他弟弟奥兰多,奥兰多也流浪到了这片森林,在这里他遇见了那位正义的伯爵并受到热情款待,于是他也留了下来。此时奥兰多心里只有罗瑟琳,他在森林里四处游荡,把她的名字刻在树上,还写了许多情诗,并把它们挂在灌木丛上,而这些都被罗瑟琳和赛利娅发现了。一天,奥兰多遇见了她们俩,觉得这个俊俏的牧羊人和他的心上人长得

很像,于是就喜欢上了他,可他并未认出女扮男装的罗瑟琳。

罗瑟琳说:"有一个傻乎乎的情痴,在这片树林中出没,并在树上挂满了情诗。如果我碰到了他,就会治好他的傻病。"

奥兰多承认他就是那个傻乎乎的情痴,于是罗瑟琳对他说道:"如果你每天都过来看我,我就会假装是罗瑟琳,扮演她的角色,并像女人那样任性那样反复无常,直到让你为愚蠢地爱她而感到羞愧。"

从那以后他每天都会去她家,把想要说给罗瑟琳的所有甜言蜜语都说给她听,并乐在其中;而她呢,也因所有的情话找对了倾诉对象而满怀喜悦。就这样他们度过了许多快乐的日子。

一天清晨,奥兰多正要去拜访甘尼米德,他看到一个年轻人正在地上酣睡,而一只雌狮就蹲在附近,等待着这个睡着的猎物醒来——据说狮子不会捕食睡着的或死去的猎物。奥兰多看了那年轻人一眼,那人正是想夺取他性命的邪恶的哥哥奥利弗。奥兰多同狮子搏斗并将其杀死,救了他哥哥的命。

奥兰多同雌狮的搏斗惊醒了奥利弗,看到他曾经刻薄对待的弟弟为了救他而冒着生命危险同野兽搏斗,他为自己的邪恶感到懊悔,并祈求得到奥兰多的原谅,此后他们又成了好兄弟。由于奥兰多的手臂被狮子伤得厉害,不能去看望牧羊人,于是他就让他哥哥把甘尼米德叫了过来。

奥利弗去了罗瑟琳那里并把事情的整个经过告诉了甘尼米德和爱丽娜,爱丽娜着迷于他这种敢于认错的男子汉气概,一下子就爱上了他。然而,当甘尼米德听到奥兰多处于危险时,她昏了过去。醒来时,她真切地说道:"实际上,我是个女人。"

奥利弗回到弟弟那里把一切讲给他听,并说道:"我爱上了爱丽娜,我愿意把我的财产都给你并和她结婚,在这儿过牧羊人的生活。"

"那你明天就举行婚礼吧,"奥兰多说道,"我去邀请公爵和他的朋友们参加。"

奥兰多告诉甘尼米德他哥哥第二天就要结婚了,并说道:"通过另一个男人的眼睛看到幸福是多么痛苦的一件事啊!"

听到这些,依然身着男装的罗瑟琳用低沉的声音问道:"如果你深爱罗瑟琳,你哥哥和爱丽娜结婚的时候,你会娶她吗?"

第二天,公爵和他的随从、奥兰多、奥利弗及爱丽娜聚集在一起等待着婚礼开始。

这时甘尼米德走了进来,对伯爵说道:"如果我把你的女儿带来,你会不会把她嫁给奥兰多呢?""当然会,"伯爵说道,"如果我有整个王国作陪嫁就好了。"

"如果我把她带来,你说你会娶她吗?"罗瑟琳问奥兰多。"我会的,"他回答道,"我将会是最幸福的人。"

于是,罗瑟琳和赛利娅走了出去,过了一会儿罗瑟琳穿着她最漂亮的女装回来了。

她转向她父亲:"我把自己交给了你,因为我是你的。""如果我看到的一切都是真的,"他说道,"你就是我的女儿。"

然后她又对奥兰多说:"我把自己交给了你,因为我是你的。""如果我看到的一切都是真的,"他说道,"你就是我的罗瑟琳。"

她对公爵说:"如果你不是我父亲,我就没有父亲。"又对奥兰多说:"如果你不是我丈夫,我就没有丈夫。"

于是,罗瑟琳嫁给了奥兰多,赛利娅嫁给了奥利弗,他们从此以后过着幸福的生活,并和公爵一起回到了王国。因为弗雷德瑞克的邪恶行为被一个圣士揭发,他把公地还给了他的哥哥,自己跑到寺庙里赎罪去了。

欢快的婚礼在森林的苔藓地上进行。一个牧羊人和牧羊女的婚礼也在当天举行,他们是罗瑟琳假扮牧羊人时的朋友,这美丽的小树林中的盛宴和快乐,在四处是高墙的地方是找不到的。

8. Twelfth Night

Viola and the Captain

Orsino①, the Duke of Illyria②, was deeply in love with a beautiful Countess named Olivia③. Yet was all his love in vain, for she disdained④ his suit; and when her brother died, she sent back a messenger from the Duke, bidding him tell his master that for seven years she would not let the very air behold⑤ her face, but that, like a nun, she would walk veiled; and all this for the sake of a dead brother's love, which she would keep fresh and lasting in her sad remembrance⑥.

The Duke longed for someone to whom he could tell his sorrow, and

---

① Orsino [ɔːˈsiːnəu] n. 奥西诺(男子名)
② Illyria [iˈliːriə] n. 伊利里亚(古代沿巴尔干半岛亚德里亚海岸的一个地区)
③ Olivia [ˈɔliviə] n. 奥丽维娅(女子名)
④ disdaine [disˈdein] v. 蔑视, 鄙弃
⑤ behold [biˈhəuld] v. 把……视为, 看
⑥ remembrance [riˈmembrəns] n. 回想, 记忆

repeat over and over again the story of his love. And chance brought him such a companion①. For about this time a goodly ship was wrecked② on the Illyrian coast, and among those who reached land in safety were the captain and a fair young maid, named Viola③. But she was little grateful for being rescued④ from the perils of the sea, since she feared that her twin brother was drowned, Sebastian, as dear to her as the heart in her bosom, and so like her that, but for the difference in their manner of dress, one could hardly be told from the other. The captain, for her comfort, told her that he had seen her brother bind himself "to a strong mast that lived upon the sea", and that thus there was hope that he might be saved.

Viola now asked in whose country she was, and learning that the young Duke Orsino ruled there, and was as noble in his nature as in his name, she decided to disguise herself in male attire, and seek for employment with him as a page⑤.

In this she succeeded, and now from day to day she had to listen to the story of Orsino's love. At first she sympathized very truly with him, but soon her sympathy grew to love. At last it occurred to Orsino that his hopeless love-suit might prosper better if he sent this pretty lad to woo Olivia for him. Viola unwillingly went on this errand⑥, but when she came to the house, Malvolio, Olivia's steward, a vain, officious⑦ man, sick, as his mistress told him, of self-love, forbade the messenger admittance. Viola, however (who was now called Cesario⑧), refused to take any denial, and vowed to have

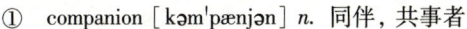

① companion [kəmˈpænjən] n. 同伴，共事者
② wreck [rek] v. 遇难，失事
③ Viola [ˈvaiələ] n. 薇奥拉（女子名）
④ rescue [ˈreskjuː] v. 援救，营救
⑤ page [peidʒ] n. 仆人
⑥ on errand 跑腿
⑦ officious [əˈfiʃəs] adj. 多管闲事的
⑧ Cesario [siːˈzɑːriəu] n. 西萨里奥（男子名）

speech with the Countess. Olivia, hearing how her instructions were defied and curious to see this daring youth, said, "We'll once more hear Orsino's embassy."

When Viola was admitted to her presence and the servants had been sent away, she listened patiently to the reproaches① which this bold messenger from the Duke poured upon her, and listening she fell in love with the supposed Cesario; and when Cesario had gone, Olivia longed to send some love-token after him. So, calling Malvolio, she bade him follow the boy.

"He left this ring behind him," she said, taking one from her finger. "Tell him I will none of it."

Malvolio did as he was bid, and then Viola, who of course knew perfectly well that she had left no ring behind her, saw with a woman's quickness② that Olivia loved her. Then she went back to the Duke, very sad at heart for her lover, and for Olivia, and for herself.

It was but cold comfort she could give Orsino, who now sought to ease the pangs of despised love by listening to sweet music, while Cesario stood by his side.

"Ah," said the Duke to his page that night, "you too have been in love."

"A little," answered Viola.

"What kind of woman is it?" he asked.

"Of your complexion③," she answered.

"What years, i' faith?" was his next question.

To this came the pretty answer, "About your years, my lord."

"Too old, by Heaven!" cried the Duke. "Let still the woman take an elder than herself."

And Viola very meekly④ said, "I think it well, my lord."

① reproach [ri'prəutʃ] v. 责备
② a woman's quickness 女人的敏感
③ complexion [kəm'plekʃən] n. 面色,肤色,情况
④ meekly ['mi:kli] adv. 温顺地,懦弱地

By and by Orsino begged Cesario once more to visit Olivia and to plead his love-suit. But she, thinking to dissuade① him, said—

"If some lady loved you as you love Olivia?"

"Ah! that cannot be," said the Duke.

"But I know," Viola went on, "what love woman may have for a man. My father had a daughter loved a man, as it might be," she added blushing②, "perhaps, were I a woman, I should love your lordship."

"And what is her history?" he asked.

"A blank, my lord," Viola answered. "She never told her love, but let concealment③ like a worm in the bud feed on her damask④ cheek: she pined in thought, and with a green and yellow melancholy⑤ she sat, like Patience on a monument, smiling at Grief. Was not this love indeed?"

"But died thy sister of her love, my boy?" the Duke asked; and Viola, who had all the time been telling her own love for him in this pretty fashion, said—

"I am all the daughters my father has and all the brothers—Sir, shall I go to the lady?"

"To her in haste," said the Duke, at once forgetting all about the story, "and give her this jewel."

So Viola went, and this time poor Olivia was unable to hide her love, and openly confessed it with such passionate⑥ truth, that Viola left her hastily, saying: "Nevermore will I deplore my master's tears to you."

But in vowing this, Viola did not know the tender pity she would feel for other's suffering. So when Olivia, in the violence of her love, sent a messenger, praying Cesario to visit her once more, Cesario had no heart to refuse the request.

～～～～～～～～～

①   dissuade [di'sweid] *v.* 劝阻
②   blushing [ˈblʌʃiŋ] *adj.* 红色的
③   concealment [kənˈsiːlmənt] *n.* 隐藏，隐蔽，隐蔽处
④   damask [ˈdæməsk] *adj.* 红玫瑰色的；缎子的
⑤   melancholy [ˈmelənkəli] *n.* 忧郁
⑥   passionate [ˈpæʃənit] *adj.* 充满热情的

But the favors which Olivia bestowed① upon this mere page aroused the jealousy of Sir Andrew Aguecheek, a foolish, rejected② lover of hers, who at that time was staying at her house with her merry old uncle Sir Toby. This same Sir Toby dearly loved a practical joke, and knowing Sir Andrew to be an arrant③ coward, he thought that if he could bring off a duel④ between him and Cesario, there would be rare sport indeed. So he induced Sir Andrew to send a challenge, which he himself took to Cesario. The poor page, in great terror, said: "I will return again to the house, I am no fighter."

"Back you shall not to the house," said Sir Toby, "unless you fight me first."

And as he looked a very fierce old gentleman, Viola thought it best to await Sir Andrew's coming; and when he at last made his appearance⑤, in a great fright, if the truth had been known, she tremblingly drew her sword, and Sir Andrew in like fear followed her example. Happily for them both, at this moment some officers of the Court came on the scene, and stopped the intended duel. Viola gladly made off with what speed she might, while Sir Toby called after her: "A very paltry⑥ boy, and more a coward than a hare!"

Now, while these things were happening, Sebastian had escaped all the dangers of the deep, and had landed safely in Illyria, where he determined to make his way to the Duke's Court. On his way thither he passed Olivia's house just as Viola had left it in such a hurry, and whom should he meet but Sir Andrew and Sir Toby. Sir Andrew, mistaking

① bestow [bi'stəu] v. 给予，安放
② reject [ri'dʒekt] v. 拒绝，抵制，否决
③ arrant ['ærənt] adj. 彻头彻尾的
④ duel ['dju(ː)əl] n. 决斗
⑤ appearance [ə'piərəns] n. 出现，露面，外貌，外观
⑥ paltry ['pɔːltri] adj. 不足取的，无价值的，琐碎的

Sebastian for the cowardly Cesario, took his courage in both hands, and walking up to him struck him, saying, "There's for you."

"Why, there's for you; and there, and there!" said Sebastian, hitting back a great deal harder, and again and again, till Sir Toby came to the rescue of his friend. Sebastian, however, tore himself free from Sir Toby's clutches, and drawing his sword would have fought them both, but that Olivia herself, having heard of the quarrel, came running in, and with many reproaches sent Sir Toby and his friend away. Then turning to Sebastian, whom she too thought to be Cesario, she besought him with many a pretty speech to come into the house with her.

Sebastian, half dazed and all delighted with her beauty and grace, readily consented, and that very day, so great was Olivia's baste①, they were married before she had discovered that he was not Cesario, or Sebastian was quite certain whether or not he was in a dream.

Meanwhile Orsino, hearing how ill Cesario sped with Olivia, visited her himself, taking Cesario with him. Olivia met them both before her door, and seeing, as she thought, her husband there, reproached him for leaving her, while to the Duke she said that his suit was as fat and wholesome to her as howling after music.

"Still so cruel?" said Orsino.

"Still so constant," she answered.

Then Orsino's anger growing to cruelty, he vowed that, to be revenged② on her, he would kill Cesario, whom he knew she loved. "Come, boy," he said to the page.

And Viola, following him as he moved away, said, "I, to do you rest, a thousand deaths would die."

A great fear took hold on Olivia, and she cried aloud, "Cesario, husband, stay!"

"Her husband?" asked the Duke angrily.

"No, my lord, not I," said Viola.

---

① baste [beist] *v.* 粗缝
② revenge [riˈvendʒ] *v.* 报仇

"Call forth the holy father," cried Olivia.

And the priest who had married Sebastian and Olivia, coming in, declared Cesario to be the bridegroom.

"O thou dissembling cub!" the Duke exclaimed. "Farewell, and take her, but go where thou and I henceforth① may never meet."

At this moment Sir Andrew came up with bleeding crown, complaining that Cesario had broken his head, and Sir Toby's as well.

"I never hurt you," said Viola, very positively, "you drew your sword on me, but I bespoke you fair, and hurt you not."

Yet, for all her protesting, no one there believed her; but all their thoughts were on a sudden changed to wonder, when Sebastian came in.

"I am sorry, madam," he said to his wife, "I have hurt your kinsman. Pardon me, sweet, even for the vows we made each other so late ago."

"One face, one voice, one habit, and two persons!" cried the Duke, looking first at Viola, and then at Sebastian.

"An apple cleft in two," said one who knew Sebastian, "is not more twin than these two creatures. Which is Sebastian?"

"I never had a brother," said Sebastian. "I had a sister, whom the blind waves and surges have devoured②." "Were you a woman," he said to Viola, "I should let my tears fall upon your cheek, and say, 'Thrice welcome, drowned Viola!'"

Then Viola, rejoicing to see her dear brother alive, confessed that she was indeed his sister, Viola. As she spoke, Orsino felt the pity that is akin to love.

"Boy," he said, "thou hast said to me a thousand times thou never shouldst love woman like to me."

"And all those sayings will I overswear," Viola replied, "and all those swearings keep true."

"Give me thy hand," Orsino cried in gladness. "Thou shalt be my

---

① henceforth [hens'fɔːθ] *adv.* 自此以后
② devour [di'vauə] *v.* 吞吃，狼吞虎咽

wife, and my fancy's queen."

Thus was the gentle Viola made happy, while Olivia found in Sebastian a constant① lover, and a good husband, and he in her a true and loving wife.

第十二夜

伊利里亚的公爵奥西诺深深爱上了一位名叫奥丽维娅的美丽的女伯爵。然而他对她的爱完全是徒劳的,因为她无视他的追求;奥丽维娅的哥哥去世后,她将公爵的信使遣送回去,请他告诉他的主人为了怀念对亡兄的爱——这份需她要时刻缅怀、铭记于心的爱——她决定在以后的七年里,像修女那样蒙着面纱走路,就连空气也见不到她的脸。

公爵渴望能够有人聆听他的忧愁,他要一遍又一遍地诉说他的爱情故事。一个偶然的机会给他带来了这么一个同伴。那时正好有一艘大船在伊利里亚海岸遇难,被救上岸的人中有一位船长,还有一位叫薇奥拉的美丽的姑娘。然而尽管她被救脱险,却并不觉得欢喜,因为她担心自己的孪生哥哥西巴斯辛会落难,她像爱自己的心肝一样爱着哥哥。兄妹俩长得很像,如果不是穿的衣服不同,简直没法把他们区分出来。船长为了安慰她,说他看见她哥哥紧抱着"一根结实的桅杆,飘在海面上",这样他就有了被救的希望。

薇奥拉问这个地方归谁管,得知这是年轻的公爵奥西诺统治的地方,并且他是一位品性和地位同样高贵的公爵,她决定女扮男装,去给奥西诺公爵当侍从。

当上侍从之后,她每天都要听奥西诺讲他的爱情故事。起初,她对他表示深切的同情,可不久后这种同情变成了爱。后来奥西诺突然想到,如果派这个俊秀的青年替他向奥丽维娅求婚的话,说不定他无望的追求会出现转机呢。薇奥拉很不情愿地去跑这个差使,到了之后,她发现奥丽维娅的管家马伏里奥是一个自负又爱管闲事的家伙,就像他的女主人说得那样,他还很自恋。马伏里奥不让薇奥拉进去,然而,薇奥拉(现在叫西萨里奥)就是不吃那一套,坚决要求和女伯爵说说话。奥丽维娅听说有人公然反抗她的指令,对这位勇敢的青年十分感兴趣,说:"我们再听听奥西诺的使者的话吧。"

薇奥拉进去后,其他的仆人就被打发走了,奥丽维娅耐心地听着奥西诺

---

① constant ['kɔnstənt] *adj.* 坚决的

派来的这个勇敢的使者滔滔不绝的责备之词;听着听着,奥丽维娅就爱上了这个假扮的西萨里奥。西萨里奥走后,奥丽维娅迫切地想送个信物给他,于是就唤来了马伏里奥,叫他跟上那个男孩。

"他把戒指忘在这里了,"她从手指上取下一枚戒指说,"告诉他我不在乎这枚戒指。"

马伏里奥按照主人的吩咐去做,薇奥拉当然非常清楚她并没有留下什么戒指,女人的直觉告诉她奥丽维娅爱上她了。于是她回到公爵那里,心里为她的爱人,为奥丽维娅,也为她自己感到难过。

她能给奥西诺的只有冷冰冰的安慰,奥西诺正为减轻那份不予理睬的爱情所带来的痛苦听着一首甜美的曲子,西萨里奥就站在他旁边。

"啊,"那晚公爵对他的侍从说,"你也恋爱了。"

"一点点。"薇奥拉回答说。

"她是个怎样的女人呢?"他问。

"肤色跟您一样。"她回答。

"她多大了?什么信仰啊?"他追问。

薇奥拉巧妙地回答:"和您年纪一样大,老爷。"

"天哪,太大了!"公爵叫嚷道。"让那个傻女人嫁一个年纪比她大的吧。"

而薇奥拉温柔地说:"我觉得还好,老爷。"

不久以后,奥西诺又恳求西萨里奥去拜访奥丽维娅并替他求婚,而她正琢磨着怎么劝阻他,说——

"如果有位女子像你爱奥丽维娅一样爱着你,你会怎么做?"

"啊!不可能有这种事。"公爵说。

"可是我知道,"薇奥拉继续说道,"这个女人多么爱这个男人。我父亲有个女儿爱上了一个男人。"她红着脸又说:"或许,如果我是个女人,我就会爱上老爷。"

"她什么来头?"他问。

"没有什么来头,老爷。"薇奥拉回答说。"她从不透露她的爱意,却让这秘密像蓓蕾中的害虫,吃她淡红的面颊来养生。哀思中她憔悴了,忧郁地坐在那里,如墓碑般有耐性,看着悲伤微笑。难道这不是真正的爱吗?"

"我的孩子,你的姐姐为爱而死了吗?"公爵问。一直以这种美好的方式对他表达爱意的薇奥拉说——

"我是我父亲全部的女儿和儿子——老爷,我现在就去小姐那里吗?"

"快点去,"公爵说,马上把这个故事忘得一干二净了,"把这个珠宝给她。"

于是薇奥拉去了奥丽维娅那里,这次奥丽维娅无法隐藏她的爱,她满怀激情,公然对薇奥拉表白,薇奥拉赶紧离开,说:"我再也不向你痛诉老爷的眼泪了。"

在说这些话的时候,薇奥拉不知她该对另外一个受伤的人怀有怎样的同情之心。怀着强烈的爱,奥丽维娅派了信使祈求西萨里奥再来看望她,西萨里奥不忍拒绝这一请求。

奥丽维娅竟然对公爵的侍从产生了好感,这激起了鲁莽的安德鲁·艾古契克爵士的妒忌,他曾经痴爱过奥丽维娅并遭到了拒绝。那时候,他住在她家里,和她快乐的老伯父托比爵士待在一起。这个托比爵士很喜欢搞恶作剧,他知道安德鲁爵士是个彻头彻尾的懦夫,心里琢磨着如果他能挑起安德鲁和西萨里奥之间的决斗,那么真的很有看头。于是他就诱劝安德鲁爵士发出挑战书,并亲自带到西萨里奥那里。这个可怜的侍从,吓得胆战心惊,说:"我会再去拜访奥丽维娅,可我绝不迎战。"

"你不能再回去了,"托比爵士说,"除非你先把我打败。"

他看起来是个很凶狠的老绅士,薇奥拉心想还是等安德鲁爵士过来为好;他终于出现了,薇奥拉非常害怕,战战兢兢地抽出剑来。实际上,安德鲁爵士同样心惊胆战。令他们二人感到高兴的是,正在这时一些宫中官员赶来,阻止了这场蓄意的决斗。薇奥拉以最快的速度跑掉了,而托比爵士在后面喊:"你这个小东西,比兔子还胆小。"

当这一切正在发生的时候,西巴斯辛也逃脱了危险,在伊利里亚安全上岸了,他决定到公爵那里去。当他经过奥丽维娅家时,薇奥拉刚刚匆忙逃离,本该遇见妹妹的他,却撞见了安德鲁爵士和托比爵士。安德鲁爵士错把西巴斯辛当做了胆小的西萨里奥,于是就紧握拳头,鼓起勇气,走上前去对西巴斯辛说:"吃我这一剑。"

"好,吃我这一剑;来吧,来吧!"西巴斯辛说着,以更大的力量一次又一次地回击,托比爵士不得不出马解救朋友。然而,西巴斯辛挣脱了托比爵士纠缠,拔出剑来要同他们二人决战。奥丽维娅听到了吵闹声就跑了过来,一边责备托比爵士和他的朋友,一边将二人打发走了。然后转向西巴斯辛(她还以为这就是西萨里奥呢)说了许多好话,请他跟她回家。

西巴斯辛被她美丽的外表和优雅的举止迷住了,满心欢喜地答应下来。奥丽维娅太粗心了,就在当天,也就是在她还没有发现眼前的这位并非西萨里奥时,就嫁给了他,而西巴斯辛很清楚他是否在做梦。

同时,奥西诺听说西萨里奥和奥丽维娅谈得非常糟糕,就带上西萨里奥

亲自去拜访她。奥丽维娅在自家门前碰到了他们,看见西萨里奥,她误以为是自己的丈夫,就嗔怪他为什么离开,而对公爵她却说他向她求婚就如同听过音乐之后的嚎叫一样令人发腻不安。

"还这么冷酷?"奥西诺说。

"还这么顽固!"她回答说。

奥西诺顿时火冒三丈,他发誓说,为了报仇他一定要杀了西萨里奥——这个奥丽维娅所爱的家伙。"小子,来吧。"他对侍从说。

在他离开的时候,薇奥拉跟上来说:"为了你,我死一千次都可以。"

奥丽维娅脸上露出惊恐之色,她大声哭喊道:"西萨里奥,我的夫君,你别走啊!"

"她的夫君?"公爵生气地问。

"不,老爷,不是我。"薇奥拉说。

"把神甫叫来。"奥利维娅哭着说。

为奥丽维娅和西巴斯辛主持婚礼的神甫走了进来,宣称西萨里奥就是新郎。

"啊,你这个虚伪的骗子!"公爵惊叫着。"好,再见,去接受她,到一个我再也见不到你们的地方去吧。"

正在这时,头破血流的安德鲁爵士进来了,抱怨说西萨里奥把他和托比爵士的头都打破了。

"我从来没有伤害过你,"薇奥拉断然说,"你拔剑跟我决斗,可是我根本没有伤害你。"

然而,尽管她一再否认,却没有一个人相信她;这时西巴斯辛走了进来,所有的人都震惊了。

"对不起,夫人,"他对他的妻子说,"我打伤了你的亲戚,宝贝原谅我,为了我们刚刚发过的那些誓言原谅我吧。"

"相同的面孔,相同的声音,相同的习惯,却是两个人。"公爵惊呼。他看了看薇奥拉,又看了看西巴斯辛。

"一个苹果分成了两半,"一个认识西巴斯辛的人说,"再没有比这两个人长得更像的双胞胎了。哪位是西巴斯辛?"

西巴斯辛说:"我从来就没有弟弟,而有个妹妹,没长眼睛的海浪吞没了她。""你是女人吗?"他问薇奥拉,"我真该让我的泪水落在你的脸庞上,对你说'非常欢迎,溺死了的薇奥拉!'"

薇奥拉很欢欣地看到亲爱的哥哥还活着,她承认说自己就是他的妹妹

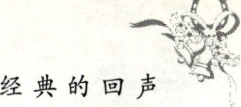

经典的回声
Echoes of Classics:Stories from Shakespeare

薇奥拉。在她说话的时候,奥西诺觉得自己对她的同情像是爱。

"孩子,"他说,"你曾对我说过千百回你永远不会像爱我这样去爱一个女人。"

"那些话都是我发过的誓言,"薇奥拉回答,"那些誓言都是真的。"

"把你的手给我,"奥西诺喜极而泣,"你就是我的妻子,我美丽的王后。"

于是温柔可人的薇奥拉非常幸福,奥丽维娅也找到了西巴斯辛这样忠贞不渝的爱人,这样的好丈夫,奥丽维娅呢,也是他贤惠温柔的好妻子。

9. Romeo and Juliet

Romeo and Juliet

Once upon a time there lived in Verona two great families named Montagu① and Capulet②. They were both rich, and I suppose they were as sensible③, in most things, as other rich people. But in one thing they were extremely silly. There was an old, old quarrel between the two families, and instead of making it up like reasonable folks, they made a sort of pet of their quarrel, and would not let it die out. So that a Montagu

---

① Montagu [ˈmɔntəgjuː] n. 蒙塔古
② Capulet [ˈkæpjulet] n. 凯普莱特
③ sensible [ˈsensəbl] adj. 有感觉的，明智的

wouldn't speak to a Capulet if he met one in the street—nor a Capulet to a Montagu—or if they did speak, it was to say rude and unpleasant things, which often ended in a fight. And their relations and servants were just as foolish, so that street fights and duels and uncomfortablenesses of that kind were always growing out of the Montagu-and-Capulet quarrel.

Now Lord Capulet, the head of that family, gave a party—a grand① supper and a dance—and he was so hospitable that he said anyone might come to it except (of course) the Montagues. But there was a young Montagu named Romeo, who very much wanted to be there, because Rosaline, the lady he loved, had been asked. This lady had never been at all kind to him, and he had no reason to love her; but the fact was that he wanted to love somebody, and as he hadn't seen the right lady, he was obliged to love the wrong one. So to the Capulet's grand party he came, with his friends Mercutio② and Benvolio③.

Old Capulet welcomed him and his two friends very kindly—and young Romeo moved about among the crowd of courtly④ folk dressed in their velvets and satins, the men with jeweled sword hilts and collars, and the ladies with brilliant gems on breast and arms, and stones of price set in their bright girdles. Romeo was in his best too, and though he wore a black mask over his eyes and nose, everyone could see by his mouth and his hair, and the way he held his head, that he was twelve times handsomer than anyone else in the room.

Presently amid⑤ the dancers he saw a lady so beautiful and so lovable that from that moment

① grand [grænd] adj. 盛大的，豪华的
② Mercutio [məˈkjuːʃiəu] n. 茂丘西奥（男子名）
③ Benvolio [benˈvɔliəu] n. 班伏里奥（男子名）
④ courtly [ˈkɔːtli] adj. 尊严而有礼貌的
⑤ amid [əˈmid] prep. 在……中

he never again gave one thought to that Rosaline whom he had thought he loved. And he looked at this other fair lady, as she moved in the dance in her white satin and pearls, and all the world seemed vain and worthless to him compared with her. And he was saying this, or something like it, when Tybalt①, Lady Capulet's nephew, hearing his voice, knew him to be Romeo. Tybalt, being very angry, went at once to his uncle, and told him how a Montagu had come uninvited to the feast; but old Capulet was too fine a gentleman to be discourteous② to any man under his own roof, and he bade Tybalt be quiet. But this young man only waited for a chance to quarrel with Romeo.

In the meantime Romeo made his way to the fair lady, and told her in sweet words that he loved her, and kissed her. Just then her mother sent for her, and then Romeo found out that the lady on whom he had set his heart's hopes was Juliet, the daughter of Lord Capulet, his sworn foe. So he went away, sorrowing indeed, but loving her none the less.

Then Juliet said to her nurse: "Who is that gentleman that would not dance?"

"His name is Romeo, and a Montagu, the only son of your great enemy," answered the nurse.

Then Juliet went to her room, and looked out of her window, over the beautiful green-grey garden, where the moon was shining. And Romeo was hidden in that garden among the trees—because he could not bear to go right away without trying to see her again. So she—not knowing him to be there—spoke her secret thought aloud, and told the quiet garden how she loved Romeo.

And Romeo heard and was glad beyond measure③. Hidden below, he looked up and saw her fair face in the moonlight, framed in the blossoming creepers that grew round her window, and as he looked and listened, he felt as though he had been carried away in a dream, and set

---

① Tybalt ['tibəlt] n. 提伯尔特（男子名）
② discourteous [dis'kɔːtjəs] adj. 失礼的，无礼貌的
③ beyond measure 无可估量，极度

down by some magician in that beautiful and enchanted① garden.

"Ah—why are you called Romeo?" said Juliet. "Since I love you, what does it matter what you are called?"

"Call me but love, and I'll be new baptized②—henceforth I never will be Romeo," he cried, stepping into the full white moonlight from the shade of the cypresses③ and oleanders④ that had hidden him.

She was frightened at first, but when she saw that it was Romeo himself, and no stranger, she too was glad, and, he standing in the garden below and she leaning from the window, they spoke long together, each one trying to find the sweetest words in the world, to make that pleasant talk that lovers use. And the tale of all they said, and the sweet music their voices made together, is all set down in a golden book, where you children may read it for yourselves some day.

And the time passed so quickly, as it does for folk who love each other and are together, that when the time came to part, it seemed as though they had met but that moment—and indeed they hardly knew how to part.

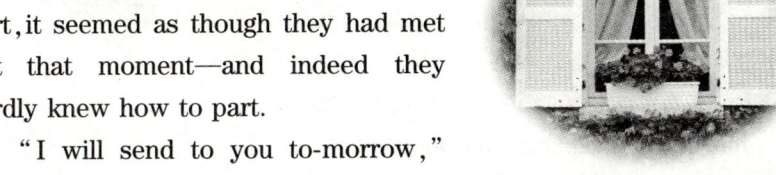

"I will send to you to-morrow," said Juliet.

And so at last, with lingering and longing, they said good-bye.

Juliet went into her room, and a dark curtain bid her bright window. Romeo went away through the still and dewy garden like a man in a dream.

The next morning, very early, Romeo went to Friar Laurence, a priest, and, telling him all the story, begged him to marry him and Juliet

---

① enchant [in'tʃɑːnt] v. 施魔法，使迷惑
② baptize [bæp'taiz] v. 给人施洗礼
③ cypress ['saipris, -prəs] n. 柏木属植物
④ oleander [ˌəuli'ændə] n. 夹竹桃

without delay①. And this, after some talk, the priest consented to do.

So when Juliet sent her old nurse to Romeo that day to know what he purposed to do, the old woman took back a message that all was well, and all things ready for the marriage of Juliet and Romeo on the next morning.

The young lovers were afraid to ask their parents' consent to their marriage, as young people should do, because of this foolish old quarrel between the Capulets and the Montagues.

And Friar Laurence was willing to help the young lovers secretly, because he thought that when they were once married their parents might soon be told, and that the match might put a happy end to the old quarrel.

So the next morning early, Romeo and Juliet were married at Friar Laurence's cell, and parted with tears and kisses. And Romeo promised to come into the garden that evening, and the nurse got ready a rope-ladder to let down from the window, so that Romeo could climb up and talk to his dear wife quietly and alone.

But that very day a dreadful thing happened.

Tybalt, the young man who had been so vexed at Romeo's going to the Capulet's feast, met him and his two friends, Mercutio and Benvolio, in the street, called Romeo a villain, and asked him to fight. Romeo had no wish to fight with Juliet's cousin, but Mercutio drew his sword, and he and Tybalt fought. And Mercutio was killed. When Romeo saw that this friend was dead, he forgot everything except anger at the man who had killed him, and he and Tybalt fought till Tybalt fell dead.

So, on the very day of his wedding, Romeo killed his dear Juliet's cousin, and was sentenced to be banished. Poor Juliet and her young husband met that night indeed; he climbed the rope-ladder among the

---

① without delay 赶快，立刻

flowers, and found her window, but their meeting was a sad one, and they parted with bitter tears and hearts heavy, because they could not know when they should meet again.

Now Juliet's father, who, of course, had no idea that she was married, wished her to wed① a gentleman named Paris, and was so angry when she refused, that she hurried away to ask Friar Laurence what she should do. He advised her to pretend to consent, and then he said:

"I will give you a draught② that will make you seem to be dead for two days, and then when they take you to church it will be to bury you, and not to marry you. They will put you in the vault③ thinking you are dead, and before you wake up Romeo and I will be there to take care of you. Will you do this, or are you afraid?"

"I will do it; talk not to me of fear!" said Juliet. And she went home and told her father she would marry Paris. If she had spoken out and told her father the truth...well, then this would have been a different story.

Lord Capulet was very much pleased to get his own way, and set about inviting his friends and getting the wedding feast ready. Everyone stayed up all night, for there was a great deal to do, and very little time to do it in. Lord Capulet was anxious to get Juliet married because he saw she was very unhappy. Of course she was really fretting④ about her husband Romeo, but her father thought she was grieving for the death of her cousin Tybalt, and he thought marriage would give her something else to think about.

Early in the morning the nurse came to call Juliet, and to dress her for her wedding; but she would not wake, and at last the nurse cried out suddenly—

"Alas! alas! help! help! my lady's dead! Oh, well-a-day that ever I was born!"

---

① wed [wed] *v.* 娶，嫁，结婚
② draught [drɑːft] *n.* 顿服药，顿服量
③ vault [vɔːlt] *n.* 地下室，(教堂下的)墓穴
④ fret [fret] *v.* (使)烦恼，(使)焦急

Lady Capulet came running in, and then Lord Capulet, and Lord Paris, the bridegroom. There lay Juliet cold and white and lifeless, and all their weeping could not wake her. So it was a burying that day instead of a marrying. Meantime Friar Laurence had sent a messenger to Mantua with a letter to Romeo telling him of all these things; and all would have been well, only the messenger was delayed, and could not go.

But ill news travels fast. Romeo's servant who knew the secret of the marriage, but not of Juliet's pretended death, heard of her funeral, and hurried to Mantua to tell Romeo how his young wife was dead and lying in the grave.

"Is it so?" cried Romeo, heart-broken. "Then I will lie by Juliet's side tonight."

And he bought himself a poison, and went straight back to Verona. He hastened① to the tomb where Juliet was lying. It was not a grave, but a vault. He broke open the door, and was just going down the stone steps that led to the vault where all the dead Capulets lay, when he heard a voice bebind him calling on him to stop.

It was the Count Paris, who was to have married Juliet that very day.

"How dare you come here and disturb the dead bodies of the Capulets, you vile Montagu?" cried Paris.

Poor Romeo, half mad with sorrow, yet tried to answer gently.

"You were told," said Paris, "that if you returned to Verona you must die."

"I must indeed," said Romeo. "I came here for nothing else. Good, gentle youth—leave me! Oh, go—before I do you any harm! I love you better than myself—go—leave me here—"

---

① hasten ['heisn] v. 催促，赶紧

Then Paris said, "I defy① you, and I arrest you as a felon②," and Romeo, in his anger and despair, drew his sword. They fought, and Paris was killed.

As Romeo's sword pierced him, Paris cried—

"Oh, I am slain! If thou be merciful, open the tomb, and lay me with Juliet!"

And Romeo said, "In faith I will."

And he carried the dead man into the tomb and laid him by the dear Juliet's side. Then he kneeled by Juliet and spoke to her, and held her in his arms, and kissed her cold lips, believing that she was dead, while all the while she was coming nearer and nearer to the time of her awakening. Then he drank the poison, and died beside his sweetheart and wife.

Now came Friar Laurence when it was too late, and saw all that had happened—and then poor Juliet woke out of her sleep to find her husband and her friend both dead beside her.

The noise of the fight had brought other folks to the place too, and Friar Laurence, hearing them, ran away, and Juliet was left alone. She saw the cup that had held the poison, and knew how all had happened, and since no poison was left for her, she drew her Romeo's dagger and thrust it through her heart—and so, falling with her head on her Romeo's breast, she died. And here ends the story of these faithful and most unhappy lovers.

And when the old folks knew from Friar Laurence of all that had befallen, they sorrowed exceedingly, and now, seeing all the mischief③ their wicked quarrel had wrought, they repented them of it, and over the bodies of their dead children they clasped hands at last, in friendship and forgiveness.

① defy [di'fai] v. 不服从，公然反抗
② felon ['felən] n. 重罪人
③ mischief ['mistʃif] n. 伤害，危害

罗密欧与朱丽叶

很久很久以前，在维罗纳有两个大家族——蒙塔古和凯普莱特。这两个家族都是有钱人家，在许多事情上他们都像其他的有钱人一样明理。可是他们就在一件事情上犯糊涂，早先这两个家族曾发生过一次争吵，非但没有像其他通情达理的人一样和好，反而越吵越凶，没完没了。如果蒙塔古家的人在街上碰到凯普莱特家的人，或是凯普莱特家的人碰到蒙塔古家的人，他们不会理睬对方；即使说话，他们也是对骂，往往还会用决斗来结束争吵。他们的亲戚和仆人们也像他们一样愚蠢可笑，因而在维罗纳大街上的殴打、决斗以及种种令人不安的举动往往是由蒙太古—凯普莱特两大家族之间的不合引起的。

这天，凯普莱特家族的首领凯普莱特大老爷举办了一个宴会——有盛大的晚餐和舞会——他非常热情好客，传出话来说只要不是蒙塔古家的人，所有来宾都将受到欢迎。可是蒙塔古家族里有一个叫罗密欧的年轻人也很想参加这个宴会，因为罗密欧所爱的罗瑟琳受到了邀请。罗瑟琳从来没有对他表示过一点点好感，他也没有理由去爱他，而实际上，他只想找个人来爱却没有找对人，而不得不错爱着她。于是他带着他的两个朋友茂丘西奥和班伏里奥去参加凯普莱特家族的盛大宴会。

老凯普莱特热情地欢迎罗密欧和他的朋友们的到来，年轻的罗密欧在穿着天鹅绒和绸缎衣服的、彬彬有礼的人群中走来走去，男士们的剑柄和衣领上镶嵌着珠宝，女士们佩戴的宝石在胸前和手腕上闪着光，价值不菲的珍奇珠宝也在她们的腰际环绕。罗密欧也身着盛装，尽管他的黑色面罩遮住了他的眼睛和鼻子，人们还是可以看见他的嘴、他的头发和他的行为举止，可以看出他要比在场的其他任何人英俊十二倍。

很快，在那些跳舞的人群中，他看见了一位美丽脱俗的女子，从那一刻起他再也不去想那个他自以为爱着的罗瑟琳了。他看着眼前这位美人，身着白色绸缎，佩戴着珍珠，舞中移步，在罗密欧眼里，与她相比，整个世界都顿时黯然失色，不值一提。正在他赞美着她的时候，凯普莱特夫人的侄子提伯尔特听见了，他从声音里辨出是罗密欧。提伯尔特非常生气，马上告诉他姑父说有个蒙塔古家的人没被邀请就来参加宴会。老凯普莱特大人是一位正派的绅士,不想对他的任何宾客失礼,就嘱咐提伯尔特冷静下来。这个年轻人只好伺机与罗密欧争吵。

这时,罗密欧走到这位美人面前,充满柔情地对她表达了爱意,并吻了她。正在那时她的母亲派人来叫她,罗密欧这才发现,这位令他倾心的女子就是与他不共戴天的仇人——凯普莱特大人的女儿朱丽叶。尽管依然爱着她,罗密欧还是难过地离开了。

后来朱丽叶问她的奶妈:"没有跳舞的那个绅士是谁啊?"

"他叫罗密欧,蒙塔古家的人,是你仇人家唯一的儿子。"奶妈回答。

朱丽叶回到她的房间,望着窗外,在美丽的、灰绿色的花园上方,一轮明月闪耀着光芒。罗密欧正藏在花园里的树丛中,因为他舍不得离开,还想再看她一眼。她呢,根本不知道罗密欧躲在那里,就对着宁静的花园大声地说出了她心中的秘密:她深深爱上了罗密欧。

听了这番话,罗密欧满心狂喜。他藏在下面抬头仰望,看见月光下她那美丽的脸庞,像是镶在四周长着开花的爬藤的窗户里。罗密欧看着、听着,感觉自己像是走进了梦境,被这个美丽而迷人的花园中的魔法师钉在那里发怔。

"啊,你为什么叫罗密欧呢?"朱丽叶说。"既然我爱你,你叫什么又有什么关系呢?"

"只管叫我爱人,我将会被重新洗礼——今后我再也不是罗密欧了。"他大声说着,从他躲藏的柏树和夹竹桃的阴影中走到了明亮的月光下。

起初,朱丽叶感到害怕,可当她看到只是罗密欧而不是陌生人时,就特别高兴。罗密欧站在下面的花园里,她从窗子里探出身,两个人都用最甜蜜的话语来表达彼此的爱意,他们情投意合,交谈了很久很久,难舍难分。他们所倾吐的话语如一只甜美的曲子,被载入金典,有一天你们这些孩子可以自己读来听。

对于两个相爱的人来说,在一起的时光总是过得飞快,到了要分别的时候,感觉好像才刚刚见面——实际上他们不知道怎么告别。

"明天我送信给你。"朱丽叶说。

两人最终还是依依不舍地告别了。

朱丽叶回到房间,用一个深色的帘子遮住了明亮的窗子。罗密欧如同一个梦游的人儿,穿过静谧而潮湿的花园离去。

第二天一大早,罗密欧就跑去修道院找劳伦斯神父,并把他和朱丽叶的事情讲给神父听,祈求他立刻为他和朱丽叶主持婚礼。交谈之后,神父答应了罗密欧的请求。

那天朱丽叶让她的奶妈去了解罗密欧的计划,这位老妇人捎信回来说一切进展顺利,为第二天举行婚礼的一切准备也都已经安排得妥妥当当。

正如年轻人应该做的那样,这对年轻的恋人却没敢征求父母的意见,因为凯普莱特家族和蒙塔古家族积怨太深。

劳伦斯神父愿意暗地里帮助这对年轻的恋人,因为他认为他们两个一旦完婚,双方父母很快就会知道了,他希望他们的结合能使两个家族言归于好。

于是第二天一早,罗密欧和朱丽叶就在劳伦斯神父的密室里举行了婚礼,然后含泪吻别。罗密欧发誓说当天晚上会到花园去见朱丽叶,奶妈也准备好了绳梯,从窗口放下,罗密欧就可以爬上去,跟他亲爱的妻子相会了。

可是就在那一天发生了一件可怕的事。

提伯尔特,就是那个对罗密欧参加凯普莱特家的宴会很恼火的年轻人,在街上遇见了罗密欧和他的两个朋友,茂丘西奥和班伏里奥,提伯尔特辱骂罗密欧是个恶棍,并要和罗密欧决斗。罗密欧根本无意和朱丽叶的表哥决斗,可茂丘西奥拔出剑和提伯尔特打了起来,结果茂丘西奥被刺死了。看见朋友死去,罗密欧实在按捺不住了,除了对杀死他朋友的这个人充满仇恨,其他一切都忘在脑后了。于是他同提伯尔特开始决斗,直到提伯尔特倒地死去。

就这样,在结婚的当天,罗密欧杀死了他挚爱的朱丽叶的表哥,被判流放。当晚,可怜的朱丽叶和他年轻的丈夫见了面;他在花丛中爬上绳梯,找到了她的窗子,可是他们的见面是悲伤的,眼含痛苦的泪水他们依依惜别,心情非常沉重,因为他们不知道何时才能再见面。

朱丽叶的父亲根本不知道她结婚的事,希望她能嫁给一个叫帕利斯的绅士,朱丽叶拒绝了,这让她父亲很生气。朱丽叶匆忙跑到劳伦斯神父那里,请他为她想个办法。他建议她假装同意,然后说:

"我会给你一瓶药,吃下去后的两天内你会看起来像死了一样,然后他们会把你带到教堂并把你埋葬,而不是把你嫁出去。因为他们认为你已经死去,就会把你放在教堂下的墓室里,在你醒来之前我和罗密欧会来照看你。你敢不敢这样做？你害怕吗？"

"我愿意做；我绝不害怕！"朱丽叶说。然后她回到家告诉父亲她愿意嫁给帕利斯。假若她对父亲说实话……那么，接下来发生的可能就是另一个故事了。

凯普莱特老爷非常高兴，开始邀请他的亲朋好友，准备结婚喜宴。有太多事情要做，每个人都要熬夜，几乎没有时间休息。看到女儿近来闷闷不乐，凯普莱特老爷急切地想把她嫁出去。当然她是为了自己的丈夫罗密欧而苦恼，而她父亲还以为她是为死去的表哥提伯尔特悲伤，认为结婚可以消除她的悲伤。

第二天一早，奶妈就过来叫朱丽叶起床，为她穿嫁衣；可是怎么也叫不醒她，最后奶妈突然哭喊起来——

"啊！啊！来人啊！来人啊！我的小姐死了！天哪！我的命怎么那么苦啊！"

凯普莱特夫人跑了进来，接着凯普莱特老爷和新郎帕利斯也跑了进来。朱丽叶躺在那里，身体冰冷，面色苍白，已无生息。所有人的哭泣也无法将她唤醒。那天，婚礼变成了葬礼。与此同时，劳伦斯神父派信使给在曼图亚的罗密欧送了一封信，告诉他这些事情的真相；若非信使拖延了送信时间或者根本没有去送，一切都将会进展顺利。

然而坏消息往往传得更快。罗密欧的仆人知道他们结婚的秘密，但并不知道朱丽叶假死的事实，听说了她的葬礼后就跑去曼图亚告诉罗密欧他年轻的妻子已经死去，躺在坟墓里。

"是真的吗？"罗密欧哭着说。他的心都碎了。"那么今晚我要和我的朱丽叶死在一起。"

于是他给自己买了一瓶毒药，直接回到了维罗纳。他急匆匆地赶向朱丽叶躺着的坟墓。这不是墓地，而是教堂下的墓室。他打开门，正要走下石梯，前往墓室，那里躺着凯普莱特家族所有的亡者，突然有个声音从身后传来让他停下了脚步。

正是那天要和朱丽叶完婚的帕利斯伯爵。

"你怎么敢来这里扰乱凯普莱特家族亡者的安宁，你这个卑鄙的蒙塔古！"帕利斯喊道。

可怜的罗密欧，伤心得近乎疯狂，然而他尽力委婉地回答。

"你知道，"帕利斯说，"如果你回到维罗纳

你只有死路一条。"

"我必须回来,"罗密欧说,"我来到这里不为别的。善良而高贵的年轻人——别管我!哦,走吧——在我伤害你之前!我爱你胜过爱自己——走吧——别管我——"

帕利斯说:"我要和你决斗,我要把你当作重罪犯逮捕。"于是愤怒和绝望的罗密欧拔出剑来,两人决斗起来,帕利斯倒下了。

当罗密欧的剑刺穿他的时候,帕利斯喊道——

"哦,我死了!如果你够仁慈的话,请打开墓穴,将我和朱丽叶放在一起!"

罗密欧说:"好,我答应你!"

他把这个死去的人抬进了坟墓,放到心爱的朱丽叶身边,然后跪在她面前,向她诉说,将她拥在怀中,亲吻着她冰冷的嘴唇,他以为她真的死了。朱丽叶就要醒来了,可他却将毒药喝了下去,倒在了他挚爱的妻子身旁。

劳伦斯神父赶到时已经太迟了,他看到了刚刚发生过的一幕。可怜的朱丽叶从昏睡中醒来,发现她的丈夫和朋友都死在她的身边。

打斗的嘈杂声引来了其他人,劳伦斯神父听到后,立即走开了,留下朱丽叶一人在那里。看到那个盛过毒药的杯子,她明白了刚才发生的一切。毒药被罗密欧喝得干干净净,于是她就抽出他的匕首刺穿了自己的胸膛,倒在了罗密欧的怀中,死了。这对坚贞不渝却又最不幸的恋人的故事就这样结束了。

两个家族的长辈们从劳伦斯神父那里得知了所发生的一切后,悲痛欲绝,亲眼看到他们两个家族之间的野蛮而恶毒的争吵所带来的恶果,双方都感到后悔难过。最后,在死去的孩子们的尸体前他们握手言和,发誓彼此宽恕,永世和好。

10. Hamlet

Polonius Killed by Hamlet

Hamlet was the only son of the King of Denmark. He loved his father and mother dearly—and was happy in the love of a sweet lady named Ophelia①. Her father, Polonius②, was the King's Chamberlain.

While Hamlet was away studying at Wittenberg, his father died. Young Hamlet hastened home in great grief to hear that a serpent③ had stung the King, and that he was dead. The young Prince had loved his father so tenderly that you may judge what he felt when he found that the

---

① Ophelia [əuˈfiːliə] n. 奥菲莉娅(女子名)
② Polonius [pəˈləuniəs] n. 波洛涅斯(男子名)
③ serpent [ˈsəːpənt] n. 大毒蛇,阴险的人

Queen, before yet the King had been laid in the ground a month, had determined to marry again—and to marry the dead King's brother.

Hamlet refused to put off① mourning for the wedding.

"It is not only the black I wear on my body," he said, "that proves my loss. I wear mourning in my heart for my dead father. His son at least remembers him, and grieves still."

Then said Claudius the King's brother, "This grief is unreasonable. Of course you must sorrow at the loss of your father, but—"

"Ah," said Hamlet, bitterly, "I cannot in one little month forget those I love."

With that the Queen and Claudius left him, to make merry over their wedding, forgetting the poor good King who had been so kind to them both.

And Hamlet, left alone, began to wonder and to question as to what he ought to do. For he could not believe the story about the snake-bite. It seemed to him all too plain that the wicked Claudius had killed the King, so as to get the crown and marry the Queen. Yet he had no proof, and could not accuse Claudius.

And while he was thus thinking came Horatio②, a fellow student of his, from Wittenberg.

"What brought you here?" asked Hamlet, when he had greeted his friend kindly.

"I came, my lord, to see your father's funeral."

"I think it was to see my mother's wedding," said Hamlet, bitterly. "My father! We shall not look upon his like again."

"My lord," answered Horatio, "I

---

① put off 推迟,拖延
② Horatio [hɔ'reiʃiəu] n. 霍拉旭(男子名)

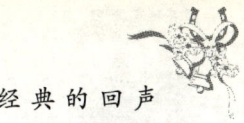

think I saw him yesternight."

Then, while Hamlet listened in surprise, Horatio told how he, with two gentlemen of the guard, had seen the King's ghost on the battlements. Hamlet went that night, and true enough, at midnight, the ghost of the King, in the armor he had been wont to① wear, appeared on the battlements in the chill moonlight. Hamlet was a brave youth. Instead of running away from the ghost he spoke to it—and when it beckoned② him he followed it to a quiet place, and there the ghost told him that what he had suspected was true. The wicked Claudius had indeed killed his good brother the King, by dropping poison into his ear as he slept in his orchard③ in the afternoon.

"And you," said the ghost, "must avenge this cruel murder—on my wicked brother. But do nothing against the Queen—for I have loved her, and she is your mother. Remember me."

Then seeing the morning approach, the ghost vanished.

"Now," said Hamlet, "there is nothing left but revenge. Remember thee—I will remember nothing else—books, pleasure, youth—let all go— and your commands alone live on my brain."

So when his friends came back he made them swear to keep the secret of the ghost, and then went in from the battlements, now gray with mingled④ dawn and moonlight, to think how he might best avenge his murdered father.

The shock of seeing and hearing his father's ghost made him feel almost mad, and for fear⑤ that his uncle might notice that he was not himself, he determined to hide his mad longing for revenge under a pretended madness in other matters.

And when he met Ophelia, who loved him—and to whom he had

① wont to 习惯于
② beckon ['bekən] v. 招手,召唤
③ orchard ['ɔːtʃəd] n. 果园
④ mingle ['miŋgl] v. 混合
⑤ for fear 以免

given gifts, and letters, and many loving words—he behaved so wildly to her, that she could not but think him mad. For she loved him so that she could not believe he would be as cruel as this, unless he were quite mad. So she told her father, and showed him a pretty letter from Hamlet. And in the letter was much folly①, and this pretty verse—

"Doubt that the stars are fire;
Doubt that the sun doth move;
Doubt truth to be a liar;
But never doubt I love."

And from that time everyone believed that the cause of Hamlet's supposed madness was love.

Poor Hamlet was very unhappy. He longed to obey his father's ghost—and yet he was too gentle and kindly to wish to kill another man, even his father's murderer. And sometimes he wondered whether, after all, the ghost spoke truly.

Just at this time some actors came to the Court, and Hamlet ordered them to perform a certain play before the King and Queen. Now, this play was the story of a man who had been murdered in his garden by a near relation, who afterwards married the dead man's wife.

You may imagine the feelings of the wicked King, as he sat on his throne, with the Queen beside him and all his Court around, and saw, acted on the stage, the very wickedness that he had himself done. And when, in the play, the wicked relation poured poison into the ear of the sleeping man, the wicked Claudius suddenly rose, and staggered from the room—the Queen and others following.

Then said Hamlet to his friends—

"Now I am sure the ghost spoke true. For if Claudius had not done this murder, he could not have been so distressed② to see it in the play."

---

① folly ['fɔli] n. 愚蠢，荒唐事
② distressed [di'strest] adj. 哀伤的

Now the Queen sent for Hamlet, by the King's desire, to scold him for his conduct during the play, and for other matters; and Claudius, wishing to know exactly what happened, told old Polonius to hide himself behind the hangings① in the Queen's room. And as they talked, the Queen got frightened at Hamlet's rough, strange words, and cried for help, and Polonius behind the curtain cried out too. Hamlet, thinking it was the King who was hidden there, thrust with his sword at the hangings, and killed, not the King, but poor old Polonius.

So now Hamlet had offended his uncle and his mother, and by bad hap killed his true love's father.

"Oh! what a rash② and bloody deed is this," cried the Queen.

And Hamlet answered bitterly, "Almost as bad as to kill a king, and marry his brother." Then Hamlet told the Queen plainly all his thoughts and how he knew of the murder, and begged her, at least, to have no more friendship or kindness of the base Claudius, who had killed the good King. And as they spoke the King's ghost again appeared before Hamlet, but the Queen could not see it. So when the ghost had gone, they parted.

When the Queen told Claudius what had passed, and how Polonius was dead, he said, "This shows plainly that Hamlet is mad, and since he has killed the Chancellor, it is for his own safety that we must carry out③ our plan, and send him away to England."

So Hamlet was sent, under charge of two courtiers who served the King, and these bore letters to the English Court, requiring that Hamlet should be put to death. But Hamlet had the good sense to get at these

---

① hanging ['hæŋiŋ] n. 悬挂物,(通常用复数)帘子、幔帐
② rash [ræʃ] adj. 轻率的,匆忙的,鲁莽的
③ carry out 完成,实现,贯彻,执行

letters, and put in others instead, with the names of the two courtiers who were so ready to betray him. Then, as the vessel went to England, Hamlet escaped on board a pirate ship, and the two wicked courtiers left him to his fate, and went on to meet theirs.

Hamlet hurried home, but in the meantime a dreadful thing had happened. Poor pretty Ophelia, having lost her lover and her father, lost her wits too, and went in sad madness about the Court, with straws①, and weeds, and flowers in her hair, singing strange scraps of songs, and talking poor, foolish, pretty talk with no heart of meaning to it. And one day, coming to a stream where willows grew, she tried to hang a flowery garland② on a willow, and fell into the water with all her flowers, and so died.

And Hamlet had loved her, though his plan of seeming madness had made him hide it; and when he came back, he found the King and Queen, and the Court, weeping at the funeral of his dear love and lady.

Ophelia's brother, Laertes③, had also just come to Court to ask justice for the death of his father, old Polonius; and now, wild with grief, he leaped into his sister's grave, to clasp her in his arms once more.

"I loved her more than forty thousand brothers," cried Hamlet, and leapt into the grave after him, and they fought till they were parted.

Afterwards Hamlet begged Laertes to forgive him.

"I could not bear," he said, "that any, even a brother, should seem to love her more than I."

But the wicked Claudius would not let them be friends. He told Laertes how Hamlet had killed old Polonius, and between them they made a plot to slay Hamlet by treachery.

Laertes challenged him to a fencing match④, and all the Court were present. Hamlet had the blunt foil always used in fencing, but Laertes had

---

① straw [strɔː] *n.* 稻草
② flowery garland 花环
③ Laertes [leiˈɔːtis] *n.* 雷尔提斯（男子名）
④ fencing match 击剑比赛

prepared for himself a sword, sharp, and tipped with poison. And the wicked King had made ready a bowl of poisoned wine, which he meant to give poor Hamlet when he should grow warm with the sword play, and should call for drink.

So Laertes and Hamlet fought, and Laertes, after some fencing, gave Hamlet a sharp sword thrust. Hamlet, angry at this treachery①—for they had been fencing, not as men fight, but as they play—closed with Laertes in a struggle; both dropped their swords, and when they picked them up again, Hamlet, without noticing it, had exchanged his own blunt sword for Laertes' sharp and poisoned one. And with one thrust of it he pierced Laertes, who fell dead by his own treachery.

At this moment the Queen cried out, "The drink, the drink! Oh, my dear Hamlet! I am poisoned!"

She had drunk of the poisoned bowl the King had prepared for Hamlet, and the King saw the Queen, whom, wicked as he was, he really loved, fall dead by his means.

Then Ophelia being dead, and Polonius, and the Queen, and Laertes, and the two courtiers who had been sent to England, Hamlet at last found courage to do the ghost's bidding and avenge② his father's murder—which, if he had braced up his heart to do long before, all these lives had been spared, and none had suffered but the wicked King, who well deserved③ to die.

Hamlet, his heart at last being great enough to do the deed he ought to, turned the poisoned sword on the false King.

"Then—venom—do thy work!" he cried, and the King died.

So Hamlet in the end kept the promise he had made his father. And all being now

---

① treachery ['tretʃəri] n. 背叛,背信弃义
② avenge [ə'vendʒ] v. 为……报复,报仇
③ deserved [di'zə:vd] adj. 应得的

accomplished, he himself died. And those who stood by saw him die, with prayers and tears, for his friends and his people loved him with their whole hearts. Thus ends the tragic tale of Hamlet, Prince of Denmark.

哈 姆 雷 特

哈姆雷特是丹麦国王唯一的儿子,他深爱着自己的父母,并沐浴在美女奥菲莉娅的爱河里。奥菲莉娅的父亲波洛涅斯是国王的御前大臣。

哈姆雷特远在温特堡学习期间,其父去世。年轻的哈姆雷特听说国王是被毒蛇咬死的,悲恸万分,急匆匆地赶回家。这位年轻的王子深爱着父亲,当他发现父亲下葬还不到一个月,母后就决意嫁给已故国王的弟弟,你可以想象他该是怎样的感受。

哈姆雷特反对因婚礼而推迟哀悼。

"我不仅要穿着黑纱来悼念我死去的父亲,"他说,"还要在心里悼念他。至少他的儿子依然记得他,依然为他感到悲恸。"

已故国王的弟弟克劳荻斯说:"你的悲伤是不理智的。当然失去父亲会使你感到难过,可是——"

"啊,"哈姆雷特痛苦地说道,"我无法在短短的一个月就忘记我爱的人。"

克劳荻斯和王后随即弃哈姆雷特而去,享受他们的婚礼,已过世的那位可怜而善良的国王曾经对他们的好心善意,他们早已忘记。

无人过问的哈姆雷特开始思索,开始考虑他应该做些什么。因为他无法相信毒蛇咬死父王的故事。他认为,显然是恶毒的克劳荻斯为了得到王位、迎娶王后而杀死了国王。可是他没有证据,因而无法谴责他。

正在他陷入沉思的时候,从温特堡一起回来的同学霍拉旭来了。

"什么风把你吹来了?"哈姆雷特温和地问候他的朋友。

"我的殿下,我来参加你父亲的葬礼。"

"我想该是来参加我母亲的婚礼吧,"

哈姆雷特痛苦地说道,"而我的父亲!我们将再也看不到他的容颜了。"

"殿下,"霍拉旭答道,"我想我昨晚看见国王了。"

于是,哈姆雷特惊讶地从霍拉旭那里得知,他和两位守城人看到先王的鬼魂出现在城垛上。哈姆雷特当晚便去了城垛,午夜时分,他真的看到了先父的鬼魂,穿着常穿的盔甲,在寒冷的月夜出现在城垛上。哈姆雷特是位很勇敢的年轻人,他非但没有逃跑,反而跟那鬼魂说话——并随着先父的鬼魂来到了一个僻静处,在那里鬼魂的话验证了他的怀疑,确实是邪恶的克劳荻斯杀死了他的好王兄。那天下午国王在果园里睡觉,克劳荻斯把毒药倒进了他的耳朵。

"你要记住,"鬼魂对哈姆雷特说道,"你一定要去找我邪恶的弟弟,那个残忍无比的凶手复仇。但不要伤害王后,因为我曾经爱过她,而且她是你的母亲。记住我说的话。"

看到黎明将至,鬼魂消失了。

"现在,"哈姆雷特说道,"我一无所有,只有复仇。我只记得你——其他什么事都不记得——什么书籍、快乐、青春——统统抛却——我的脑海里只有你的嘱托。"

朋友们回来后,哈姆雷特让他们发誓不要说出鬼魂的秘密,然后从城垛中走了出来。月光和晨曦交汇的时刻,天微微泛白,哈姆雷特开始思索如何为被杀害的父亲报仇。

看到先父的鬼魂并听到他讲话,这突如其来的惊吓几乎使哈姆雷特发疯,为避免叔父怀疑他的反常,他决定假装发疯来隐藏自己复仇的迫切心情。

哈姆雷特见到了深爱着他的奥菲莉娅,他曾经为他心爱的人儿赠送礼物,并为她写了一封封有着甜言蜜语的情书,而今他的粗野行为使奥菲莉娅误以为他真的疯癫了。因深爱着他,除非他真的疯掉,否则她无法相信他会像现在这么残酷。于是她告诉了她父亲,并让他看了哈姆雷特写给她的情书。这封情书言辞傻气,并附有一首小诗——

可怀疑星辰如火焚;

可怀疑太阳不恒定;

可怀疑真理是谎言;

决不怀疑我的深情。

此后,所有人都认为哈姆雷特所谓的疯癫,究其原因是爱情。

可怜的哈姆雷特闷闷不乐,他渴望遵循父亲鬼魂的意愿,然而,他性情

善良温和而不忍心杀害其他人,即使是杀害他父亲的凶手。有时,他还会怀疑鬼魂说得是否属实。

恰恰在这个时候,皇宫里来了一些演员,哈姆雷特就让他们给国王和王后表演他编排的戏剧。在这个故事里,一个男人在他的花园里被他的一位近亲谋杀,后来这位凶手又娶了死去男人的遗孀为妻。

你可以想象一下这个邪恶的国王有着怎样的感受!他坐在王座上,旁边坐着王后,还有所有的大臣,观看着舞台上表演的自己的邪恶行径。当表演到邪恶的亲戚往熟睡者的耳朵里灌毒药时,邪恶的克劳狄斯突然起身,跌跌撞撞地走出了房间——王后和其他人紧跟其后。

于是,哈姆雷特对他的朋友们说——

"现在我确信那个鬼魂说的是真的了。因为如果克劳狄斯不是凶手的话,他今天看到戏中的表演时就不会这么神情不对。"

王后奉国王的旨意训导哈姆雷特,责备了他编排演出,以及其他的一些行为;克劳狄斯想知道他们母子谈话的内容,就吩咐御前大臣老波洛涅斯躲在王后寝宫的帷幕后面偷听。在他们母子交谈的时候,哈姆雷特的言辞激烈,尖锐刻薄,王后听了非常害怕,就大呼救命,帷幕后面的波洛涅斯也大声呼喊了起来。哈姆雷特听到后,以为是国王藏在那里,就拔出剑来,朝那个发出声音的地方刺去,结果杀死的不是国王,而是可怜的老波洛涅斯。

如今哈姆雷特不仅冒犯了叔叔和母亲,又意外地将自己心上人的父亲杀死了。

"哎呀!"王后嚷道,"你干了一件多么鲁莽残忍的事呀!"

哈姆雷特痛苦地说:"残忍得像杀了一个国王,然后嫁给他的弟弟。"接着哈姆雷特坦白地告诉了王后他的想法以及他怎样查出了凶手,并祈求她不要再亲近克劳狄斯,不要再对那个卑鄙的人好了,是他亲手杀死了善良的国王。正在那时,已死国王的鬼魂再次出现了,而王后却看不见他。鬼魂消失以后,他们也分开了。

王后把发生的事情和波洛涅斯是怎么死的告诉了克劳狄斯,克劳狄斯说:"很显然,哈姆雷特真的疯了,既然他杀死了我的这位大臣,为了哈姆雷特的安全起见,我们必须执行我们的计划,把他送往英格兰。"

于是在国王的两个大臣的押送下,哈姆雷特被送往英格兰。他们给英格兰王宫带了国王的亲笔信,信中要求将哈姆雷特处死。哈姆雷特疑心这里面有阴谋,夜里偷偷拿到那封信,巧妙地把要处死的人改成押送他的两个朝臣的名字,然后又把信封起来放回原来的地方。当船快要抵达英格兰时,哈姆雷特逃到了一只海盗船上,那两个邪恶的大臣把他丢下,让他听凭命运的摆布,他俩则带着那封被篡改过的信去英格兰领命了。

哈姆雷特急匆匆地往家赶,可这时一件更可怕的事情发生了。可怜的奥菲莉娅失去了爱人和父亲后,因悲伤过度也变得神经错乱。她疯狂地在宫中跑来跑去,头发上插着稻草、杂草和野花,唱着一些奇怪的歌,傻乎乎地说着一些毫无意义的疯话。一天,她来到一个周围种着柳树的小溪边,想把花环挂到一棵柳树上,结果这个美丽可爱的姑娘和她采摘的花草一起跌进水里淹死了。

哈姆雷特深爱着她,可是他装疯的计划使他不得不掩藏他的悲伤;回来后,他看到国王和王后,以及宫中大臣正在他心爱的姑娘的葬礼上哭泣。

奥菲莉娅的哥哥雷尔提斯也来到王宫为他死去的父亲波洛涅斯讨公道。他悲伤欲绝,跳进他妹妹的坟墓里,再次紧紧地将她抱在怀中。

"我对她的爱比她四万个哥哥对她的爱还要深。"哈姆雷特哭喊着,也随他跳进了坟墓,两人扭打起来,直到被人拉开。

后来哈姆雷特请求雷尔提斯原谅他。

"我无法忍受,"哈姆雷特说,"连一个哥哥都看起来比我还爱她。"

然而,邪恶的克劳荻斯不愿意让他们俩成为朋友,他告诉雷尔提斯哈姆雷特是怎样将老波洛涅斯杀死的,他们又密谋了一个将哈姆雷特杀死的计划。

雷尔提斯向哈姆雷特挑战击剑比赛,朝中所有的大臣都前去观战。哈姆雷特使用的是一把经常在比赛中使用的钝剑,而雷尔提斯却准备了一把锋利无比的剑,并且在剑锋上涂上了毒药。邪恶的国王还备了一碗毒酒,准备让哈姆雷特在比赛中热得想喝水时喝。

于是两人交起手来,几个回合后,雷尔提斯刺了哈姆雷特一剑,哈姆雷特对他这种背信弃义的举止感到气愤——因为他们是在比剑术,而非决斗。厮战中两人的剑都掉在了地上,当他们拾起剑继续比赛时,哈姆雷特无意中

将自己那把钝剑和雷尔提斯那把有毒的利剑换了过来,然后又用雷尔提斯的那把剑回刺了他一下,这样,他随即死于他自己的奸计。

正在这时,王后大叫道:"酒,酒!哦,我亲爱的哈姆雷特!我中毒了!"

她喝下了国王为哈姆雷特准备的毒酒。尽管国王卑鄙无耻,却深爱着王后,就这样他看着自己心爱的王后惨死在自己手中。

奥菲莉娅、波洛涅斯、王后、雷尔提斯,还有派往英格兰的两位大臣都已经死去,哈姆雷特终于鼓起勇气去执行那个鬼魂的命令为父亲复仇。如果他早这样做,这些生命就不会白白死去,而只有这个罪有应得的国王会受到惩罚。

哈姆雷特终于鼓起勇气做他应该做的事了,他手持那把毒剑转向这个假国王。

"来吧,你这条毒蛇,受死吧!"他喊着,把国王杀死了。

哈姆雷特最终完成了为父王复仇的使命。遗愿实现了,他也死了。那些看着他死去的人都流下了眼泪,并为他祈祷,因为他的朋友和他的人民都全心全意地爱着他。丹麦王子哈姆雷特的悲剧故事到此结束。

11. Othello

Othello Telling Desdemona His Adventures

Four hundred years ago there lived in Venice an ensign① named Iago②, who hated his general, Othello③, for not making him a lieutenant④. Instead of Iago, who was strongly recommended, Othello had chosen Michael Cassio, whose smooth tongue had helped him to win the heart of Desdemona⑤. Lago had a friend called Roderigo⑥, who supplied him with money and felt he could not be happy unless Desdemona was

---

① ensign [ˈensain, ˈensn] n. 海军少尉，这里指掌旗官
② Iago [ˈiɑːgəu] n. 伊阿古（男子名）
③ Othello [əuˈθeləu] n. 奥赛罗（男子名）
④ lieutenant [lefˈtenənt; leˈtenənt; ljuːˈtenənt] n. 陆军中尉，海军上尉
⑤ Desdemona [ˌdezdəˈməunə] n. 苔丝狄蒙娜（女子名）
⑥ Roderigo [ˌrəudəˈriːgəu] n. 罗德利哥（男子名）

his wife.

Othello was a Moor, but of so dark a complexion① that his enemies called him a Blackamoor②. His life had been hard and exciting. He had been vanquished③ in battle and sold into slavery; and he had been a great traveler and seen men whose shoulders were higher than their heads. Brave as a lion, he had one great fault—jealousy. His love was a terrible selfishness. To love a woman meant with him to possess her as absolutely as he possessed something that did not live and think. The story of Othello is a story of jealousy.

One night Iago told Roderigo that Othello had carried off Desdemona without the knowledge of her father, Brabantio④. He persuaded Roderigo to arouse Brabantio, and when that senator appeared Iago told him of Desdemona's elopement in the most unpleasant way. Though he was Othello's officer, he termed him a thief and a Barbary⑤ horse.

Brabantio accused Othello before the Duke of Venice of using sorcery⑥ to fascinate⑦ his daughter, but Othello said that the only sorcery he used was his voice, which told Desdemona his adventures and hair-breadth escapes. Desdemona was led into the council-chamber, and she explained how she could love Othello despite his almost black face by saying, "I saw Othello's visage⑧ in his mind."

As Othello had married Desdemona, and she was glad to be his wife, there was no

---

① complexion [kəmˈplekʃən] n. 面色,肤色
② blackamoor [ˈblækəmuə] n. 皮肤黑的人
③ vanquish [ˈvæŋkwiʃ] v. 征服
④ Brabantio [brəˈbæntiəu] n. 勃拉班修(男子名)
⑤ Barbary [ˈbɑːbəri] n. 巴巴里(北非伊斯兰教地区,濒地中海海岸,在埃及与大西洋之间)
⑥ sorcery [ˈsɔːsəri] n. 巫术,魔术
⑦ fascinate [ˈfæsineit] v. 使着迷,使神魂颠倒
⑧ visage [ˈvizidʒ] n. 面貌,容貌

more to be said against him, especially as the Duke wished him to go to Cyprus① to defend it against the Turks. Othello was quite ready to go, and Desdemona, who pleaded to go with him, was permitted to join him at Cyprus.

Othello's feelings on landing in this island were intensely joyful. "Oh, my sweet," he said to Desdemona, who arrived with Iago, his wife, and Roderigo before him, "I hardly know what I say to you. I am in love with my own happiness."

News coming presently that the Turkish② fleet was out of action, he proclaimed a festival in Cyprus from five to eleven at night.

Cassio was on duty in the Castle where Othello ruled Cyprus, so Iago decided to make the lieutenant drink too much. He had some difficulty, as Cassio knew that wine soon went to his head, but servants brought wine into the room where Cassio was, and Iago sang a drinking song, and so Cassio lifted a glass too often to the health of the general.

When Cassio was inclined to be quarrelsome③, Iago told Roderigo to say something unpleasant to him. Cassio cudgeled Roderigo, who ran into the presence of Montano④, the ex-governor. Montano civilly interceded⑤ for Roderigo, but received so rude an answer from Cassio that he said, "Come, come, you're drunk!" Cassio then wounded him, and Iago sent Roderigo out to scare the town with a cry of mutiny⑥.

The uproar aroused Othello, who, on learning its cause, said, "Cassio, I love thee, but never more be officer of mine."

On Cassio and Iago being alone together, the disgraced man moaned about his reputation. Iago said reputation and humbug⑦ were the same thing. "O God," exclaimed Cassio, without heeding him, "that men

① Cyprus ['saiprəs] n. 塞浦路斯(地中海东部的一个岛国,位于土耳其以南)
② Turkish ['tə:kiʃ] adj. 土耳其的,土耳其人的,土耳其语的
③ quarrelsome ['kwɔr(ə)lsəm] adj. 喜欢吵架的,好争论的
④ Montano [mɔn'tænəu] n. 蒙太诺(男子名)
⑤ intercede [ˌintə(:)'si:d] v. 调解
⑥ mutiny ['mju:tini] n. 兵变,反抗
⑦ humbug ['hʌmbʌg] n. 欺骗

should put an enemy in their mouths to steal away their brains!"

Iago advised him to beg Desdemona to ask Othello to pardon him. Cassio was pleased with the advice, and next morning made his request to Desdemona in the garden of the castle. She was kindness itself, and said, "Be merry, Cassio, for I would rather die than forsake① your cause."

Cassio at that moment saw Othello advancing with Iago, and retired hurriedly.

Iago said, "I don't like that."

"What did you say?" asked Othello, who felt that he had meant something unpleasant, but Iago pretended he had said nothing. "Was not that Cassio who went from my wife?" asked Othello, and Iago, who knew that it was Cassio and why it was Cassio, said, "I cannot think it was Cassio who stole away② in that guilty manner."

Desdemona told Othello that it was grief and humility③ which made Cassio retreat at his approach. She reminded him how Cassio had taken his part when she was still heart-free, and found fault with④ her Moorish lover. Othello was melted, and said, "I will deny thee nothing", but Desdemona told him that what she asked was as much for his good as dining.

Desdemona left the garden, and Iago asked if it was really true that Cassio had known Desdemona before her marriage.

"Yes," said Othello.

"Indeed," said Iago, as though something that had mystified⑤ him was now very clear.

"Is he not honest?" demanded Othello, and Iago repeated the adjective inquiringly, as though he were afraid to say "No."

---

① forsake [fə'seik] v. 放弃,抛弃
② steal away 溜走
③ humility [hju(:)'militi] n. 谦卑
④ find fault with 找茬
⑤ mystify ['mistifai] v. 迷惑

"What do you mean?" insisted Othello.

To this Iago would only say the flat opposite of what he said to Cassio. He had told Cassio that reputation was humbug. To Othello he said, "Who steals my purse steals trash, but he who filches from me my good name ruins me."

At this Othello almost leapt into the air, and Iago was so confident of his jealousy that he ventured to warn him against it. Yes, it was no other than Iago who called jealousy "the green-eyed monster which doth mock① the meat it feeds on."

Iago having given jealousy one blow, proceeded to feed it with the remark that Desdemona deceived her father when she eloped with Othello. "If she deceived him, why not you?" was his meaning.

Presently Desdemona re-entered to tell Othello that dinner was ready. She saw that he was ill at ease. He explained it by a pain in his forehead. Desdemona then produced a handkerchief, which Othello had given her. A prophetess, two hundred years old, had made this handkerchief from the silk of sacred silkworms, dyed it in a liquid prepared from the hearts of maidens, and embroidered② it with strawberries. Gentle Desdemona thought of it simply as a cool, soft thing for a throbbing brow; she knew of no spell upon it that would work destruction for her who lost it. "Let me tie it round your head," she said to Othello; "you will be well in an hour." But Othello pettishly③ said it was too small, and let it fall. Desdemona and he then went indoors to dinner, and Emilia picked up the handkerchief which Iago had often asked her to steal.

She was looking at it when Iago came in. After a few words about it he snatched it from her, and bade her leave him.

In the garden he was joined by Othello,

---

① mock [mɔk] v. 嘲笑,骗
② embroider [imˈbrɔidə] v. 刺绣
③ pettishly [ˈpetiʃli] adv. 易怒地

who seemed hungry for the worst lies he could offer. He therefore told Othello that he had seen Cassio wipe his mouth with a handkerchief, which, because it was spotted with① strawberries, he guessed to be one that Othello had given his wife.

The unhappy Moor went mad with fury, and Iago bade the heavens witness that he devoted his hand and heart and brain to Othello's service. "I accept your love," said Othello. "Within three days let me hear that Cassio is dead."

Iago's next step was to leave Desdemona's handkerchief in Cassio's room. Cassio saw it, and knew it was not his, but he liked the strawberry pattern on it, and he gave it to his sweetheart Bianca and asked her to copy it for him.

Iago's next move was to induce Othello, who had been bullying Desdemona about the handkerchief, to play the eavesdropper② to a conversation between Cassio and himself. His intention was to talk about Cassio's sweetheart, and allow Othello to suppose that the lady spoken of was Desdemona.

"How are you, lieutenant?" asked Iago when Cassio appeared.

"The worse for being called what I am not," replied Cassio, gloomily③.

"Keep on reminding Desdemona, and you'll soon be restored," said Iago, adding, in a tone too low for Othello to hear, "If Bianca could set the matter right, how quickly it would mend!"

"Alas! poor rogue," said Cassio, "I really think she loves me." And like the talkative coxcomb④ he was, Cassio was led on to boast of Bianca's fondness for him, while Othello imagined, with choked rage, that he prattled of Desdemona, and thought, "I see your nose, Cassio, but not the dog I shall throw it to."

---

① spot with 布满
② eavesdropper [ˈiːvzˌdrɔpə(r)] n. 偷听者
③ gloomily [ˈgluːmili] adv. 沮丧地
④ coxcomb [ˈkɔkskəum] n. 花花公子,纨绔子弟,鸡冠花

Othello was still spying when Bianca entered, boiling over① with the idea that Cassio, whom she considered her property, had asked her to copy the embroidery on the handkerchief of a new sweetheart. She tossed him the handkerchief with scornful words, and Cassio departed with her.

Othello had seen Bianca, who was in station lower, in beauty and speech inferior far, to Desdemona and he began in spite of himself to praise his wife to the villain before him. He praised her skill with the needle, her voice that could "sing the savageness out of a bear," her wit, her sweetness, the fairness of her skin. Every time he praised her Iago said something that made him remember his anger and utter it foully②, and yet he must needs praise her, and say, "The pity of it, Iago! O Iago, the pity of it, Iago!"

There was never in all Iago's villainy one moment of wavering. If there had been he might have wavered then.

"Strangle③ her," he said; and "Good, good!" said his miserable dupe④.

The pair were still talking murder when Desdemona appeared with a relative of Desdemona's father, called Lodovico, who bore a letter for Othello from the Duke of Venice. The letter recalled Othello from Cyprus, and gave the governorship to Cassio.

Luckless Desdemona seized this unhappy moment to urge once more the suit of Cassio.

"Fire and brimstone!" shouted Othello.

"It may be the letter agitates⑤ him," explained Lodovico to Desdemona, and he told her what it contained.

"I am glad," said Desdemona. It was the first bitter speech that Othello's unkindness had wrung out of her.

---

① boil over 生……的气，发怒
② foully ['faulli] *adv.* 下流地，卑鄙地
③ strangle ['stræŋgl] *v.* 扼死
④ dupe [dju:p] *n.* 易受骗的人，易受愚弄的人
⑤ agitate ['ædʒiteit] *v.* 搅动，摇动

"I am glad to see you lose your temper," said Othello.

"Why, sweet Othello?" she asked, sarcastically; and Othello slapped her face.

Now was the time for Desdemona to have saved her life by separation, but she knew not her peril—only that her love was wounded to the core. "I have not deserved this," she said, and the tears rolled slowly down her face.

Lodovico was shocked and disgusted. "My lord," he said, "this would not be believed in Venice. Make her amends;" but, like a madman talking in his nightmare①, Othello poured out his foul thought in ugly speech, and roared, "Out of my sight!"

"I will not stay to offend you," said his wife, but she lingered even in going, and only when he shouted "Avaunt②!" did she leave her husband and his guests.

Othello then invited Lodovico to supper, adding, "You are welcome, sir, to Cyprus. Goats and monkeys!" Without waiting for a reply he left the company.

Distinguished visitors detest being obliged to look on at family quarrels, and dislike being called either goats or monkeys, and Lodovico asked Iago for an explanation.

True to himself, Iago, in a roundabout way, said that Othello was worse than he seemed, and advised them to study his behavior and save him from the discomfort of answering any more questions.

He proceeded to tell Roderigo to murder Cassio. Roderigo was out of tune with his friend. He had given Iago quantities of jewels for Desdemona without effect; Desdemona had seen none of them, for Iago was a thief.

Iago smoothed him with a lie, and when Cassio was leaving Bianca's house, Roderigo wounded him, and was wounded in return. Cassio shouted, and Lodovico and a friend came running up. Cassio pointed out

---

① nightmare ['naitmeə(r)] *n.* 梦魇, 噩梦
② avaunt [ə'vɔːnt] *adv.* 滚, 走开

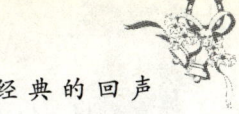

Roderigo as his assailant, and Iago, hoping to rid himself of an inconvenient friend, called him "Villain!" and stabbed him, but not to death.

At the Castle, Desdemona was in a sad mood. She told Emilia that she must leave her; her husband wished it. "Dismiss me!" exclaimed Emilia. "It was his bidding," said Desdemona; "we must not displease him now."

She sang a song which a girl had sung whose lover had been base to her—a song of a maiden crying by that tree whose boughs droop① as though it weeps, and she went to bed and slept.

She woke with her husband's wild eyes upon her. "Have you prayed tonight?" he asked; and he told this blameless and sweet woman to ask God's pardon for any sin she might have on her conscience. "I would not kill thy soul," he said.

He told her that Cassio had confessed, but she knew Cassio had nought to confess that concerned her. She said that Cassio could not say anything that would damage her. Othello said his mouth was stopped.

Then Desdemona wept, but with violent words, in spite of all her pleading, Othello pressed upon her throat and mortally hurt her.

Then with boding heart came Emilia, and besought② entrance at the door, and Othello unlocked it, and a voice came from the bed saying, "A guiltless death I die."

"Who did it?" cried Emilia; and the voice said, "Nobody—I myself. Farewell!"

"Twas I that killed her," said Othello.

He poured out his evidence by that sad bed to the people who came running in, Iago among them; but when he spoke of the handkerchief, Emilia told the truth.

---

① droop [druːp] v. 低垂,凋萎
② besought [bi'sɔːt] v. beseech 的过去式和过去分词,恳求,哀求

And Othello knew. "Are there no stones in heaven but thunderbolts?" he exclaimed, and ran at Iago, who gave Emilia her deathblow and fled.

But they brought him back, and the death that came to him later on was a relief from torture.

They would have taken Othello back to Venice to try him there, but he escaped them on his sword. "A word or two before you go," he said to the Venetians in the chamber. "Speak of me as I was—no better, no worse. Say I cast away the pearl of pearls①, and wept with these hard eyes; and say that, when in Aleppo years ago I saw a Turk beating a Venetian, I took him by the throat and smote him thus."

With his own hand he stabbed himself to the heart; and ere he died his lips touched the face of Desdemona with despairing② love.

奥 赛 罗

四百年前，威尼斯有一个名叫伊阿古的掌旗官，他特别讨厌他的将军奥赛罗，因为奥赛罗没让他当上上尉。尽管伊阿古受到极力推荐，奥赛罗却选中了迈克尔·凯西奥，因为他的伶牙俐齿帮助奥赛罗博取了苔丝狄蒙娜的芳心。伊阿古有个朋友叫罗德利哥，给了伊阿古许多钱财，他感到除非苔丝狄蒙娜嫁给他，否则他就不会感到幸福快乐。

奥赛罗是摩尔人，因为皮肤黝黑，他的敌人称他为黑人。他早年的生活艰苦而惊险，曾因战败被俘而被卖去做奴隶；他曾是一位伟大的旅行家，见过肩膀高过脑袋的人。他像狮子一样勇猛，却有一大缺点——嫉妒。他的爱自私得可怕，对他来说爱一个女人就意味着要完全拥有她的一切，就像拥有那些没有生命、不会思考的东西一样。奥赛罗的故事就是一个有关嫉妒的故事。

一天夜里，伊阿古告诉他的朋友罗德利哥，在苔丝狄蒙娜的父亲勃拉班修不知晓的情况下，奥赛罗就把她带走了。他劝说罗德利哥去提醒勃拉班修，于是当见到这位元老院议员时，伊阿古告诉他苔丝狄蒙娜以最不光彩的

---

① the pearl of pearls 宝中宝
② despairing [dɪsˈpɛərɪŋ] adj. 绝望的，失望的

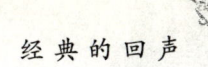

经典的回声
Echoes of Classics:Stories from Shakespeare

方式与人私奔了。尽管他是奥赛罗的手下,他还是骂奥赛罗是强盗,是巴巴里马。

勃拉班修来到威尼斯公爵面前控诉奥赛罗用巫术迷惑了他的女儿,而奥赛罗却说他的巫术只不过是他的声音——他给苔丝狄蒙娜讲述了他的冒险故事和九死一生的逃跑经历。苔丝狄蒙娜被带进了会议室,她解释说尽管奥赛罗的皮肤黝黑,可她是那么爱他。她说:"我看见了他的心灵。"

苔丝狄蒙娜嫁给了奥赛罗,并且非常高兴做他的妻子,再也没有人说反对奥赛罗的话了,尤其是公爵想派他去塞浦路斯抵御突厥人的进攻。奥赛罗要立即出发,请求跟着他的苔丝狄蒙娜也被应允随夫一起去塞浦路斯。

一登上这个岛,奥赛罗就分外高兴。随他同行的有伊阿古和他的妻子,还有走在前面的罗德利哥。"哦,宝贝,"他对苔丝狄蒙娜说,"我不知道该对你说什么,我恋上了自己的幸福。"

很快,有消息传来,说突厥舰队失去了战斗力,于是奥赛罗宣布从下午五点到夜里十一点在塞浦路斯举行庆祝。

当时在奥赛罗管辖下的塞浦路斯的一个城堡里,凯西奥正在值班,伊阿古想要把这个上尉灌醉。起初他的劝酒不怎么顺利,因为凯西奥知道自己一喝酒就上头,然而仆人们把酒送到了凯西奥的房间,同时伊阿古也唱起了祝酒歌,凯西奥于是频频为将军的健康举杯。

凯西奥喝醉想找茬的时候,伊阿古就吩咐罗德利哥对他说些难听的话。凯西奥用棍子打了罗德利哥,于是罗德利哥就跑去前总督蒙太诺那里诉苦。蒙太诺谦恭地为罗德利哥求情,却被凯西奥粗鲁地回绝了,蒙太诺生气地说:"嗨,嗨,你这个醉鬼!"凯西奥又将他刺伤。于是伊阿古趁机吩咐罗德利哥出去在街上大喊发生兵变了。

嘈杂声惊醒了奥赛罗,得知事情的原委后,他说:"凯西奥,我器重你,可是你永远都别想在我的手下干了。"

凯西奥和伊阿古单独在一起时,这个颜面丢尽的人哀叹着自己失去的名誉。伊阿古对他说名誉和欺骗是一样的。没有留意到伊阿古在身边,凯西奥慨叹道:"哦,天哪,人就应该把敌人放在嘴中,然后取走他们的脑髓。"

伊阿古建议他请求苔丝狄蒙娜在奥赛罗面前为他求情,凯西奥觉得这个主意不错,于是第二天一早就去城堡的花园里向苔丝狄蒙娜求情了。苔丝狄蒙娜亲切地说:"不用难过,凯西奥,我宁死也不会不管你托付的事。"

这时,凯西奥看到奥赛罗和伊阿古过来了,便匆忙回避。

伊阿古说:"我不喜欢那样。"

143

"你说什么?"奥赛罗问。他觉得伊阿古是在暗示某种令人不快的事情,而伊阿古假装自己并没有说什么。"从我妻子身边溜走的不正是凯西奥吗?"奥赛罗问。而伊阿古明明知道那就是凯西奥,并且知道他为什么在那里,却说:"我无法想象凯西奥竟然那样偷偷摸摸地溜走。"

苔丝狄蒙娜告诉奥赛罗说,凯西奥因伤心谦卑才会在他到来时如此匆匆离去,并提醒他说,当初她还不知爱的滋味,当她对她的摩尔情人挑剔时,凯西奥是怎样替他辩护。奥赛罗动了心,说:"我答应你的请求。"而苔丝狄蒙娜说她向他要求的不过如一顿美餐一样简单。

苔丝狄蒙娜离开花园后,伊阿古问奥赛罗在苔丝狄蒙娜嫁给他之前凯西奥认不认识她。

"认识。"奥赛罗说。

"真的吗?"伊阿古故弄玄虚地说,似乎一件让他迷惑不解的事情突然清晰明了了。

"难道他不诚实吗?"奥赛罗质问道。伊阿古却一直似有疑虑地重复着这个形容词,似乎害怕说出"是"。

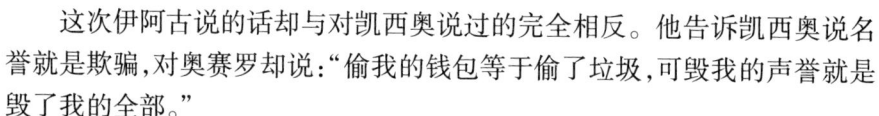

"你什么意思?"奥赛罗继续问。

这次伊阿古说的话却与对凯西奥说过的完全相反。他告诉凯西奥说名誉就是欺骗,对奥赛罗却说:"偷我的钱包等于偷了垃圾,可毁我的声誉就是毁了我的全部。"

听了这些奥赛罗气得火冒三丈,伊阿古对奥赛罗的妒忌之心了如指掌,就大胆地警告他要防备着凯西奥。伊阿古把嫉妒称作"绿眼睛的魔鬼,它还嘲笑它所吃的肉。"

给了嫉妒一击之后,伊阿古继续添油加醋地说苔丝狄蒙娜在和奥赛罗私奔的时候欺骗了她的父亲,言外之意是:"她能欺骗她父亲,为什么就不能欺骗你呢?"

不一会儿,苔丝狄蒙娜又进来告诉奥赛罗说晚餐准备好了,却看到他坐立不安的样子,他解释说有点头疼。于是苔丝狄蒙娜拿出了奥赛罗送给她的手帕。这个手帕是一个二百岁的女巫用神蚕的丝织成的,然后又用从处女的心中取出来的染汁染过,上面还绣着草莓的图案。温柔的苔丝狄蒙娜只简单地把它看作凉凉的、柔软的、用来减轻疼痛的东西;却没有想到上面有魔咒,谁弄丢了它这个人就会有灾难临头。"让我把它绑在你头上,"她对奥赛罗说,"一个小时后你的头就不疼了。"可是奥赛罗却生气地说太小了,把它扔到了地上。苔丝狄蒙娜和他进屋吃饭去了,于是爱米利娅就将手帕捡了起来,因为伊阿古一直让她偷的就是这块手帕。

她正盯着手帕看,伊阿古走了进来。还没有说上几句话,他就把它夺去并匆匆打发她走了。

伊阿古走到花园里,奥赛罗又跟了上来,看起来特别想听他所说的恶毒的谎言。于是他就趁机告诉奥赛罗,他曾见凯西奥用一块手帕擦嘴,因为那个手帕上绣着草莓图案,他猜那可能是奥赛罗送给他妻子的那块。

这个郁闷的摩尔人气得发疯,伊阿古向天发誓说,他的双手、他的心脏和他的大脑随时愿为奥赛罗效劳。"我接受你的忠诚,"奥赛罗说,"三天之内我要听到凯西奥死亡的消息。"

伊阿古的下一步计划就是把苔丝狄蒙娜的那块手帕丢进凯西奥的房间。凯西奥看见了手帕,并且知道那不是他的,可他特别喜欢上面的草莓图案,于是就给了他的情人比恩卡,并让她为他绣一块一模一样的。

伊阿古的下一步计划就是诱使奥赛罗(他已经为丢失的手帕责难了苔丝狄蒙娜)偷听他和凯西奥之间的谈话。他的目的就是让凯西奥说一说他的情人,并让奥赛罗误以为他说的情人就是苔丝狄蒙娜。

"你好啊,上尉!"见到凯西奥时,伊阿古跟他打招呼。

"糟糕的是,我现在已经不是你称呼的上尉了。"凯西奥闷闷不乐地说。

"继续提醒苔丝狄蒙娜,不久你就会复职的,"伊阿古说,然后他又用奥赛罗听不见的声音补充道,"如果比恩卡着手,那手帕很快就会缝好!"

"啊!可怜的人儿,"凯西奥说,"我真的认为她爱着我。"他像个健谈的花花公子,继续吹嘘着比恩卡对他的迷恋。然而在一旁怒火中烧的奥赛罗却想着他说的就是苔丝狄蒙娜,心想:"我看清你的嘴脸了,凯西奥,真想把你扔去喂狗。"

奥赛罗还在偷听时,比恩卡走了进来。她总以为凯西奥为自己所有,一想到凯西奥要让她仿绣一块他的新欢送给他的手帕,气就不打一处来。她一边说着冷嘲热讽的话一边把手帕丢给了他,凯西奥转身离开了。

奥赛罗见过比恩卡,她地位低下,论相貌、论谈吐都比苔丝狄蒙娜差远了。他开始在这个恶棍面前称赞起自己的妻子了,他称赞她娴熟的针线活,称赞她的声音能"唤出熊的野性来",称赞她的聪明才智,她的温柔甜美,还有她美丽白皙的皮肤。每次称赞她时伊阿古总会说些令他愤怒的事情,让他的脏话脱口而出,可他还是要称赞她:"多遗憾啊,伊阿古!哦,伊阿古,多

遗憾啊,伊阿古!"

对于他自己的卑鄙行径,伊阿古从来没有一刻的动摇,如果有的话,当时他就应该动摇了。

"勒死她。"他说。"好,好!"他可怜的受骗者说。

苔丝狄蒙娜带着她父亲的一位亲戚走进来的时候,他们俩还在商讨着谋杀的事。这位亲戚叫罗多维科,他捎来一封威尼斯公爵给奥赛罗的亲笔信,信中说要把奥赛罗从塞浦路斯召回,并将总督职位交给凯西奥。

不幸的苔丝狄蒙娜在这个不幸的时刻再次为凯西奥求情。

"你可真够热心的啊!"奥赛罗吼道。

"可能是信的内容惹火了他。"罗多维科对她说,并告诉了她信的内容。

"我很高兴。"苔丝狄蒙娜说。奥赛罗的刻薄使她第一次说了这么难听的话。

"我也很高兴看到你发火。"奥赛罗说。

"为什么,亲爱的奥赛罗?"她挖苦地问。奥赛罗却给了她一巴掌。

这个时候,苔丝狄蒙娜应该离开这里来挽救自己的生命,可是她对自己所面临的危险一无所知——只知道她的爱彻底受伤了。"你不该这样对我。"她说着,眼泪慢慢滑过她的脸颊。

罗多维科感到非常震惊也很生气。"大人,"他说,"这种事情在威尼斯都让人不敢相信,快点儿道歉吧!"可是,奥赛罗却像一个做着噩梦的疯子,说着龌龊不堪的脏话,倾倒出了他心里所有污秽的想法,并咆哮着:"别再让我看见你!"

"我不会留下来冒犯你的。"他的妻子说着蹒跚离去,他刚喊完"滚!"她就已经离开了她的丈夫和客人。

奥赛罗后来邀请罗多维科一起吃晚饭,并说:"爵士,欢迎你来到塞浦路斯。臭羊猴。"还没有听到回答,他就把客人撂在一旁离开了。

尊贵的客人可不愿意看家庭纠纷,也不喜欢被人叫做羊或者猴子,于是罗多维科让伊阿古给他一个解释。

伊阿古又露出了真面目,绕着圈子说奥赛罗要比他表面上坏得多,然后建议他多观察奥赛罗的举止,不要再问他问题了,以免他让大家不愉快。

伊阿古继续吩咐罗德利哥谋杀凯西奥。罗德利哥这次没有和他的朋友保持一致。为了追求苔丝狄蒙娜他曾送了伊阿古许多珠宝,却没起一点儿作用;而苔丝狄蒙娜又没有将他们二人放在眼里,因为伊阿古是一个贼。

伊阿古用谎言说动了他,凯西奥离开比恩卡的房间后,罗德利哥将他刺伤，可自己也受了伤。凯西奥大声呼叫，罗多维科和他的一位朋友跑了过来。凯西奥说罗德利哥是个刺客，而伊阿古呢，为了摆脱这个麻烦的朋友，也称他是"恶棍"，还刺了他一剑，但并没有把他刺死。

苔丝狄蒙娜在城堡里忧伤难过。她告诉爱米利娅她必须离开她，她丈夫希望她这么做。"解雇我！"爱米利娅大吃一惊。"是他的命令，"苔丝狄蒙娜说，"我们现在千万不要惹他不开心。"

她唱了一首歌，是一首因爱人卑鄙丑恶的行为而受伤害的女孩唱过的歌。歌中的少女在树下痛哭，树枝低垂，好像也跟着哭泣似的。然后，她上床睡去了。

醒来时，她看到丈夫正用狂怒的眼睛盯着她。"今晚祈祷了没有？"他问。他让这个清白无辜、温柔甜美的女人祈祷，恳请上帝宽恕她良心上的任何罪恶。"我不想杀害你的灵魂。"他说。

他告诉她凯西奥已经坦白，可她知道关于她凯西奥没有什么可坦白的。她争辩说凯西奥不会说什么伤害她的话，奥赛罗却说凯西奥已经不会再说话了。

于是苔丝狄蒙娜哭了，尽管她极力哀求，可奥赛罗一边说着尖刻的话，一边掐住她的喉咙，活活地将她掐死了。

突然爱米利娅有种不祥的预感，恳求进去。奥赛罗把门打开，从床上传来微弱的声音："我死得冤枉。"

"谁干的？"爱米利娅哭着问。这个声音说："没有人——是我自己，永别了！"

"是我杀死了她。"奥赛罗说。

他站在那个令人伤心的床前向跑进来的人诉说着杀死妻子的理由，伊阿古也在场；当他提及那个手帕的时候，爱米利娅道出了实情。

奥赛罗这才恍然大悟，惊呼道："天上只有霹雳，没有石头吗？"说着就冲向伊阿古，而伊阿古给了爱米利娅致命的一击后就逃走了。

伊阿古被逮回来后立即被处死，他的死是对痛苦的一丝安慰。

他们要把奥赛罗带回威尼斯审问，可是他却挥舞着剑奋力挣脱。"在你们临行之前我说几句，"他对威尼斯元老院的议员们说，"说我这个人怎么样呢，没有比我更好的，也没有比我更坏的了。比如，我扔掉了宝中之宝，又用我这双无情的眼睛哭泣；比如，多年前，我在阿勒颇看到一个突厥人鞭笞着一个威尼斯人，我掐住他的喉咙，将他活活打死。"

说完，他把剑刺入了自己的心脏；临死时，他用绝望的爱将双唇贴在了苔丝狄蒙娜的脸上。

12. King Lear

Goneril and Regan

King Lear was old and tired. He was aweary of① the business of his kingdom, and wished only to end his days quietly near his three daughters. Two of his daughters were married to the Dukes of Albany② and Cornwall③; and the Duke of Burgundy④ and the King of France were both suitors for the hand of Cordelia⑤, his youngest daughter.

Lear called his three daughters together, and told them that he

---

① be aweary of 厌倦做某事
② Albany [ˈɔːlbəni] n. 奥本尼
③ Cornwall [ˈkɔːnwɔːl] n. 康沃尔(英国郡名)
④ Burgundy [ˈbəːgəndi] n. 勃艮第(法国东南部地方的地名)
⑤ Cordelia [kɔːˈdiːliə] n. 考狄利亚(女子名)

proposed to divide his kingdom between them. "But first," said he, "I should like to know how much you love me."

Goneril①, who was really a very wicked woman, and did not love her father at all, said she loved him more than words could say; she loved him dearer than eyesight, space or liberty, more than life, grace, health, beauty, and honor.

"I love you as much as my sister and more," professed Regan, "since I care for nothing but my father's love."

Lear was very much pleased with Regan's professions②, and turned to his youngest daughter, Cordelia. "Now, our joy, though last not least," he said, "the best part of my kingdom have I kept for you. What can you say?"

"Nothing, my lord," answered Cordelia.

"Nothing can come of nothing. Speak again," said the King.

And Cordelia answered, "I love your Majesty according to my duty—no more, no less."

And this she said, because she was disgusted with the way in which her sisters professed love, when really they had not even a right sense of duty to their old father.

"I am your daughter," she went on, "and you have brought me up and loved me, and I return you those duties back as are right and fit, obey you, love you, and most honor you."

Lear, who loved Cordelia best, had wished her to make more extravagant③ professions of love than her sisters. "Go," he said, "be forever a stranger to my heart and me."

The Earl of Kent, one of Lear's favorite courtiers④ and captains, tried to say a word for Cordelia's sake, but Lear would not listen. He

---

① Goneril [ˈɡɔnəril] n. 贡纳莉（女子名）
② profession [prəˈfeʃən] n. 表白
③ extravagant [iksˈtrævəɡənt] adj. 奢侈的，浪费的
④ courtier [ˈkɔːtjə] n. 朝臣

divided the kingdom between Goneril and Regan, and told them that he should only keep a hundred knights at arms, and would live with his daughters by turns.

When the Duke of Burgundy knew that Cordelia would have no share of the kingdom, he gave up his courtship of her. But the King of France was wiser, and said, "Thy dowerless① daughter, King, is Queen of us—of ours, and our fair France."

"Take her, take her," said the King, "for I will never see that face of hers again."

So Cordelia became Queen of France, and the Earl of Kent, for having ventured to take her part, was banished from② the kingdom. The King now went to stay with his daughter Goneril, who had got everything from her father that he had to give, and now began to grudge③ even the hundred knights that he had reserved for himself. She was harsh and undutiful④ to him, and her servants either refused to obey his orders or pretended that they did not hear them.

Now the Earl of Kent, when he was banished, made as though he would go into another country, but instead he came back in the disguise of a servingman and took service with the King. The King had now two friends—the Earl of Kent, whom he only knew as his servant, and his Fool, who was faithful to him. Goneril told her father plainly that his knights only served to fill her Court with riot⑤ and feasting; and so she begged him only to keep a few old men about him such as himself.

"My train are men who know all parts of duty," said Lear. "Goneril, I will not trouble you further—yet I have left for another daughter."

And his horses being saddled, he set out with his followers for the castle of Regan. But she, who had formerly outdone her sister in

---

① dowerless ['dauəlis] adj. 没有嫁妆的
② be banished from 从……驱逐出去
③ grudge [grʌdʒ] v. 不给予
④ undutiful ['ʌn'djuːtifəl] adj. 未尽职的,不顺从的,不孝的
⑤ riot ['raiət] n. 暴乱,骚动

professions of attachment to the King, now seemed to outdo her in undutiful conduct, saying that fifty knights were too many to wait on① him, and Goneril (who had hurried thither to prevent Regan showing any kindness to the old King) said five were too many, since her servants could wait on him.

Then when Lear saw that what they really wanted was to drive him away②, he left them. It was a wild and stormy night, and he wandered about the heath③ half mad with misery④, and with no companion but the poor Fool. But presently his servant, the good Earl of Kent, met him, and at last persuaded him to lie down in a wretched little hovel. At daybreak the Earl of Kent removed his royal master to Dover, and hurried to the Court of France to tell Cordelia what had happened.

Cordelia's husband gave her an army and with it she landed at Dover. Here she found poor King Lear, wandering about the fields, wearing a crown of nettles and weeds. They brought him back and fed and clothed him, and Cordelia came to him and kissed him.

"You must bear with⑤ me," said Lear; "forget and forgive. I am old and foolish."

And now he knew at last which of his children it was that had loved him best, and who was worthy of his love.

Goneril and Regan joined their armies to fight Cordelia's army, and were successful; and Cordelia and her father were thrown into prison. Then Goneril's husband, the Duke of Albany, who was a good man, and had not known how wicked his wife was, heard the truth of the whole story; and when Goneril found that her husband knew her for the wicked

① wait on 服侍
② drive away 赶走
③ heath [hi:θ] n. 石南,石南树丛
④ misery ['mizəri] n. 痛苦,苦恼,悲惨
⑤ bear with 宽恕

woman she was, she killed herself, having a little time before given a deadly poison to her sister, Regan, out of a spirit of jealousy.

But they had arranged that Cordelia should be hanged in prison, and though the Duke of Albany sent messengers at once, it was too late. The old King came staggering into the tent of the Duke of Albany, carrying the body of his dear daughter Cordelia, in his arms.

And soon after, with words of love for her upon his lips, he fell with her still in his arms, and died.

李 尔 王

李尔王年迈体衰,处理国事已力不从心,只希望能在三个女儿身边安享晚年。大女儿和二女儿分别嫁给了奥本尼公爵和康沃尔公爵,至于小女儿考狄利亚,勃艮第公爵和法兰西国王都在向她求婚。

李尔把三个爱女叫到一起,告诉她们他打算将领土分给她们三人掌管。"首先,"他说,"我想知道你们有多爱我。"

大女儿贡纳莉是个十分邪恶的女人,她根本不爱她的父亲,却说她对他的爱无法用语言来表达,她爱父亲胜过爱自己的目光、空间和自由,胜过爱生命、优雅、健康、美丽和荣誉。

二女儿里根说:"我比姐姐还要爱你,因为除了父亲您的爱,其他的我什么都不在乎。"

李尔对里根的表白非常满意,然后转向他的小女儿考狄利亚,说:"我的小'开心果',你是最后一个,但不是最不重要的,我会把国土最好的一部分给你,你对我说些什么呢?"

"什么都不说,父王。"考狄利亚回答说。

"什么都不说就什么都没有。再给你一次机会。"国王说。

于是考狄利亚回答说:"我会尽做女儿的本分去爱陛下,不多也不少。"

她之所以这么说是因为她讨厌姐姐们的虚伪奉承,其实她们对老父亲根本没有责任感。

"我是您的女儿,"她继续说,"您抚育我成人,给予我父爱,我将正确地、恰当地回报您,听您的话、爱您、尊敬您。"

李尔最疼爱考狄利亚,同她的两个姐姐相比,希望她的表白辞藻更华丽,表达更有力。"走吧,"他说,"你在我心里永远是个陌生人了。"

李尔王的宠臣肯特伯爵想为考狄利亚说句公道话,可李尔根本听不进去。于是他把领土分给了贡纳莉和里根,并告诉她俩他只留一百名骑士在身边,并在她们两家轮流居住。

勃艮第公爵得知考狄利亚没有分到疆土后,便放弃了求婚。而聪明的法兰西国王却说:"陛下,您没有嫁妆的女儿是我的王后,我们锦绣法兰西的王后。"

"带她走吧,带她走吧,"国王说,"因为我再也不想看见她了。"

于是,考狄利亚成了法兰西王后,肯特伯爵因冒险替考狄利亚说情而被驱除出国。现在国王住在大女儿贡纳莉那里,她从她父亲那里得到了她想要的一切,却对父亲为自己保留的百名骑士抱怨不已。她刻薄地对待父亲,不尽孝道,连她的仆人也都要么不服从他的命令,要么对他的吩咐充耳不闻。

而肯特伯爵在被流放的时候,假装去了另一个国家,实际上又乔装成男仆回来在国王身边照顾他。国王现在只有两个朋友,一个是照顾着他、他以为是仆人的肯特伯爵,另一个就是一直忠于他的佛儿。贡纳莉直截了当地告诉她父亲说他的百名骑士只会在她的宫中饮酒享乐,惹是生非,请求他只留几个老仆人在他身边就行了。

"我的手下都是安分守己的人,"李尔说,"贡纳莉,我不再打扰你了,我到另一个女儿那里去。"

于是李尔王驱马前行,带着随从去了二女儿里根的城堡。里根先前曾对父亲表白说比起姐姐她更深爱着父亲,可现在看来与她姐姐相比,她的不孝行为倒是更胜一筹。她竟然向父亲抱怨说用五十名骑士来服侍他就已经太多了,贡纳莉(她匆匆赶到前头去阻止里根对父亲好)说五个也太多,因为她的仆人可以服侍他。

这时李尔终于明白了她们这样做的真正目的就是将他赶走,于是他就径直离开了。那是一个狂风肆虐、暴雨淋漓的夜晚,他满怀悲愤,疯癫地徘徊在丛林里,只有可怜的佛儿陪着他。不久他遇见了老仆人,善良的肯特伯爵,在他的劝说下去了一个破旧的小屋。黎明时分,肯特伯爵又带着他的老主人去了多佛,并急忙赶到法兰西把国王的遭遇告诉了考狄利亚。

考狄利亚的丈夫让她带着一队人马到了多佛。在那里,她看到可怜的父亲头上戴着用荨麻稻草编织成的王冠,在荒野里徘徊。他们将他带回法兰西,喂他饭吃,给他衣穿。考狄利亚走到父亲身边,亲吻着他。

"你要宽恕我,"李尔王说,"原谅我,原谅我,我真是老糊涂。"

现在他终于知道哪个孩子最爱他,最值得他爱了。

贡纳莉和里根的军队联合起来同考狄利亚的军队作战,结果战胜;考狄利亚和父亲都被投入了监牢。贡纳莉的丈夫,也就是奥本尼公爵,是一个善良的人,他根本不知道自己的妻子有多邪恶,后来方知事情的真相。贡纳莉得知她丈夫知道了自己恶劣的行径后便自杀了,由于她妒忌妹妹里根,在死之前她又将毒酒给她喝。

然而她们已经安排在狱中绞死考狄利亚,尽管奥本尼公爵派信使过去阻止行刑,但为时已晚。老国王怀抱着爱女考狄利亚的尸体,蹒跚地走进了奥本尼公爵的帐篷。

他怀抱着女儿并诉说着对她的爱,不久就倒了下去,死了。

13. Macbeth

The Three Witches

When a person is asked to tell the story of Macbeth①, he can tell two stories. One is of a man called Macbeth who came to the throne of Scotland by a crime in the year of our Lord 1039, and reigned justly and well, on the whole, for fifteen years or more. This story is a part of Scottish history. The other story issues from a place called Imagination; it is gloomy and wonderful, and you shall hear it.

A year or two before Edward the Confessor② began to rule England, a battle was won in Scotland against a Norwegian King by two generals named Macbeth and Banquo③. After the battle, the generals walked

---

① Macbeth [mək'beθ] n. 麦克白(苏格兰国王,在一次战斗中杀死其表兄国王邓肯后即位。他夺权和统治的传说构成了莎士比亚《麦克白》的主要基础)

② Edward the Confessor 忏悔者爱德华(英格兰国王)

③ Banquo ['bæŋkwəu] n. 班柯(男子名)

together towards Forres, in Elginshire, where Duncan, King of Scotland, was awaiting them.

While they were crossing a lonely heath, they saw three bearded① women, sisters, hand in hand, withered in appearance and wild in their attire.

"Speak, who are you?" demanded Macbeth.

"Hail, Macbeth, chieftain② of Glamis," said the first woman.

"Hail, Macbeth, chieftain of Cawdor," said the second woman.

"Hail, Macbeth, King that is to be," said the third woman.

Then Banquo asked, "What of me?" and the third woman replied, "Thou shalt be the father of kings."

"Tell me more," said Macbeth. "By my father's death I am chieftain of Glamis, but the chieftain of Cawdor lives, and the King lives, and his children live. Speak, I charge you!"

The women replied only by vanishing, as though suddenly mixed with the air.

Banquo and Macbeth knew then that they had been addressed by witches, and were discussing their prophecies③ when two nobles approached. One of them thanked Macbeth, in the King's name, for his military services, and the other said, "He bade me call you chieftain of Cawdor."

Macbeth then learned that the man who had yesterday borne that title was to die for treason④, and he could not help thinking, "The third witch called me, 'King that is to be.'"

"Banquo," he said, "you see that the witches spoke truth concerning me. Do you not believe, therefore, that your child and grandchild will be kings?"

---

① bearded ['biədid] *adj.* 有须的，有胡子的
② chieftain ['tʃiːftən] *n.* 酋长，首领
③ prophecy ['prɔfisi] *n.* 预言
④ treason ['triːzn] *n.* 叛逆，通敌，背信

经典的回声
Echoes of Classics:Stories from Shakespeare

Banquo frowned. Duncan had two sons, Malcolm① and Donalbain②, and he deemed③ it disloyal to hope that his son Fleance should rule Scotland. He told Macbeth that the witches might have intended to tempt them both into villainy④ by their prophecies concerning the throne. Macbeth, however, thought the prophecy that he should be King too pleasant to keep to himself, and he mentioned it to his wife in a letter.

Lady Macbeth was the grand-daughter of a King of Scotland who had died in defending his crown against the King who preceded Duncan, and by whose order her only brother was slain. To her, Duncan was a reminder of bitter wrongs. Her husband had royal blood in his veins, and when she read his letter, she was determined that he should be King.

When a messenger arrived to inform her that Duncan would pass a night in Macbeth's castle, she nerved herself for a very base action.

She told Macbeth almost as soon as she saw him that Duncan must spend a sunless morrow. She meant that Duncan must die, and that the dead are blind. "We will speak further," said Macbeth uneasily, and at night, with his memory full of Duncan's kind words, he would fain have spared his guest.

"Would you live a coward?" demanded Lady Macbeth, who seems to have thought that morality⑤ and cowardice⑥ were the same.

"I dare do all that may become a man," replied Macbeth; "who dare do more is none."

"Why did you write that letter to me?" she inquired fiercely, and with bitter words she egged him on to

———

① Malcolm ['mælkəm] n. 马尔康(男子名)
② Donalbain ['dɔnəlbein] n. 道纳本(男子名)
③ deem [di:m] v. 认为
④ villainy ['viləni] n. 邪恶,坏事,恶行
⑤ morality [mə'ræliti] n. 道德
⑥ cowardice ['kauədis] n. 怯懦,胆小

murder, and with cunning words she showed him how to do it.

After supper Duncan went to bed, and two grooms were placed on guard at his bedroom door. Lady Macbeth caused them to drink wine till they were stupefied.① She then took their daggers② and would have killed the King herself if his sleeping face had not looked like her father's.

Macbeth came later, and found the daggers lying by the grooms; and soon with red hands he appeared before his wife, saying, "Methought I heard a voice cry, 'Sleep no more! Macbeth destroys the sleeping.' "

"Wash your hands," said she. "Why did you not leave the daggers by the grooms? Take them back, and smear the grooms with blood."

"I dare not," said Macbeth.

His wife dared, and she returned to him with hands red as his own, but a heart less white, she proudly told him, for she scorned his fear.

The murderers heard a knocking, and Macbeth wished it was a knocking which could wake the dead. It was the knocking of Macduff, the chieftain of Fife, who had been told by Duncan to visit him early. Macbeth went to him, and showed him the door of the King's room.

Macduff entered, and came out again crying, "O horror! horror! horror!"

Macbeth appeared as horror-stricken③ as Macduff, and pretending that he could not bear to see life in Duncan's murderers, he slew the two grooms with their own daggers before they could proclaim their innocence.

These murders did not shriek out, and Macbeth was crowned at Scone. One of Duncan's sons went to Ireland, the other to England.

---

① stupefy [ˈstjuːpifai] v. 麻木,使惊奇
② dagger [ˈdæɡə] n. 短剑,匕首
③ horror-stricken adj. 吓坏的

Macbeth was King. But he was discontented①. The prophecy concerning Banquo oppressed his mind. If Fleance were to rule, a son of Macbeth would not rule. Macbeth determined, therefore, to murder both Banquo and his son. He hired two ruffians②, who slew Banquo one night when he was on his way with Fleance to a banquet which Macbeth was giving to his nobles. Fleance escaped.

Meanwhile Macbeth and his Queen received their guests very graciously③, and he expressed a wish for them which has been uttered thousands of times since his day—"Now good digestion④ wait on appetite⑤, and health on both."

"We pray your Majesty to sit with us," said Lennox, a Scotch noble; but ere Macbeth could reply, the ghost of Banquo entered the banqueting hall and sat in Macbeth's place.

Not noticing the ghost, Macbeth observed that, if Banquo were present, he could say that he had collected under his roof the choicest chivalry of Scotland. Macduff, however, had curtly declined his invitation.

The King was again pressed to take a seat, and Lennox, to whom Banquo's ghost was invisible, showed him the chair where it sat.

But Macbeth, with his eyes of genius, saw the ghost. He saw it like a form of mist and blood, and he demanded passionately, "Which of you have done this?"

Still none saw the ghost but he, and to the ghost Macbeth said, "Thou canst not say I did it."

The ghost glided out, and Macbeth was impudent⑥ enough to raise a

---

① discontented [ˈdiskənˈtentid] adj. 不满的,不快的
② ruffian [ˈrʌfjən,-fiən] n. 流氓,恶棍
③ graciously [ˈgreiʃəsli] adv. 和蔼地,优雅地
④ digestion [diˈdʒestʃən, daiˈdʒestʃən] n. 消化力,领悟
⑤ appetite [ˈæpitait] n. 食欲,胃口,欲望
⑥ impudent [ˈimpjudənt] adj. 放肆无礼的,厚颜无耻的

glass of wine, "to the general joy of the whole table, and to our dear friend Banquo, whom we miss."

The toast was drunk as the ghost of Banquo entered for the second time.

"Begone!" cried Macbeth. "You are senseless, mindless! Hide in the earth, thou horrible shadow."

Again none saw the ghost but he.

"What is it your Majesty sees?" asked one of the nobles.

The Queen dared not permit an answer to be given to this question. She hurriedly begged her guests to quit a sick man who was likely to grow worse if he was obliged to talk.

Macbeth, however, was well enough next day to converse with the witches whose prophecies had so depraved① him.

He found them in a cavern on a thunderous② day. They were revolving round a cauldron③, in which were boiling particles of many strange and horrible creatures, and they knew he was coming before he arrived.

"Answer me what I ask you," said the King.

"Would you rather hear it from us or our masters?" asked the first witch.

"Call them," replied Macbeth.

Thereupon the witches poured blood into the cauldron and grease into the flame that licked it, and a helmeted head appeared with the visor on, so that Macbeth could only see its eyes.

He was speaking to the head, when the first witch said gravely, "He knows thy thought," and a voice in the head said, "Macbeth, beware Macduff, the chieftain of Fife." The head then descended into the cauldron till it disappeared.

① deprave [diˈpreiv] v. 堕落
② thunderous [ˈθʌndərəs] adj. 打雷的,像打雷的
③ cauldron [ˈkɔːldrən] n. (= caldron) 大锅炉

"One word more," pleaded Macbeth.

"He will not be commanded," said the first witch, and then a crowned child ascended① from the cauldron bearing a tree in his hand. The child said—

"Macbeth shall be unconquerable till
The Wood of Birnam climbs Dunsinane Hill."

"That will never be," said Macbeth; and he asked to be told if Banquo's descendants② would ever rule Scotland.

The cauldron sank into the earth; music was heard, and a procession of phantom③ kings filed past Macbeth; behind them was Banquo's ghost. In each king, Macbeth saw a likeness to Banquo, and he counted eight kings.

Then he was suddenly left alone.

His next proceeding was to send murderers to Macduff's castle. They did not find Macduff, and asked Lady Macduff where he was. She gave a stinging answer, and her questioner called Macduff a traitor. "Thou liest!" shouted Macduff's little son, who was immediately stabbed, and with his last breath entreated④ his mother to fly. The murderers did not leave the castle while one of its inmates remained alive.

Macduff was in England listening, with Malcolm, to a doctor's tale of cures wrought by Edward the Confessor when his friend Ross came to tell him that his wife and children were no more. At first Ross dared not speak the truth, and turn Macduff's bright sympathy with sufferers into sorrow and hatred. But when Malcolm said that England was sending an army into Scotland against Macbeth, Ross blurted out his news, and Macduff cried, "All dead, did you say? All my pretty ones and their mother? Did you say all?"

① ascend [ə'send] v. 攀登,上升
② descendant [di'sendənt] n. 子孙,后代
③ phantom ['fæntəm] n. 幻影
④ entreat [in'triːt] v. 恳求,乞求

His sorry hope was in revenge, but if he could have looked into Macbeth's castle on Dunsinane Hill, he would have seen at work a force more solemn than revenge. Retribution① was working, for Lady Macbeth was mad. She walked in her sleep amid ghastly② dreams. She was wont to wash her hands for a quarter of an hour at a time; but after all her washing, would still see a red spot of blood upon her skin. It was pitiful to hear her cry that all the perfumes of Arabia could not sweeten her little hand.

"Canst thou not minister to a mind diseased?" inquired Macbeth of the doctor, but the doctor replied that his patient must minister to her own mind. This reply gave Macbeth a scorn of medicine. "Throw physic③ to the dogs," he said; "I'll none of it."

One day he heard a sound of women crying. An officer approached him and said, "The Queen, your Majesty, is dead."

"Out, brief candle," muttered Macbeth, meaning that life was like a candle, at the mercy of a puff of air④. He did not weep; he was too familiar with death.

Presently a messenger told him that he saw Birnam Wood on the march. Macbeth called him a liar and a slave, and threatened to hang him if he had made a mistake. "If you are right you can hang me," he said.

From the turret windows of Dunsinane Castle, Birnam Wood did indeed appear to be marching. Every soldier of the English army held aloft⑤ a bough which he had cut from

① retribution [ˌretrɪˈbjuːʃən] n. 报应
② ghastly [ˈɡɑːstlɪ] adj. 苍白的，死人般的，可怕的
③ physic [ˈfɪzɪk] n. 医术，药
④ a puff of air 一缕空气
⑤ aloft [əˈlɒft] adv. 在高处，在上

a tree in that wood, and like human trees they climbed Dunsinane Hill.

Macbeth had still his courage. He went to battle to conquer or die, and the first thing he did was to kill the English general's son in single combat①. Macbeth then felt that no man could fight him and live, and when Macduff came to him blazing for revenge, Macbeth said to him, "Go back; I have spilt too much of your blood already."

"My voice is in my sword," replied Macduff, and hacked at him and bade him yield.

"I will not yield!" said Macbeth, but his last hour had struck. He fell.

Macbeth's men were in retreat when Macduff came before Malcolm holding a King's head by the hair.

"Hail, King!" he said; and the new King looked at the old.

So Malcolm reigned after Macbeth; but in years that came afterwards the descendants of Banquo were kings.

麦 克 白

若要某个人讲讲麦克白的故事,他可以讲两个故事。一个是麦克白通过不正当的手段于1039年登上苏格兰国王的王位;他在位15年多,治国公正严明,井然有序。这个故事也是苏格兰的一段历史。而另外一个故事则源于一个叫做幻想的地方,这个故事忧伤而又令人惊叹,你可以用心聆听。

在忏悔者爱德华国王统治英国前的一两年,苏格兰的两员虎将麦克白和班柯使苏格兰在对挪威的战争中取得了胜利。战争过后,两位将军一起去埃尔金郡的福瑞斯,苏格兰国王邓肯正在那里等候他们。

当二人穿过一片荒原时,看到三个长着大胡子的女人,像是姐妹,她们手牵着手,面容憔悴,服装怪异。

"说,你们是什么人?"麦克白命令道。

"万福,麦克白,葛莱米斯的首领。"第一个女人说。

"万福,麦克白,考特的首领。"第二个女人说。

"万福,麦克白,未来的君王。"第三个女人说。

---

① combat ['kɔmbət] n. 战斗

于是,班柯问道:"我呢?"第三个女人回答说:"你的子孙将会君临一国。"

"再多告诉我些吧,"麦克白说,"我父亲死后我就是葛莱米斯的首领,可是考特的首领还活着,国王也活着,他们的子孙都活着。快说,不然就杀了你。"

这三个女人没有回答就消失了,她们似乎在空气中突然蒸发了。

班柯和麦克白这才明白跟他们俩说话的人是女巫,他们正谈论着有关她们的预言,两位贵族向他们走来。其中一位贵族以国王的名义感谢麦克白参加战事,另一位则说:"他让我称呼您考特的首领,"

麦克白后来得知,有那个头衔称呼的人于昨日死于叛国罪,他不由得想:"第三个女巫称我为'未来的君王'。"

他对班柯说:"你瞧,女巫们所说的有关我的事居然都一一应验了,难道你不希望你的子子孙孙也做国王吗?"

班柯皱了皱眉头。想到邓肯有两个儿子,马尔康和道纳本,如果希望自己的儿子弗里恩斯统治苏格兰就是不忠。于是他告诉麦克白说,或许女巫们想通过告诉他们有关王位的事情而诱使他们作恶。然而,麦克白一想到他会成为国王的预言就高兴得不能自已,在给他妻子的信中也提到了此事。

麦克白夫人的爷爷曾是苏格兰的国王,在捍卫自己的王位时死去,那是邓肯之前的国王的所作所为。她唯一的哥哥也被那个篡权的国王下令处死,对她来说,邓肯就是辛酸往事的痛苦记忆。她的丈夫也是皇家血脉,当她读到这封信时,更确定他应该是国王。

这时,有个信使报告说国王邓肯要到麦克白的城堡住一晚,想到自己打算做的卑劣行径,她寝食难安。

她一见到麦克白就告诉他说,邓肯绝对不能见着第二天的太阳。她的意思就是邓肯必须死,并且要死得神不知鬼不觉。"以后再说吧。"麦克白不安地说。到了晚上,他的脑子里全是邓肯对他说过的善言,就不想伤害他的客人了。

"你愿意像懦夫一样活着吗?"麦克白夫人质问道,她认为道德和懦弱如出一辙。

"我敢做成就男人的一切,"麦克白回答说,"可做过了火就什么都不是了。"

"那你为什么写那封信给我?"她恶狠狠地问,然后一边说着恶毒的话挑唆他去谋杀邓肯,一边用甜言蜜语教他谋杀的方法。

晚饭后邓肯去就寝,在他的卧室门口有两个男仆守卫。麦克白夫人将他俩灌得酩酊大醉,抽出他们的匕首,本想杀死国王,可是那张熟睡的脸太像她的父亲了。

后来麦克白进去了,发现匕首正放在男仆身旁;不久后他双手沾满鲜血,回到妻子面前,说:"我想我听到了一个声音在叫喊'不要再睡了!麦克白破坏了睡眠'。"

"去洗洗手吧,"她说,"你怎么不把匕首放回男仆身边呢?快放回去,把血抹在男仆身上。"

"我不敢。"麦克白说。

他的妻子特别胆大,尽管和他一样回来时双手沾满了鲜血,但她并不害怕,并骄傲地告诉丈夫她蔑视他的恐惧。

这对凶手突然听到一阵敲门声,麦克白希望这声音能够唤醒死去的人。敲门的正是费福的首领——麦克德夫,国王让他早些时间来参见。麦克白把他带到国王休憩的房间门前。

麦克德夫进去,随即又跑了出来,喊叫着:"噢,太可怕了!太可怕了!太可怕了!"

麦克白假装像麦克德夫一样被吓坏了,并佯装发怒地说他无法容忍看见凶手活着。两位男仆还没有来得及争辩他们的清白,麦克白就用他们的匕首将其杀死了。

这些凶手并没有叫喊,麦克白在苏格兰加冕。邓肯的一个儿子去了爱尔兰,另一个儿子逃往英格兰。麦克白虽然做了国王,但还是不满,因为有关班柯的预言一直在他的脑海盘桓。如果弗里恩斯将统治苏格兰,那么麦克白的儿子就没有王权。因此,麦克白决定将班柯和他的儿子一块儿置于死地。为达到此目的,麦克白特设了宴席,请来了所有的贵族,那天晚上他又雇了两个刺客埋伏在班柯和弗里恩斯前去赴宴的路上。班柯被刺死,弗里恩斯逃脱了。

与此同时,在宴席上麦克白和王后对待客人彬彬有礼,十分周道,并一再表达对他们的祝愿:"胃口好、消化好、身体好。"这句话他从即位以来已说了千百遍了。

"我们请求陛下和我们一起入座。"一位苏格兰贵族列诺克斯说。可是,还没等麦克白说话,班柯的鬼魂进了宴会大厅,并坐在麦克白的位置上。

麦克白没有注意到鬼魂就在身边,他对其他大臣们说,假若班柯列席,那就真可以说是本国所有的贤士都聚集一堂了。然而,麦克德夫却拒绝了他的邀请。

国王再次被请求就座,列诺克斯看不见班柯的鬼魂,将国王带到鬼魂坐的椅子前。

而麦克白天生就有双能瞧见鬼魂的眼睛。鬼魂呈血雾状,哽咽地问道:"是谁干的?"

仍然只有麦克白看见了鬼魂,他对鬼魂说:"你不能说是我干的。"

鬼魂悄无声息地离去了,而麦克白厚颜无耻地举杯说:"为在座众人的快乐干杯,为我们最亲爱的缺席的朋友班柯干杯。"

刚喝完第一杯,班柯的鬼魂又进来了。

"走开!"麦克白喊叫着,"你没有知觉,没有思维!你这个可怕的影子,躲到地下去吧!"

还是只有他能看得见鬼魂。

"陛下瞧见了什么?"一个贵族问道。

王后不敢让国王回答这个问题,托辞麦克白旧病复发,继续说下去会让他的病情变得更糟糕,于是将客人们打发走了。

然而,到了第二天麦克白就恢复正常了,他决定去找女巫们谈谈,是她们的预言将他变得如此邪恶。

在一个雷声隆隆的日子里,他在山洞里找到了她们。她们正绕着一个大锅炉转来转去,里面煮着一些奇怪而可怕的动物,她们已经预知了他的到来。

"回答我的问题。"国王说。

"你愿意听我们回答还是听我们的主人回答?"第一个女巫问他。

"把他们唤出来吧。"麦克白回答说。

于是女巫们将血倒入大锅炉,把油脂倒入锅炉下面的火苗。于是一个戴着头盔的脑袋出现了,麦克白只能看见他的眼睛。

麦克白正要跟这个脑袋说话,第一个女巫严肃地说:"他知道你的心思。"他听到那脑袋说:"麦克白,当心费福的首领麦克德夫。"说完那个脑袋就潜入锅炉消失了。

"再多说些啊。"麦克白祈求着。

"他是不受命令的。"第一个女巫说。接着一个戴着王冠的孩子从锅炉里浮了出来,手里拿着一棵树。孩子说——

"麦克白永远不会被击败,
除非勃南姆树林爬上邓西嫩山。"

"那是永远不会发生的事情。"麦克白说。他想知道班柯的后代会不会统治苏格兰。

正在此时,那个大锅炉沉到地下去了;音乐响起,一队国王的幻影从麦克白面前走过;班柯的鬼魂紧随其后。麦克白看到每个国王都有和班柯相像的地方,他数了数共有八个。

突然剩下他孤零零的一个人。

他的下一步计划就是派杀手去麦克德夫的城堡。可是他们连麦克德夫的人影也未见到,于是就审问其夫人他去了哪里,她的回答像刀一样尖锐。这些审问者称麦克德夫是叛国贼。"你们撒谎!"麦克德夫的小儿子大声喊道,话音未落就被刺死了,临终时他祈求母亲快逃,然而这城堡里没有留下一个活口。

麦克德夫正与马尔康在英格兰听一位医生讲述忏悔者爱德华国王治疗疾病的故事,他的朋友罗斯赶来告诉他,他的爱妻和孩子都已不在人世了。起初罗斯不敢说出真相,不想让麦克德夫对受害者的同情转变成悲伤和仇恨。可是当马尔康说到英格兰要向苏格兰派军攻打麦克白时,罗斯才突然说出了这个消息,麦克德夫哭喊着:"都死了,是你说的吗?我可爱的儿女和他们的母亲都死了?是你说的吗?"

他可怜的愿望就是复仇,如果他留意观察,就会发现比复仇更可怕的力量笼罩着坐落在邓西嫩山上的麦克白的城堡。报应已经开始,麦克白夫人疯了,她每每从噩梦中惊醒就来来回回走个不停,每次洗手要花上一刻钟;即使洗完后,她还会看见皮肤上有鲜红的血点。人们会听到她令人同情的哭喊,阿拉伯所有的香水都无法让她的小手变得有香味。

"难道你无法治愈有精神疾病的人吗?"麦克白问医生,医生却回答说心病还需心药医。听到这个回答麦克白知道王后已无药可医了。"把药扔给狗吧,"他说,"我已无计可施了。"

有一天,他听到了女人们的哭声。一名军官走上前来告诉他说:"陛下,王后去世了。"

"出去吧,生命短暂如烛。"麦克白嘟囔着。他的意思是生命如同蜡烛,任凭空气的摆布。他没有哭泣,因为他早就知道死

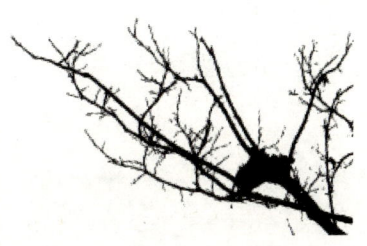

亡是怎么一回事了。

不久,一个信使跑来告诉麦克白,说他看到勃南姆树林正在移动。麦克白骂他是撒谎的狗奴才,威胁他说如果再撒谎就吊死他,接着又说:"要是你说的是真话,你就把我吊死吧。"

透过邓西嫩城堡炮楼的窗户可以看到,勃南姆树林真的像在移动。英格兰军队在穿过树林时,每个士兵按照命令都要砍下一个树枝高举在手中,就好像树林爬上了邓西嫩山。

麦克白仍留有最后一丝勇气,他破釜沉舟地加入了激战,他遇上了英格兰将军的儿子,并在短兵相接中将其杀死。麦克白感到无人能与他匹敌,当麦克德夫来到他面前声称要复仇时,麦克白对他说:"你走吧,我手上已沾满了你家族的鲜血。"

"这把剑就是我的回答。"麦克德夫说着一剑砍过去让他投降。

"我决不会投降!"麦克白说。可是他的死期已经到来,他倒下了。

麦克德夫提着国王的头颅来到马尔康面前,麦克白的人马已经在撤退了。

"万岁,国王!"他喊道。新国王看着老国王的头。

就这样马尔康将被篡权的王位夺了回来,统治着苏格兰;然而多年以后,班柯的子孙又成为苏格兰的国王。

14. Timon of Athens

Poet Reading to Timon

Four hundred years before the birth of Christ, a man lived in Athens whose generosity① was not only great, but absurd②. He was very rich, but no worldly wealth was enough for a man who spent and gave like Timon③. If anybody gave Timon a horse, he received from Timon twenty better horses. If anybody borrowed money of Timon and offered to repay it, Timon was offended④. If a poet had written a poem and Timon had time to read it, he would be sure to buy it; and a painter had only to hold up his canvas in front of Timon to receive double its market price.

---

① generosity [ˌdʒenəˈrɔsiti] n. 慷慨，宽大
② absurd [əbˈsəːd] adj. 荒谬的，可笑的
③ Timon [ˈtaimən] n. 泰门（男子名）
④ offend [əˈfend] v. 犯罪，冒犯

Flavius①, his steward②, looked with dismay at his reckless mode of life. When Timon's house was full of noisy lords drinking and spilling costly wine, Flavius would sit in a cellar and cry. He would say to himself, "There are ten thousand candles burning in this house, and each of those singers braying③ in the concert-room costs a poor man's yearly income a night;" and he would remember a terrible thing said by Apemantus④, one of his master's friends, "O what a number of men eat Timon, and Timon sees them not!"

Of course, Timon was much praised.

A jeweler who sold him a diamond pretended that it was not quite perfect till Timon wore it. "You mend the jewel by wearing it," he said. Timon gave the diamond to a lord called Sempronius⑤, and the lord exclaimed, "O, he's the very soul of bounty⑥." "Timon is infinitely dear to me," said another lord, called Lucullus, to whom he gave a beautiful horse; and other Athenians paid him compliments⑦ as sweet.

But when Apemantus had listened to some of them, he said, "I'm going to knock out an honest Athenian's brains."

"You will die for that," said Timon.

"Then I shall die for doing nothing," said Apemantus. And now you know what a joke was like four hundred years before Christ.

This Apemantus was a frank despiser of mankind, but a healthy one, because he was not unhappy. In this mixed world anyone with a number of acquaintances knows a person who talks bitterly of men, but does not shun them, and boasts that he is never deceived by their fine speeches, and is inwardly cheerful and proud. Apemantus was a man like that.

Timon, you will be surprised to hear, became much worse than

---

① Flavius ['flevjəs] n. 弗莱维斯(男子名)
② steward ['stjuəd] n. 管家,总管
③ bray [brei] v. 叫,乱哄哄地演奏
④ Apemantus [æpi'mæntəs] n. 艾帕曼特斯(男子名)
⑤ Sempronius ['semprɔniəs] n. 辛普洛涅斯(男子名)
⑥ bounty ['baunti] n. 慷慨,宽大
⑦ compliment ['kɔmplimənt] n. 称赞,恭维

Apemantus, after the dawning of a day which we call Quarter Day.

Quarter Day is the day when bills pour in. The grocer, the butcher, and the baker are all thinking of their debtors on that day, and the wise man has saved enough money to be ready for them. But Timon had not; and he did not only owe money for food. He owed it for jewels and horses and furniture; and, worst of all, he owed it to money-lenders, who expected him to pay twice as much as he had borrowed.

Quarter Day is a day when promises to pay are scorned, and on that day Timon was asked for a large sum of money. "Sell some land," he said to his steward. "You have no land," was the reply. "Nonsense! I had a hundred, thousand acres," said Timon. "You could have spent the price of the world if you had possessed it," said Flavius.

"Borrow some then," said Timon, "try Ventidius①." He thought of Ventidius because he had once got Ventidius out of prison by paying a creditor of this young man. Ventidius was now rich. Timon trusted in his gratitude②. But not for all; so much did he owe! Servants were despatched③ with requests for loans of money to several friends.

One servant (Flaminius) went to Lucullus④. When he was announced Lucullus said, "A gift, I warrant. I dreamt of a silver jug⑤ and basin last night." Then, changing his tone, "How is that honorable, free-hearted, perfect gentleman, your master, eh?"

"Well in health, sir," replied Flaminius.

"And what have you got there under your cloak?" asked Lucullus, jovially.

"Faith, sir, nothing but an empty box, which, on my master's behalf, I beg you to fill with money, sir."

"La! la! la!" said Lucullus, who could not pretend to mean, "Ha!

---

① Ventidius ['ventidjəs] n. 文提狄斯(男子名)
② gratitude ['grætitjuːd] n. 感谢的心情
③ despatch [disˈpætʃ] v. 派遣
④ Lucullus [luːˈkʌləs] n. 路库勒斯(男子名)
⑤ jug [dʒʌg] n. 水壶

ha! ha! Your master's one fault is that he is too fond of giving parties. I've warned him that it was expensive. Now, look here, Flaminius, you know this is no time to lend money without security①, so suppose you act like a good boy and tell him that I was not at home. Here's three solidares for yourself."

"Back, wretched money," cried Flaminius, "to him who worships you!"

Others of Timon's friends were tried and found stingy②. Amongst them was Sempronius.

"Hum," he said to Timon's servant, "has he asked Ventidius? Ventidius is beholden to him."

"He refused."

"Well, have you asked Lucullus?"

"He refused."

"A poor compliment to apply to me last of all," said Sempronius, in affected③ anger. "If he had sent to me at first, I would gladly have lent him money, but I'm not going to be such a fool as to lend him any now."

"Your lordship makes a good villain," said the servant.

When Timon found that his friends were so mean, he took advantage of a lull④ in his storm of creditors to invite Ventidius and Company to a banquet. Flavius was horrified, but Ventidius and Company, were not in the least ashamed, and they assembled accordingly in Timon's house, and said to one another that their princely host had been jesting⑤ with them.

① security [siˈkjuəriti] *n.* 安全
② stingy [ˈstindʒi] *adj.* 吝啬的,小气的
③ affected [əˈfektid] *adj.* 假装的
④ lull [lʌl] *n.* 暂停,麻痹
⑤ jest [ˈdʒest] *v.* 开玩笑,戏弄

"I had to put off an important engagement in order to come here," said Lucullus, "but who could refuse Timon?"

"It was a real grief to me to be without ready money① when he asked for some," said Sempronius.

"The same here," chimed in a third lord.

Timon now appeared, and his guests vied with one another in apologies and compliments. Inwardly sneering, Timon was gracious to them all.

In the banqueting hall was a table resplendent② with covered dishes. Mouths watered. These summer-friends loved good food.

"Be seated, worthy friends," said Timon. He then prayed aloud to the gods of Greece. "Give each man enough," he said, "for if you, who are our gods, were to borrow of men they would cease to adore③ you. Let men love the joint more than the host. Let every score of guests contain twenty villains. Bless my friends as much as they have blessed me. Uncover the dishes, dogs, and lap!"

The hungry lords were too much surprised by this speech to resent④ it. They thought Timon was unwell, and, although he had called them dogs, they uncovered the dishes.

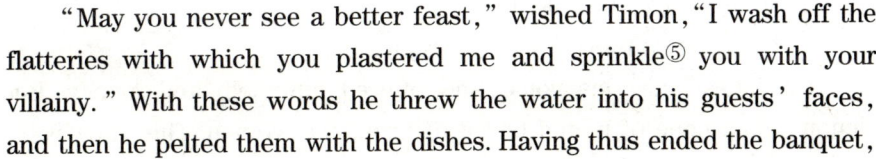

There was nothing in them but warm water.

"May you never see a better feast," wished Timon, "I wash off the flatteries with which you plastered me and sprinkle⑤ you with your villainy." With these words he threw the water into his guests' faces, and then he pelted them with the dishes. Having thus ended the banquet,

---

① ready money 现钱
② resplendent [ris'plendənt] adj. 辉煌的,灿烂的,光辉的
③ adore [ə'dɔː] v. 崇拜,爱慕
④ resent [ri'zent] v. 愤恨,怨恨
⑤ sprinkle ['spriŋkl] v. 撒(某物)于(某物之表面),洒,喷撒

he went into an outhouse, seized a spade, and quitted Athens for ever.

His next dwelling was a cave near the sea.

Of all his friends, the only one who had not refused him aid was a handsome soldier named Alcibiades①, and he had not been asked because, having quarreled with the Government of Athens, he had left that town. The thought that Alcibiades might have proved a true friend did not soften Timon's bitter feeling. He was too weak-minded② to discern the fact that good cannot be far from evil in this mixed world. He determined to see nothing better in all mankind than the ingratitude③ of Ventidius and the meanness of Lucullus.

He became a vegetarian④, and talked pages to himself as he dug in the earth for food.

One day, when he was digging for roots near the shore, his spade struck gold. If he had been a wise man he would have enriched himself quickly, and returned to Athens to live in comfort. But the sight of the gold vein⑤ gave no joy but only scorn to Timon. "This yellow slave," he said, "will make and break religions. It will make black white and foul fair. It will buy murder and bless the accursed."

He was still ranting⑥ when Alcibiades, now an enemy of Athens, approached with his soldiers and two beautiful women who cared for nothing but pleasure.

Timon was so changed by his bad thoughts and rough life that Alcibiades did not recognize him at first.

"Who are you?" he asked.

"A beast, as you are," was the reply.

Alcibiades knew his voice, and offered him help and money. But Timon would none of it, and began to insult the women. They, however,

---

① Alcibiades [ˌælsɪˈbaɪədiːz] n. 艾西巴第斯（男子名）
② weak-minded [miːkˈmaɪndɪd] adj. 优柔寡断的，低能的，怯懦的
③ ingratitude [ɪnˈɡrætɪtjuːd] n. 忘恩，不知恩
④ vegetarian [ˌvedʒɪˈtɛərɪən] n. 素食者，食草动物
⑤ vein [veɪn] n. 血管，静脉
⑥ rant [rænt] v. 咆哮，激昂地说

when they found he had discovered a gold mine, cared not a jot for his opinion of them, but said, "Give us some gold, good Timon. Have you more?"

With further insults, Timon filled their aprons① with gold ore.

"Farewell," said Alcibiades, who deemed② that Timon's wits were lost; and then his disciplined soldiers left without profit the mine which could have paid their wages, and marched towards Athens.

Timon continued to dig and curse, and affected great delight when he dug up③ a root and discovered that it was not a grape.

Just then Apemantus appeared. "I am told that you imitate me," said Apemantus. "Only," said Timon, "because you haven't a dog which I can imitate."

"You are revenging yourself on your friends by punishing yourself," said Apemantus. "That is very silly, for they live just as comfortably as they ever did. I am sorry that a fool should imitate me."

"If I were like you," said Timon, "I should throw myself away."

"You have done so," sneered Apemantus. "Will the cold brook make you a good morning drink, or an east wind warm your clothes as a valet④ would?"

"Off with you!" said Timon; but Apemantus stayed a while longer and told him he had a passion for extremes, which was true. Apemantus even made a pun, but there was no good laughter to be got out of Timon.

Finally, they lost their temper like two schoolboys, and Timon said he was sorry to lose the stone which he flung at Apemantus, who left him with an evil wish.

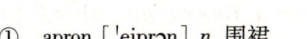

① apron ['eiprən] n. 围裙
② deem [diːm] v. 认为,相信
③ dig up 挖出,掘起
④ valet ['vælit, 'væli] n. (男人的)贴身男仆

This was almost an "at home" day for Timon, for when Apemantus had departed, he was visited by some robbers. They wanted gold.

"You want too much," said Timon. "Here are water, roots and berries."

"We are not birds and pigs," said a robber.

"No, you are cannibals," said Timon. "Take the gold, then, and may it poison you! Henceforth rob one another."

He spoke so frightfully to them that, though they went away with full pockets, they almost repented① of their trade. His last visitor on that day of visits was his good steward Flavius. "My dearest master!" cried he.

"Away! What are you?" said Timon.

"Have you forgotten me, sir?" asked Flavius, mournfully.

"I have forgotten all men," was the reply; "and if you'll allow that you are a man, I have forgotten you."

"I was your honest servant," said Flavius.

"Nonsense! I never had an honest man about me," retorted Timon.

Flavius began to cry.

"What! shedding tears?" said Timon. "Come nearer, then. I will love you because you are a woman, and unlike men, who only weep when they laugh or beg."

They talked awhile; then Timon said, "Yon gold is mine. I will make you rich, Flavius, if you promise me to live by yourself and hate mankind. I will make you very rich if you promise me that you will see the flesh slide off the beggar's bones before you feed him, and let the debtor die in jail before you pay his debt."

Flavius simply said, "Let me stay to comfort you, my master."

"If you dislike cursing, leave me," replied Timon, and he turned his back on Flavius, who went sadly back to Athens, too much accustomed to② obedience to force his services upon his ailing master.

The steward had accepted nothing, but a report got about that a

---

① repent [ri'pent] v. 后悔,悔改
② accustom to 习惯于

mighty nugget of gold had been given him by his former master, and Timon therefore received more visitors. They were a painter and a poet, whom he had patronized① in his prosperity.

"Hail, worthy Timon!" said the poet. "We heard with astonishment how your friends deserted you. No whip's large enough for their backs!"

"We have come," put in the painter, "to offer our services."

"You've heard that I have gold," said Timon.

"There was a report," said the painter, blushing; "but my friend and I did not come for that."

"Good honest men!" jeered② Timon. "All the same, you shall have plenty of gold if you will rid me of two villains."

"Name them," said his two visitors in one breath. "Both of you!" answered Timon. Giving the painter a whack③ with a big stick, he said, "Put that into your palette④ and make money out of it." Then he gave a whack to the poet, and said, "Make a poem out of that and get paid for it. There's gold for you."

They hurriedly withdrew.

Finally Timon was visited by two senators who, now that Athens was threatened by Alcibiades, desired to have on their side this bitter noble whose gold might help the foe.

"Forget your injuries," said the first senator. "Athens offers you dignities whereby you may honorably live."

"Athens confesses that your merit was overlooked, and wishes to atone⑤, and more than atone, for her forgetfulness," said the second senator.

"Worthy senators," replied Timon, in his grim way, "I am almost weeping;

① patronize ['pætrənaiz] v. 资助
② jeer [dʒiə] v. 嘲弄, 戏弄
③ whack [(h)wæk] n. & v. 重击
④ palette ['pælit] n. 调色板
⑤ atone [ə'təun] v. 弥补

you touch me so! All I need are the eyes of a woman and the heart of a fool."

But the senators were patriots. They believed that this bitter man could save Athens, and they would not quarrel with him. "Be our captain," they said, "and lead Athens against Alcibiades, who threatens to destroy her."

"Let him destroy the Athenians too, for all I care," said Timon; and seeing an evil despair in his face, they left him.

The senators returned to Athens, and soon afterwards trumpets① were blown before its walls. Upon the walls they stood and listened to Alcibiades, who told them that wrong-doers should quake in their easy chairs. They looked at his confident army, and were convinced that Athens must yield if he assaulted② it, therefore they used the voice that strikes deeper than arrows.

"These walls of ours were built by the hands of men who never wronged you, Alcibiades," said the first senator.

"Enter," said the second senator, "and slay every tenth man, if your revenge needs human flesh."

"Spare the cradle," said the first senator.

"I ask only justice," said Alcibiades. "If you admit my army, I will inflict③ the penalty④ of your own laws upon any soldier who breaks them."

At that moment a soldier approached Alcibiades, and said, "My noble general, Timon is dead." He handed Alcibiades a sheet of wax, saying, "He is buried by the sea, on the beach, and over his grave is a stone with letters on it

---

① trumpet ['trʌmpit] n. 喇叭
② assault [ə'sɔːlt] v. 袭击
③ inflict [in'flikt] v. 加以(处罚或判刑);给予(打击)
④ penalty ['penlti] n. 处罚,罚款

which I cannot read, and therefore I have impressed them on wax."

Alcibiades read from the sheet of wax this couplet①—

"Here lie I, Timon, who, alive,

all living men did hate.

Pass by and say your worst; but pass,

and stay not here your gait②."

"Dead, then, is noble Timon," said Alcibiades; and be entered Athens with an olive branch instead of a sword.

So it was one of Timon's friends who was generous in a greater matter than Timon's need; yet are the sorrow and rage of Timon remembered as a warning lest another ingratitude should arise to turn love into hate.

雅典的泰门

公元前400年前，在雅典有一个叫泰门的人，他慷慨大方得近乎荒谬。他非常富有，可是再多的财富也经不起他这样的挥霍和馈赠。倘若有人给他一匹马，这个人就会收到比这匹马更好的二十匹马的回赠。任何人向泰门借钱，若要还钱就会得罪他。倘若有位诗人写了首诗，而他刚好看到了，他就会将那首诗买下；如果某个画家在泰门面前哪怕仅是支起画布，他就会得到高于市场价两倍的报酬。

泰门的管家弗莱维斯为他这种漫无节制的生活方式发愁。泰门的家里挤满了吵吵闹闹的食客，他们喝着名贵的酒，并把酒洒得满地都是。弗莱维斯躲在地窖里哭泣，他自言自语地说："这座房子里点着成千上万只蜡烛，演奏厅里所请的每一个戏子一夜所花的费用就是一个穷人一年的收入啊。"他还记得主人的一位朋友艾帕曼特斯说过的一件可怕的事："这么多人在这里吃泰门，他怎么就熟视无睹呢！"

当然，泰门听到了许多恭维话。

一个珠宝商卖给他一颗钻石，虚伪地说只有泰门戴上它这颗钻石才称得上完美。"你戴上这颗珠宝让它更趋完美。"他说。泰门把这颗钻石赠给

---

① couplet [kʌplit] n. 对句，对联
② gait [geit] n. 步态，步法

了一个叫辛普洛涅斯的贵族,这个贵族惊呼:"噢,他真豪爽慷慨。""泰门真的对我很好。"另外一个叫路库勒斯的贵族说泰门给了他一匹漂亮的马。其他雅典人也不断地对泰门大献殷勤。

可当艾帕曼特斯听了他们的话以后,说:"我要去敲碎一个诚实的雅典人的脑袋。"

"那你要偿命的。"泰门说。

"我不会偿命的,因为我已找不到诚实的人了。"艾帕曼特斯说。现在你明白公元前400年前的玩笑是怎么一回事了吧。

这个艾帕曼特斯心直口快,鄙视不公,但他的心理很健康,因为他很快乐。在这个错综复杂的世界上,任何拥有很多朋友的人都知道,那个虽狠狠挖苦人的人并没有躲避他们,并吹嘘着从来不会为他们的花言巧语所迷惑,内心也感到高兴和自豪。艾帕曼特斯就是那样的人。

听到下面的话你会感到很惊讶,在我们称作结算日的凌晨,泰门的情况比艾帕曼特斯的还要糟。

结算日那天是账单涌入的日子,杂货店老板、屠夫、还有面包师都会在那一天想起他们的债主,精明的人会在那天为他们准备好足够的钱。而泰门却未准备好,他不仅欠食品的钱,还欠珠宝、马匹及家具的钱;更糟糕的是,他还欠那些放高利贷人的钱,他们则希望从他那里得到的钱会是借出去的两倍。

结算日那天是泰门被耻笑的日子,那天他要还一大笔钱,可他答应要还的账却还不上。"卖些地吧。"他对管家说。"没有地可卖了。"管家说。"胡说!我有上百亩、上千亩的地。"泰门说。"就算整个世界都属于您,您也会把它挥霍掉啊!"弗莱维斯说。

"那么去借些钱吧,"泰门说,"试着从文提狄斯那里借些。"他之所以想起文提狄斯是因为他曾经为文提狄斯还了一大笔债,这个年轻人才被释放出狱。文提狄斯现在很富有,泰门相信他会心存感激之情。可是根本不是那样;他欠的债务太多了!仆人们都被派去向他的几个朋友借钱了。

有一个仆人(弗莱米涅斯)去了路库勒斯家。得知他的到来,路库勒斯说:"肯定是给我送礼物来了,昨晚我梦见了一只银壶和一只银杯。"然后就换了口气说:"那位令人尊敬的、慷慨大方的、完美的绅士,也就是你家主人,他近来可好?"

"身体非常好,阁下。"弗莱米涅斯回答说。

"那么你斗篷下面拿的是什么?"路库勒斯高兴地问。

"说实话,阁下,只是一个空盒子,我替我的主人来向您借些钱。"

"你看看,你看看!"路库勒斯说,他假装不懂他的意思,"哈!哈!哈!你家主人的一大毛病就是太喜欢举行宴会,我已经警告他这样太奢侈了。弗莱米涅斯,你瞧!现在他不能保障还钱,我也不能借给他。我想你会好好表现的,来,拿着这三枚硬币,这是给你的赏钱,告诉你家主人,就说我不在家。"

"去你的,肮脏的钱,"弗莱米涅斯叫道,"把你的臭钱扔给乖乖服帖你的人吧!"

泰门也试着叫仆人到其他朋友那里借钱,结果他们个个都很小气。他们之中有个叫辛普洛涅斯的贵族。

"嗯,"他对泰门的仆人说,"他去文提狄斯那里借了没有?他有恩于文提狄斯啊。"

"他拒绝了。"

"有没有去路库勒斯那里借啊?"

"他拒绝了。"

"最后想到来找我了,这可不好,"辛普洛涅斯假装生气地说,"如果他第一个来找我,我会很高兴地借钱给他,现在要借给他,我才没有那么傻呢。"

"阁下您做了一回好恶人!"仆人说。

泰门终于发现了他的朋友们个个小气吝啬,于是就借债务风波稍稍停息的空儿,再次宴请文提狄斯等人参加宴会。令弗莱维斯感到震惊的是文提狄斯一伙人一点儿也不感到羞耻,仍然聚集到泰门的家中来,彼此说着他们高贵大方的主人原来是在跟他们开玩笑。

"为了来这里,我推掉了一个很重要的约会,"路库勒斯说,"可是谁敢拒绝泰门呢?"

"他问我借钱的时候正好没有现钱,为此我真的很难过。"辛普洛涅斯说。

"和我的情况一样。"第三个人插进话来说。

这时泰门进来了,他的客人们争相道歉和恭维。尽管内心嘲笑他们的行为举止,泰门表面却对他们如同往常那样和蔼亲切。

在宴会大厅里的桌子上摆着考究的宴席,令人馋涎欲滴。他这些酒肉朋友们还是喜欢美食的。

"就座吧,我真正的朋友们。"泰门说。然后他向希腊诸神大声祈祷。

"让每个人都饱餐一顿吧,"他说,"诸神啊,如果你们向人类借钱,他们就不会再敬仰你们了。让他们爱酒食胜于爱赏赐他们酒食的主人。让每十对客人中就有二十个恶棍。保佑我的朋友吧,就像他们曾经保佑过我一样。开席吧,狗崽子,你们就进食吧!"

这些饥饿的贵族们只是惊讶于他的这番话,并没有任何反感之意。想着泰门可能有些不正常,尽管被称为狗崽子,他们还是揭开了盘子。

里面只有温热的水。

"但愿你们再也看不到更好的宴席,"泰门说,"我冲掉你们黏附在我身上的诏媚,把你们的邪恶洒在你们自己身上。"说着这些话,泰门把水泼在了他们脸上,又把杯盘往他们身上摔。宴会就这样结束了,他去外屋拿了一个铁锹,永远地离开了雅典。

他在海边的一个岩洞住了下来。

在他所有的朋友中,只有一个人没有拒绝帮助他,就是一位叫艾西巴第斯的英俊士兵,泰门之所以没有求助于他是因为他和雅典衙门吵了一架后就离开了那里。有人认为即使艾西巴第斯是个真正的朋友也温暖不了泰门痛苦的心。他脆弱的内心让他在这个纷扰复杂的世界中难以辨别善恶是非。现在他的眼里只有文提狄斯的忘恩负义和路库勒斯的卑鄙无耻,人类再也没有什么好的了。

他成了一个素食主义者,他挖地找食物时总是自言自语地说上一大段。

一天,当他在海边挖树根时,他的铁锹挖到了金子。如果他是个聪明人,他就会再次暴富,回到雅典过舒适安逸的生活。但是泰门瞅见这些金子不但不觉得快乐,反而深感恶心。"这个黄色的奴隶,"他说,"制造并破坏了宗教,让黑变白,让恶变善。它会收买凶手,保佑被诅咒的人。"

他正慷慨激昂地说着,艾西巴第斯,这时他已是雅典的敌人,带着他的士兵走了过来,还有两个只会寻欢作乐的美女。

恶劣的思想和简陋的生活把泰门改变得太多,艾西巴第斯起初并没有认出他来。

"你是谁?"他问。

"和你一样,是个野兽。"泰门回答说。

艾西巴第斯听出了泰门的声

音,马上给予他帮助,并给了他一些钱。可是泰门什么也不要,并开始凌辱那两个女人。然而当她们知道泰门发现了一个金矿时,一点儿也不在乎他对她们的态度,说:"好泰门,给我们一些金子吧,还有吗?"

泰门又将那两个女人凌辱了一番,然后把她们的围裙装满了金子。

"再见。"艾西巴第斯说。他认为泰门已经失去理智了;尽管艾西巴斯可以用这金矿来支付士兵的薪水,但他的这支纪律严明的军队并没有带走任何金子,而继续向雅典进军。

泰门继续挖掘,继续诅咒,挖到一个树根时一阵狂喜,结果却发现那并不是葡萄树根。

正在那时,艾帕曼特斯来了。"听说你在模仿我,"艾帕曼特斯说。"只是,"泰门没好气地说,"如果你有一条狗的话,我就会模仿狗也不愿模仿你了。"

"你通过惩罚你自己来报复你的朋友,"艾帕曼特斯说,"那样做非常愚蠢,因为他们依然过着舒适安逸的生活。我真的很难过,一个傻子在模仿我。"

"如果我是你,"泰门说,"我就会将自己丢弃。"

"你已经这样做了,"艾帕曼特斯讥笑着说,"你以为这冰冷的溪水能为你做一顿美味的粥汤,这凛冽的寒风能像贴身仆人一样温暖你的衣裳吗?"

"你走吧!"泰门说。艾帕曼特斯又多待了一会,说泰门的感情太极端了。泰门确实如此。艾帕曼特斯甚至说了一个俏皮话,而泰门却并没有觉得很好笑。

最后,他们像两个小学生一样发了火,泰门说他很难过的是他没用石头砸中艾帕曼特斯,艾帕曼特斯也边诅咒边离泰门而去。

这天对于泰门来说有种"在家"的感觉,因为艾帕曼特斯刚走,又来了一些强盗,他们想要金子。

"你们要的太多了,"泰门说,"这里有水、树根和草莓。"

"我们不是鸟也不是猪。"一个强盗说。

"对,你们是吃人的人,"泰门说,"那么就把金子拿走吧,让它毒害你!然后彼此争抢。"

尽管他们满载而归,可泰门说得如此吓人,他们几乎为他们的所作所为感到后悔。那天他最后一个拜访者就是他的好管家弗莱维斯。"我亲爱的主人!"他哭着说。

"走开!你是谁?"泰门说。

"你忘了我了吗,老爷?"弗莱维斯难过地问。

"我已经把所有的人都忘了,"他回答说,"如果你说你是人的话,我已经把你忘记了。"

"我是你忠诚的仆人啊。"弗莱维斯说。

"胡说!从来没有人对我忠诚过。"泰门反驳说。

弗莱维斯哭了起来。

"什么!你哭了吗?"泰门说,"那么过来吧,我会爱你的,因为你是一个女人,不像男人,他们只有在大笑或乞求时才会哭。"

他们聊了一会;然后泰门说:"这金子是我的。弗莱维斯,我会让你变得富有,如果你答应我独自生活并痛恨人类;我会让你变得更富有,如果你答应我任那空腹的乞丐形销骨立,也不丢给他们一点食物,让那些欠债的人死于狱中也不替他们还一分一文。"

弗莱维斯只是简单地说:"我的主人,让我留下来服侍你吧。"

"如果你不喜欢诅咒,就离开我。"泰门回答。然后他转过身背对着弗莱维斯。弗莱维斯难过地回到了雅典,他已经习惯于顺从他的主人而不愿意强行留下来照顾体弱的主人。

这个管家什么也没有接受,却有人说他从老主人那里得到一个大金块,于是拜访泰门的人越来越多,有画家,还有那个他有钱时曾赞助过的诗人。

"万福!令人敬仰的泰门!"诗人说。"听说您的朋友将你遗弃,我们感到非常震惊。用鞭子抽他们,怎么抽也不过分!"

画家插嘴说:"我们专程来此,想为您效劳。"

"你们听说我有金子了吧?"泰门说。

"是有这样的说法,"画家红着脸说,"可我和我的朋友并不是为此而来的。"

"真是善良诚实的人啊!"泰门嘲弄着说,"一样,如果你们愿意为我除掉两个恶棍,你们就会得到许多金子。"

"他们是谁?"两位来客异口同声地问。"就是你们两个!"泰门回答说。然后他用棒子狠狠地揍了画家一下,说:"把它放进你的颜料里就可以挣钱了。"接着又给了诗人一棒子,说:"用它做一首诗吧,会有人付钱给你,那就是你的金子。"

他们二人慌忙逃脱。

最后有两个元老院议员来拜访泰门,雅典正遭受着艾西巴第斯的威胁,他们希望能够劝说这位充满仇恨的贵族站在他们这边,因为他的金子可能会助敌人一臂之力。

"忘记你受到的伤害吧,"第一位议员说,"雅典将给予你可以体面生活

的尊严和荣誉。"

"雅典承认忽视了你的价值,希望能够补偿,并且加倍地补偿她曾经的遗忘。"第二位议员说。

"尊敬的议员啊,"泰门冷冰冰地回答,"我几乎被你们感动得流泪了!我所需要的是一双女人的眼睛和一颗傻子的心。"

可是这两位议员是爱国的人,他们相信泰门可以拯救雅典,因而没有和他争吵。"做我们的统帅吧,"他们说,"带领雅典打败艾西巴第斯,他快要把雅典毁灭了。"

"我关心的是,他也要把雅典人毁灭。"泰门说。看到他脸上邪恶的神情,他们离开了。

这两位议员回到了雅典,不久就听见了号角在雅典城墙前面响起。他们站在城墙上听着艾西巴第斯的演说,他告诉他们那些做尽坏事的人别想再坐稳安乐椅了。他们看着他气宇轩昂的军队,确信他们的进攻会迫使雅典投降,因而他们用了比利箭还要有力的声音。

"我们这座城墙,并不是建立于得罪于你的那些人之手,艾西巴第斯。"第一个议员说。

"进来吧,"第二个议员说,"如果你的复仇需要人类的血肉,那就在十人中杀死一人。"

"留下那些在摇篮里的孩子吧。"第一个议员说。

"我只要求公正,"艾西巴第斯说,"如果你们承认我的军队,我会按照你们的法律惩罚我那些违法乱纪的士兵。"

正在那时,有个士兵来到艾西巴第斯面前说:"我高贵的将军,泰门死了。"他递给艾西巴第斯一张蜡纸,说:"他被埋葬在海边的沙滩上,在他坟墓上的石头上刻着一些字,我看不懂,就把它们印在了蜡纸上。"

艾西巴第斯读出了蜡纸上的对句——

此处躺着我泰门,

生前憎恨所有人;

路人请说恶毒语,

勿在此地停脚步。

"高尚的泰门就这样死去了。"艾西巴第斯说。于是他带着一个橄榄枝而非一把利剑进入了雅典。

这就是泰门的一个朋友,他的大度在很大程度上超出了泰门的需要;然而,泰门的悲伤与愤怒也是一个警钟,以免忘恩负义会将爱转变成仇恨。

· 185 ·

15. The Comedy of Errors

Antipholus and Dromio

Egeon① was a merchant of Syracuse②, which is a seaport in Sicily. His wife was Emilia③, and they were very happy until Egeon's manager died, and he was obliged to go by himself to a place called Epidamnum④ on the Adriatic⑤. As soon as she could Emilia followed him, and after they had been together some time two baby boys were born to them. The babies were exactly alike; even when they were dressed differently they looked the same.

---

① Egeon [iːˈdʒiːɔn] n. 伊勤(男子名)
② Syracuse [ˈsaiərəkjuːz] n. 叙拉古(古代希腊人的城邦,位于西西里岛东部)
③ Emilia [iːˈmiliə] n. 伊米莉娅(女子名)
④ Epidamnum [epiˈdæmnəm] n. 厄匹达姆纽姆
⑤ Adriatic [ˌeidriˈætik] n. 亚得里亚海

And now you must believe a very strange thing. At the same inn where these children were born, and on the same day, two baby boys were born to a much poorer couple than Emilia and Egeon; so poor, indeed, were the parents of these twins that they sold them to the parents of the other twins.

Emilia was eager to show her children to her friends in Syracuse, and in treacherous① weather she and Egeon and the four babies sailed homewards.

They were still far from Syracuse when their ship sprang a leak, and the crew left it in a body by the only boat, caring little what became of their passengers.

Emilia fastened one of her children to a mast and tied one of the slave-children to him; Egeon followed her example with the remaining children. Then the parents secured themselves to the same masts, and hoped for safety.

The ship, however, suddenly struck a rock and was split in two, and Emilia, and the two children whom she had tied, floated away from Egeon and the other children. Emilia and her charges were picked up by some people of Epidamnum, but some fishermen of Corinth took the babies from her by force, and she returned to Epidanmum alone, and very miserable②. Afterwards she settled in Ephesus③, a famous town in Asia Minor④.

Egeon and his charges were also saved; and, more fortunate than Emilia, he was able to return to Syracuse and keep them till

---

① treacherous [ˈtretʃərəs] adj. 背叛的，背信弃义的
② miserable [ˈmizərəbl] adj. 痛苦的，悲惨的
③ Ephesus [ˈefisəs] n. 以弗所（古希腊小亚细亚西岸的一个重要贸易城市）
④ Asia Minor n. 小亚细亚（黑海与地中海之间亚洲西部的一个半岛）

they were eighteen. His own child he called Antipholus①, and the slavechild he called Dromio②; and, strangely enough, these were the names given to the children who floated away from him.

At the age of eighteen the son who was with Egeon grew restless with a desire to find his brother. Egeon let him depart with his servant, and the young men are henceforth③ known as Antipholus of Syracuse and Dromio of Syracuse.

Let alone, Egeon found his home too dreary④ to dwell in, and traveled for five years. He did not, during his absence, learn all the news of Syracuse, or he would never have gone to Ephesus.

As it was, his melancholy⑤ wandering ceased in that town, where he was arrested almost as soon as he arrived. He then found that the Duke of Syracuse had been acting in so tyrannical a manner to Ephesians unlucky enough to fall into his hands, that the Government of Ephesus had angrily passed a law which punished by death or a fine of a thousand pounds any Syracusan who should come to Ephesus. Egeon was brought before Solinus, Duke of Ephesus, who told him that he must die or pay a thousand pounds before the end of the day.

You will think there was fate in this when I tell you that the children who were kidnaped⑥ by the fishermen of Corinth were now citizens of Ephesus, whither they had been brought by Duke Menaphon, an uncle of Duke Solinus. They will henceforth be called Antipholus of Ephesus and Dromio of Ephesus.

Moreover, on the very day when Egeon was arrested, Antipholus of Syracuse landed in Ephesus and pretended that he came from Epidamnum in order to avoid a penalty⑦. He handed his money to his

---

① Antipholus ['æntəfələs] n. 安提福勒斯(男子名)
② Dromio ['drəumiəu] n. 德洛米奥(男子名)
③ henceforth [hens'fɔ:θ] adv. 自此以后,今后
④ dreary ['driəri] adj. 沉闷的
⑤ melancholy ['melənkəli] n. 忧郁
⑥ kidnap ['kidnæp] v. 诱拐
⑦ penalty ['penlti] n. 处罚,罚款

servant Dromio of Syracuse, and bade him take it to the Centaur Inn and remain there till he came.

In less than ten minutes he was met on the Mart by Dromio of Ephesus, his brother's slave, and immediately mistook him for his own Dromio. "Why are you back so soon? Where did you leave the money?" asked Antipholus of Syracuse.

This Dromio knew of no money except sixpence, which he had received on the previous① Wednesday and given to the saddler②; but he did know that his mistress was annoyed because his master was not in to dinner, and he asked Antipholus of Syracuse to go to a house called The Phoenix without delay. His speech angered the hearer, who would have beaten him if he had not fled. Antipholus of Syracuse then went to The Centaur, found that his gold had been deposited③ there, and walked out of the inn.

He was wandering about Ephesus when two beautiful ladies signaled to him with their hands. They were sisters, and their names were Adriana and Luciana. Adriana was the wife of his brother Antipholus of Ephesus, and she had made up her mind, from the strange account given her by Dromio of Ephesus, that her husband preferred another woman to his wife. "Ay, you may look as if you did not know me," she said to the man who was really her brother-in-law, "but I can remember when no words were sweet unless I said them, no meat flavorsome④ unless I carved it."

"Is it I you address?" said Antipholus of Syracuse stiffly. "I do not know you."

"Fie, brother," said Luciana. "You know perfectly well that she sent Dromio to you to bid you come to dinner"; and Adriana said, "Come, come; I have been made a fool of long enough.

① previous [ˈpriːvjəs] adj. 在前的, 早先的
② saddler [ˈsædlə] n. 制造马鞍的人, 马具商
③ deposit [diˈpɔzit] v. 存放, 堆积
④ flavorsome [ˈfleivəsəm] adj. 有香味的

My truant husband shall dine with me and confess his silly pranks① and be forgiven."

They were determined ladies, and Antipholus of Syracuse grew weary of disputing with them, and followed them obediently② to The Phoenix, where a very late "mid-day" dinner awaited them.

They were at dinner when Antipholus of Ephesus and his slave Dromio demanded admittance. "Maud, Bridget, Marian, Cecily, Gillian, Ginn!" shouted Dromio of Ephesus, who knew all his fellow-servants' names by heart.

From within came the reply, "Fool, dray-horse, coxcomb, idiot!" It was Dromio of Syracuse unconsciously insulting his brother.

Master and man did their best to get in, short of using a crowbar③, and finally went away; but Antipholus of Ephesus felt so annoyed with his wife that he decided to give a gold chain which he had promised her, to another woman.

Inside The Phoenix, Luciana, who believed Antipholus of Syracuse to be her sister's husband, attempted, by a discourse in rhyme, when alone with him, to make him kinder to Adriana. In reply he told her that he was not married, but that he loved her so much that, if Luciana were a mermaid④, he would gladly lie on the sea if he might feel beneath him her floating golden hair.

Luciana was shocked and left him, and reported his lovemaking to Adriana, who said that her husband was old and ugly, and not fit to be seen or heard, though secretly she was very fond of him.

① prank [præŋk] n. 胡闹，开玩笑，恶作剧
② obediently [əˈbiːdiəntli] adv. 服从地，顺从地，忠顺地
③ crowbar [ˈkrəʊbɑː(r)] n. 撬棍，铁撬
④ mermaid [ˈmɜːmeɪd] n. (传说中的)美人鱼

Antipholus of Syracuse soon received a visitor in the shape of Angelo the goldsmith①, of whom Antipholus of Ephesus had ordered the chain which he had promised his wife and intended to give to another woman.

The goldsmith handed the chain to Antipholus of Syracuse, and treated his "I bespoke it not" as mere fun, so that the puzzled merchant took the chain as good-humoredly as he had partaken of Adriana's dinner. He offered payment, but Angelo foolishly said he would call again.

The consequence was that Angelo was without money when a creditor② of the sort that stands no nonsense, threatened him with arrest unless he paid his debt immediately. This creditor had brought a police officer with him, and Angelo was relieved to see Antipholus of Ephesus coming out of the house where he had  been dining because he had been locked out of The Phoenix. Bitter was Angelo's dismay③ when Antipholus denied receipt of the chain.

At this moment up came Dromio of Syracuse and told the wrong Antipholus that he had shipped his goods, and that a favorable wind was blowing. To the ears of Antipholus of Ephesus this talk was simple nonsense. He would gladly have beaten the slave, but contented himself with crossly telling him to hurry to Adriana and bid her send to her arrested husband a purse of money which she would find in his desk.

Though Adriana was furious④ with her husband because she thought he had been making love to her sister, she did not prevent Luciana from getting the purse, and she bade Dromio of Syracuse bring home his master immediately.

---

① goldsmith ['gəuldsmiθ] n. 金匠
② creditor ['kreditə] n. 债权人
③ dismay [dis'mei] n. 沮丧,惊慌
④ furious ['fjuəriəs] adj. 狂怒的,狂暴的

Unfortunately, before Dromio of syracuse could reach the police station he met his real master, who had never been arrested, and did not understand what he meant by offering him a purse. Antipholus of Syracuse was further surprised when a lady whom he did not know asked him for a chain that he had promised her. She was, of course, the lady with whom Antipholus of Ephesus had dined when his brother was occupying his place at table. "Avaunt, thou witch!" was the answer which, to her astonishment, she received.

Meanwhile Antipholus of Ephesus waited vainly for the money which was to have released him. Never a good-tempered man, he was crazy with anger when Dromio of Ephesus, who, of course, had not been instructed to fetch a purse, appeared with nothing more useful than a rope. He beat the slave in the street despite the remonstrance① of the police officer; and his temper did not mend when Adriana, Luciana, and a doctor arrived under the impression that he was mad and must have his pulse felt. He raged so much that men came forward to bind him. But the kindness of Adriana spared him this shame. She promised to pay the sum demanded of him, and asked the doctor to lead him to The Phoenix.

Angelo's merchant creditor being paid, the two were friendly again, and might soon have been seen chatting before an abbey② about the odd behavior of Antipholus of Ephesus. "Softly," said the merchant at last, "that's he, I think."

It was not; it was Antipholus of Syracuse with his servant Dromio, and he wore Angelo's chain round his neck! The reconciled pair fairly pounced upon him to know what he meant by denying the receipt of the chain he had the impudence to wear. Antipholus of Syracuse lost his temper, and drew his sword, and at that moment Adriana and several others appeared. "Hold!" shouted the careful wife. "Hurt him not; he is mad. Take his sword away. Bind him—and Dromio too."

Dromio of Syracuse did not wish to be bound, and he said to his

---

① remonstrance [ri'mɔnstrəns] n. 抗议
② abbey ['æbi] n. 修道院

master, "Run, master! Into that abbey, quick, or we shall be robbed!"

They accordingly retreated into the abbey.

Adriana, Luciana, and a crowd remained outside, and the Abbess came out, and said, "People, why do you gather here?"

"To fetch my poor distracted① husband," replied Adriana.

Angelo and the merchant remarked that they had not known that he was mad.

Adriana then told the Abbess rather too much about her wifely worries, for the Abbess received the idea that Adriana was a shrew, and that if her husband was distracted he had better not return to her for the present.

Adriana determined, therefore, to complain to Duke Solinus, and, lo and behold! A minute afterwards the great man appeared with officers and two others. The others were Egeon and the headsman. The thousand pounds had not been found, and Egeon's fate seemed sealed.

Ere the Duke could pass the abbey Adriana knelt before him, and told a woeful tale of a mad husband rushing about stealing jewelry and drawing his sword, adding that the Abbess refused to allow her to lead him home.

The Duke bade the Abbess be summoned, and no sooner had he given the order than a servant from The Phoenix ran to Adriana with the tale that his master had singed② off the doctor's beard.

"Nonsense!" said Adriana, "he's in the abbey."

"As sure as I live I speak the truth," said the servant.

Antipholus of Syracuse had not come out of the abbey, before his brother of Ephesus prostrated himself in front of the Duke, exclaiming, "Justice, most gracious Duke, against that woman." He pointed to Adriana. "She has treated another man like her husband in my own house."

---

① distracted [dɪsˈtræktɪd] *adj.* 精神错乱的,心烦意乱的
② singe [sɪndʒ] *v.* 烧焦,烤焦

Even while he was speaking Egeon said, "Unless I am delirious①, I see my son Antipholus."

No one noticed him, and Antipholus of Ephesus went on to say how the doctor, whom he called "a threadbare juggler②," had been one of a gang who tied him to his slave Dromio, and thrust them into a vault whence he had escaped by gnawing③ through his bonds.

The Duke could not understand how the same man who spoke to him was seen to go into the abbey, and he was still wondering when Egeon asked Antipholus of Ephesus if he was not his son. He replied, "I never saw my father in my life;" but so deceived was Egeon by his likeness to the brother whom he had brought up, that he said, "Thou art ashamed to acknowledge me in misery."

Soon, however, the Abbess advanced with Antipholus of Syracuse and Dromio of Syracuse.

Then cried Adriana, "I see two husbands or mine eyes deceive me;" and Antipholus, espying④ his father, said, "Thou art Egeon or his ghost."

It was a day of surprises, for the Abbess said, "I will free that man by paying his fine, and gain my husband whom I lost. Speak, Egeon, for I am thy wife Emilia."

The Duke was touched. "He is free without a fine," he said.

So Egeon and Emilia were reunited, and Adriana and her husband reconciled⑤; but no one was happier than Antipholus of Syracuse, who, in the Duke's presence, went to Luciana and said, "I told you I loved you. Will

---

① delirious [di'liriəs] *adj.* 神志不清的
② juggler ['dʒʌglə] *n.* 变戏法者,行骗者
③ gnaw [nɔː] *v.* 咬,啃
④ espy [is'pai] *v.* 看到
⑤ reconcile ['rekənsail] *v.* 使和解,使和谐

you be my wife?"

Her answer was given by a look, and therefore is not written.

The two Dromios were glad to think they would receive no more beatings.

错误的喜剧

在西西里的海港叙拉古有位叫伊勤的商人，他的妻子叫伊米莉娅，他们夫妻俩一直过着幸福快乐的日子。伊勤的管家去世后，情况就变了，只要有事，伊勤就不得不亲自去亚得里亚海的厄匹达姆纽姆。不久后伊米莉娅就追随他而去，过了一段时日后生下两个男孩。这两个孩子长得很像，即使穿着不同的衣服他们看起来也一模一样。

现在你必须相信一件怪事，在这两个孩子出生的当天，在同一个客栈里，另外一对夫妇也生了一对双胞胎男孩，可这对夫妇要比伊勤和伊米莉娅穷得多。于是这对贫穷的夫妇就把两个孩子卖给了伊勤和伊米莉娅。

伊米莉娅迫切地想要叙拉古的朋友们看看她的孩子，于是在一个恶劣的天气里，她和伊勤带上四个孩子起航回家了。

在距离叙拉古还很远的地方，他们搭乘的船进了水，水手们离开了大船跳进唯一的小船逃生，根本顾不上他们的乘客们的安危了。

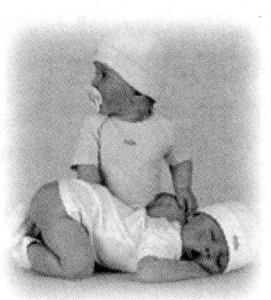

伊米莉娅将她的一个孩子绑在桅杆上，并将其中的一个奴隶孩子和他绑在一起；伊勤也仿效她的方法把另外两个孩子绑在同一个桅杆上。然后这对父母把自己也系在桅杆上以期获救。

然而，这只船突然撞到了礁石上，被撞成了两半。伊米莉娅和她捆绑的两个孩子漂离了伊勤和他照看的另外两个孩子。伊米莉娅和她照顾的那两个孩子被一些厄匹达姆纽姆人救了起来，可是科林斯的一些渔民却把孩子从她怀里抢走了，于是她孤身一人伤心地回到了厄匹达姆纽姆。从此，她就在小亚细亚的一个著名小城以弗所定居下来。

伊勤和他照顾的那两个孩子也获救了，只是要比伊米莉娅幸运得多，他回到了叙拉古并将两个孩子抚养到十八岁。他给自己的孩子取名为安提福勒斯，给那个奴隶小孩取名为德洛米奥。不可思议的是，这两个名字又分别

是另外两个丢失的孩子的名字。

到了十八岁的时候,留在伊勤身边的那个儿子急切地想找到他的哥哥,于是伊勤就让他带上他的仆人去寻找。下面我们就称这两个年轻人为叙拉古的安提福勒斯和叙拉古的德洛米奥。

儿子走后,伊勤感觉家里太沉闷而待不下去了,于是他就出去旅行,一走就是五个年头。在此期间,他没有听说有关叙拉古的任何消息,否则的话,他决不会去以弗所。

像过去那样,这位闷闷不乐的商人漂泊到了以弗所,可刚到那里就被捕了。原来,叙拉古的公爵对落入他手中的以弗所人非常残暴,因而愤怒的以弗所政府就通过了一项法律,即规定如果在以弗所发现叙拉古人,除

非他能交出一千磅的赎金,不然就会被处死。伊勤被带到以弗所公爵索列纳斯面前,公爵告诉他如果在一天的时间内凑不齐一千磅的赎金,他就必死无疑。

如果我告诉你被科林斯的渔民抢走的那两个孩子现在是以弗所的居民,你会认为这就是命运。这两个孩子被卖给了索列纳斯公爵的叔叔,也就是麦纳弗昂公爵。以后就称呼他们俩为以弗所的安提福勒斯和以弗所的德洛米奥。

此外,在伊勤被捕的当天,叙拉古的安提福勒斯来到了以弗所,为了逃避处罚,他们假装是厄匹达姆纽姆人。他给了他的仆人叙拉古的德洛米奥一些钱让他去森陶尔客栈等他回来。

还不到十分钟他在市场看到了哥哥的仆人,以弗所的德洛米奥,误以为他就是自己的德洛米奥。叙拉古的安提福勒斯就问他:"为什么这么快又回来了?你把钱放在哪里了?"

这个德洛米奥对钱的事一无所知,除了上周三得到的六便士并且又给了马具商,他就知道他家太太因为主人没有去吃饭正生气呢,于是他就叫叙拉古的安提福勒斯马上去一个叫做"凤凰"的地方。他的一番话惹恼了叙拉古的安提福勒斯,若不是他及时逃走了,叙拉古的安提福勒斯就会狠狠地揍他一顿。叙拉古的安提福勒斯去了森陶尔客栈后看到他的金子就存放在那里,于是就出去了。

他正在以弗所闲逛的时候,两位美丽的女士朝他挥手打招呼。她们是

姐妹俩,分别叫阿德里安娜和露西安娜。阿德里安娜就是他的哥哥以弗所的安提福勒斯的妻子,听了以弗所的德洛米奥的一番奇谈后,她就认为自己的丈夫喜欢上了别的女人。"啊,你现在看起来像不认识我似的,"她对她的丈夫(实际上是她的小叔子)说,"可是我仍然记得'无语柔而甜,除非是我言;无肉香味浓,除非我烹饪'的话呢。"

"你是在跟我说话吗?"叙拉古的安提福勒斯冷冰冰地说,"我不认识你啊。"

"呸,姐夫,"露西安娜说,"你很清楚她让德洛米奥叫你过来吃饭。"阿德里安娜接着说:"好了,好了,原来我一直被你愚弄着,以为我离家的丈夫会和我们一起就餐,然后再承认自己开的愚蠢玩笑就原谅你啦。"

她们两个特别固执,叙拉古的安提福勒斯也不愿意和她们争执了,就乖乖地跟着她们到了"凤凰"去吃那顿迟到的"午餐"。

在他们就餐的时候,以弗所的安提福勒斯和仆人德洛米奥在外面叫门。"莫德、布里奇特、玛丽安、赛西莉、吉莉安、吉恩!"以弗所的德洛米奥大声叫着这些人的名字,他早已把这些帮佣者的名字牢记于心。

里面的回答却是:"傻瓜、笨蛋、蠢货、白痴!"叙拉古的德洛米奥无意中辱骂着自己的哥哥。

主仆二人想方设法进去,就差没有用铁锹了,可最后还是走开了;以弗所的安提福勒斯非常生他妻子的气,决定要把答应送给她的金项链送给另外一个女人。

而在"凤凰"里,露西安娜认为叙拉古的安提福勒斯就是自己的姐夫,和他单独相处时她试着用委婉的语气告诉他要对姐姐好些。他却告诉露西安娜他仍然是单身,并深深爱上了她,假若露西安娜是个美人鱼,他会很高兴地躺在大海里,如同感受到身体下面是她飘动的金发。

露西安娜对他的这番话感到很震惊,马上离开了他,并告诉姐姐阿德里安娜姐夫向自己求爱了。阿德里安娜说她的丈夫又老又丑,不值得见也不值得听,尽管她在心里暗暗地喜欢他。

不久,叙拉古的安提福勒斯又招待了一位叫安吉罗的金匠,以弗所的安提福勒斯在他那里定做了一条项链,这条项链本来是他答应送给妻子的,现在却想送给另外一个女人了。

金匠把项链给了叙拉古的安提福勒斯,并把他说的"我没有预订"的话当作玩笑。于是这个稀里糊涂的商人拿着这条项链感觉跟吃过阿德里安娜的那顿饭一样莫名其妙。他要付钱给金匠,而安吉罗憨厚地说下次再付吧。

　　结果安吉罗没有钱还债,而那位放款人毫不含糊,带来了一位警官,并威胁说如果他不马上还债就逮捕他。因被妻子关在"凤凰"的门外,以弗所的安提福勒斯在饭店里吃完饭出来。安吉罗瞧见了他,一下子觉得轻松了。可是以弗所的安提福勒斯却否认他收下了那条项链,这让安吉罗很沮丧。

　　正在那时,叙拉古的德洛米奥走了过来,告诉以弗所的安提福勒斯他已经用船将货物运走了,风向大吉。以弗所的安提福勒斯觉得仆人在说胡话,恨不得好好揍他一顿,但幸好有他在,就吩咐他赶快去告诉阿德里安娜让她快点从他的桌子里拿一袋钱来赎她被捕的丈夫。

　　尽管阿德里安娜因为丈夫向妹妹求爱而感到非常恼火,可她还是没有阻止露西安娜拿出钱袋,并让叙拉古的德洛米奥尽快带主人回家。

　　不幸的是,以弗所的德洛米奥还没有到警局就遇到了他真正的主人,他没有被捕,更不明白他的仆人为什么给他一袋钱。令叙拉古的安提福勒斯更为惊讶的是,一位素不相识的女子竟然向他索要一条金项链,并且说那是他曾经答应要给她的。当然她就是那位和以弗所的安提福勒斯一起就餐的女子,那时他弟弟正取代着他的位置就餐呢。让这个女子吃惊的是,她听到的回答却是:"走开,你这个神经病!"

　　与此同时,以弗所的安提福勒斯还在那里徒劳地等着那笔救命钱。他本来就不是个好脾气的人,当看见以弗所的德洛米奥手里拿着没什么用的东西走来了——尽管这个德洛米奥并不知道去拿钱这回事,他更是怒火冲天。不顾警官的阻拦,他在大街上揍了仆人一顿;他的怒气还没有消下去,却看见阿德里安娜、露西安娜带着医生来了,她们以为他疯了,需要把把脉象治疗一下,更令他气愤的是那些人竟然过来绑他。善良的阿德里安娜宽恕了他做的这件丢脸的事,答应偿还他要求的钱,然后让医生带他回"凤凰"去。

　　安吉罗将钱还给了放款人,两人又成了朋友,不久后他们在一个修道院门口聊天时又提起以弗所的安提福勒斯的异常行为。"小声点,"那个商人最后说,"我确定那个人就是他。"

　　其实他们俩认错了;那是叙拉古的安提福勒斯和他的仆人德洛米奥,他的脖子上竟然戴着安吉罗的那条项链!这对和好如初的朋友突然走到他面前,想知道他为什么否认他已收下项链并且还不知羞耻地戴着。叙拉古的安提福勒斯听了大怒,并拔出剑来,正在那时阿德里安娜带着其他人赶来了。"住手!"这个细心的妻子喊道。"不要伤害他;他疯了。把他的剑拿走,再把他绑起来,还有德洛米奥。"

叙拉古的德洛米奥不愿被绑起来,就对他主人说:"快跑,主人!快去那个修道院,否则我们就要遭抢劫了!"

接着,他们跑进了修道院。

阿德里安娜、露西安娜还有那伙人留在了外面,修道院院长走了出来,问:"大家为什么聚集在这里啊?"

"要把我那位可怜的神经错乱的丈夫带回家。"阿德里安娜回答。

安吉罗和那个放款人说他们并不知道他已经疯了。

阿德里安娜告诉院长她作为妻子的种种担心,而院长却认为她是个泼妇,如果她丈夫神经错乱了,现在就不该让他回到她身边。

因此,阿德里安娜决定向索列纳斯公爵诉说此事。瞧!一会儿工夫,这个大人物就带着军官和另外两个人来了。另外两个人就是伊勤和刽子手。那一千磅还没有着落,看来伊勤的期限要到了。

公爵刚要走过修道院,阿德里安娜跪在他的面前。对他说了她疯癫的丈夫怎么偷取珠宝,怎么拔剑伤人,又说修道院院长不让她把丈夫带回家。

公爵派人叫院长出来问话,刚下完命令,就有个仆人从"凤凰"跑来告诉阿德里安娜说老爷刚刚把医生的胡子烧掉了。

"胡说!"阿德里安娜说,"他在修道院里。"

"我从来不说谎的。"这个仆人说。

叙拉古的安提福勒斯还没有从修道院里出来,他以弗所的哥哥已经跑倒公爵面前了,大声嚷道:"最仁慈的公爵啊,请您主持公道惩罚那个女人。"他指着阿德里安娜说:"在我自己的家里,她竟然像对待丈夫一样对待别的男人。"

在他对公爵说话的空儿,伊勤说道:"我不是老眼昏花了吧,我看到我的儿子安提福勒斯了。"

没人注意他,以弗所的安提福勒斯继续说医生(他称他是"陈腐的骗子")一伙怎样把他和德洛米奥绑在一起,怎样把他俩塞进地窖里,他又怎样咬断镣铐从那里跑出来的。

公爵也不明白眼前跟他说话的这个人是怎么被认定进了修道院。在伊勤问以弗所的安提福勒斯是否是他的儿子时,他还在想着这件事呢。安提福勒斯说:"我从来没有见过我的生父。"伊勤误以为这个孩子就是他抚养成人的那一个,于是说:"我的处境如此糟糕,

你也羞于认我这个父亲吧。"

然而,不一会儿院长带着叙拉古的安提福勒斯和叙拉古的德洛米奥走了出来。

阿德里安娜哭着说:"我看见了两个丈夫,是不是我的眼睛在欺骗我?"叙拉古的安提福勒斯看到了他的父亲,问道:"你是伊勤,还是他的鬼魂?"

这是个充满惊喜的日子,因为修道院院长说:"我愿意支付罚金将那个人释放,以期得到我失散已久的丈夫。伊勤,说话啊,我是你的妻子伊米莉娅啊。"

公爵被这一幕感动了,说:"他自由了,无需交罚金。"

就这样伊勤和伊米莉娅团聚了,阿德里安娜和她的丈夫和好了;然而再也没有谁比叙拉古的安提福勒斯更幸福的了,当着公爵的面,他走到露西安娜面前,说:"我告诉过你我爱你,你愿意做我妻子吗?"

她的答复只可意会,不可言传了。

两个德洛米奥一想到他们以后再也不会挨打了,真是高兴极了。

经典的回声
Echoes of Classics: Stories from Shakespeare

16. Measure for Measure

"Your Friar Is Now Your Prince."

More centuries ago than I care to say, the people of Vienna were governed too mildly. The reason was that the reigning Duke Vicentio① was excessively good-natured, and disliked to see offenders made unhappy.

The consequence was that the number of ill-behaved persons in Vienna was enough to make the Duke shake his head in sorrow when his chief secretary showed him it at the end of a list. He decided, therefore, that wrongdoers must be punished. But popularity was dear to him. He knew that, if he were suddenly strict after being lax, he would cause

---

① Vicentio ['visentiəu] n. 维森提奥(男子名)

people to call him a tyrant①. For this reason he told his Privy Council② that he must go to Poland on important business of state. "I have chosen Angelo to rule in my absence," said he.

Now this Angelo, although he appeared to be noble, was really a mean③ man. He had promised to marry a girl called Mariana, and now would have nothing to say to her, because her dowry④ had been lost. So poor Mariana lived forlornly⑤, waiting every day for the footstep of her stingy lover, and loving him still.

Having appointed Angelo his deputy, the Duke went to a friar called Thomas and asked him for a friar's dress and instruction in the art of giving religious counsel, for he did not intend to go to Poland, but to stay at home and see how Angelo governed.

Angelo had not been a day in office when he condemned⑥ to death a young man named Claudio for an act of rash selfishness which nowadays would only be punished by severe reproof⑦.

Claudio had a queer⑧ friend called Lucio, and Lucio saw a chance of freedom for Claudio if Claudio's beautiful sister Isabella would plead with Angelo.

Isabella was at that time living in a nunnery⑨. Nobody had won her heart, and she thought she would like to become a sister, or nun.

Meanwhile Claudio did not lack an advocate.

An ancient lord, Escalus⑩, was for leniency⑪. "Let us cut a little, but

---

① tyrant ['taiərənt] n. 暴君
② Privy Council 枢密院
③ mean [miːn] adj. 卑鄙的
④ dowry ['dauəri] n. 嫁妆
⑤ forlornly [fə'lɔːnli] adv. 被遗弃地
⑥ condemn [kən'de] v. 宣告有罪
⑦ reproof [ri'pruːf] n. 谴责,非难
⑧ queer [kwiə] adj. 奇怪的,特殊的
⑨ nunnery ['nʌnəri] n. 女修道院
⑩ Escalus ['eskələs] n. 爱斯卡勒斯(男子名)
⑪ leniency ['liːnjənsi] n. 宽厚,仁慈

not kill," he said. "This gentleman had a most noble father."

Angelo was unmoved. "If twelve men find me guilty, I ask no more mercy than is in the law."

Angelo then ordered the Provost to see that Claudio was executed at nine the next morning.

After the issue of this order Angelo was told that the sister of the condemned man desired to see him.

"Admit her," said Angelo.

On entering with Lucio, the beautiful girl said, "I am a woeful suitor to your Honor."

"Well?" said Angelo.

She colored at his chill monosyllable and the ascending red increased the beauty of her face. "I have a brother who is condemned to die," she continued. "Condemn the fault, I pray you, and spare my brother."

"Every fault," said Angelo, "is condemned before it is committed. A fault cannot suffer. Justice would be void if the committer of a fault went free."

She would have left the court if Lucio had not whispered to her, "You are too cold; you could not speak more tamely① if you wanted a pin."

So Isabella attacked Angelo again, and when he said, "I will not pardon him," she was not discouraged, and when he said, "He's sentenced; 'tis too late," she returned to the assult. But all her fighting was with reasons, and with reasons she could not prevail② over the Deputy.

She told him that nothing becomes power like mercy. She told him

---

① tamely [ˈteimli] *adv.* 温顺地，没骨气地
② prevail [priˈveil] *v.* 流行，盛行，获胜

that humanity receives and requires mercy from Heaven, that it was good to have gigantic① strength, and had to use it like a giant. She told him that lightning rives the oak and spares the myrtle. She bade him look for fault in his own breast, and if he found one, to refrain from making it an argument against her brother's life.

Angelo found a fault in his breast at that moment. He loved Isabella's beauty, and was tempted to do for her beauty what he would not do for the love of man.

He appeared to relent, for he said, "Come to me to-morrow before noon."

She had, at any rate, succeeded in prolonging② her brother's life for a few hours.

In her absence Angelo's conscience rebuked him for trifling with his judicial③ duty.

When Isabella called on him the second time, he said, "Your brother cannot live."

Isabella was painfully astonished, but all she said was, "Even so. Heaven keep your Honor."

But as she turned to go, Angelo felt that his duty and honor were slight in comparison with④ the loss of her.

"Give me your love," he said, "and Claudio shall be freed."

"Before I would marry you, he should die if he had twenty heads to lay upon the block," said Isabella, for she saw then that he was not the just man he pretended to be.

So she went to her brother in prison, to inform him that he must die. At first he was boastful⑤, and promised to hug⑥ the darkness of death. But when he clearly understood that his sister could buy his life by

---

① gigantic [dʒaiˈɡæntik] adj. 巨人般的, 巨大的
② prolonging [prəˈlɔŋ] v. 延长, 拖延
③ judicial [dʒu(ː)ˈdiʃəl] adj. 司法的, 法院的, 明断的
④ in comparison with 与……比较
⑤ boastful [ˈbəustful] adj. 自负的, 喜夸耀的, 自夸的
⑥ hug [hʌɡ] n. 拥抱

marrying Angelo, he felt his life more valuable than her happiness, and he exclaimed, "Sweet sister, let me live."

"O faithless coward! O dishonest wretch!" she cried.

At this moment the Duke came forward, in the habit of a friar, to request some speech with Isabella. He called himself Friar Lodowick.

The Duke then told her that Angelo was affianced to Mariana, whose love-story he related. He then asked her to consider this plan. Let Mariana, in the dress of Isabella, go closely veiled to Angelo, and say, in a voice resembling Isabella's, that if Claudio were spared she would marry him. Let her take the ring from Angelo's little finger, that it might be afterwards proved that his visitor was Mariana.

Isabella had, of course, a great respect for friars, who are as nearly like nuns as men can be. She agreed, therefore, to the Duke's plan. They were to meet again at the moated grange①, Mariana's house.

In the street the Duke saw Lucio, who, seeing a man dressed like a friar, called out, "What news of the Duke, friar?" "I have none," said the Duke.

Lucio then told the Duke some stories about Angelo. Then he told one about the Duke. The Duke contradicted② him. Lucio was provoked, and called the Duke "a shallow③, ignorant fool", though he pretended to love him. "The Duke shall know you better if I live to report you," said the Duke, grimly④. Then he asked Escalus, whom he saw in the street,

---

① grange [greindʒ] n. 农庄
② contradict [ˌkɒntrəˈdɪkt] v. 同……矛盾
③ shallow [ˈʃæləʊ] adj. 浅的,浅薄的
④ grimly [ˈɡrɪmli] adv. 严格地,可怕地,冷酷地

what he thought of his ducal master. Escalus, who imagined he was speaking to a friar, replied, "The Duke is a very temperate① gentleman, who prefers to see another merry to being merry himself."

The Duke then proceeded to call on Mariana.

Isabella arrived immediately afterwards, and the Duke introduced the two girls to one another, both of whom thought he was a friar. They went into a chamber apart from him to discuss the saving of Claudio, and while they talked in low and earnest tones, the Duke looked out of the window and saw the broken sheds and flower-beds black with moss, which betrayed Mariana's indifference to her country dwelling. Some women would have beautified their garden: not she. She was for the town; she neglected the joys of the country. He was sure that Angelo would not make her unhappier.

"We are agreed, father," said Isabella, as she returned with Mariana.

So Angelo was deceived by the girl whom he had dismissed from his love, and put on her finger a ring he wore, in which was set a milky stone which flashed in the light with secret colors.

Hearing of her success, the Duke went next day to the prison prepared to learn that an order had arrived for Claudio's release. It had not, however, but a letter was handed to the Provost while he waited. His amazement was great when the Provost read aloud these words, "Whatsoever you may hear to the contrary, let Claudio be executed by four of the clock. Let me have his head sent me by five."

But the Duke said to the Provost, "You must show the Deputy another head," and he held out a letter and a signet②. "Here," he said, "are the hand and seal of the Duke. He is to return, I tell you, and Angelo

---

① temperate ['tempərit] *adj.* 温和的
② signet ['signit] *n.* 图章,印

knows it not. Give Angelo another head."

The Provost thought, "This friar speaks with power. I know the Duke's signet and I know his hand."

He said at length, "A man died in prison this morning, a pirate of the age of Claudio, with a beard of his color. I will show his head."

The pirate's head was duly shown to Angelo, who was deceived by its resemblance① to Claudio's.

The Duke's return was so popular that the citizens removed the city gates from their hinges to assist his entry into Vienna. Angelo and Escalus duly presented themselves, and were profusely praised for their conduct of affairs in the Duke's absence.

It was, therefore, the more unpleasant for Angelo when Isabella, passionately angered by his treachery, knelt before the Duke, and cried for justice.

When her story was told, the Duke cried, "To prison with her for a slanderer of our right hand! But stay, who persuaded you to come here?"

"Friar Lodowick," said she.

"Who knows him?" inquired the Duke.

"I do, my lord," replied Lucio. "I beat him because he spake against your Grace."

A friar called Peter here said, "Friar Lodowick is a holy man."

Isabella was removed by an officer, and Mariana came forward. She took off her veil, and said to Angelo, "This is the face you once swore was worth looking on."

Bravely he faced her as she put out her hand and said, "This is the hand which wears the ring you thought to give another."

"I know the woman," said Angelo. "Once there was talk of marriage between us, but I found her frivolous②."

---

① resemblance [ri'zembləns] n. 类同之处
② frivolous ['frivələs] adj. 轻佻的, 琐碎的

Mariana here burst out that they were affianced by the strongest vows. Angelo replied by asking the Duke to insist on the production of Friar Lodowick.

"He shall appear," promised the Duke, and bade Escalus examine the missing witness thoroughly while he was elsewhere.

Presently the Duke re-appeared in the character of Friar Lodowick, and accompanied by Isabella and the Provost. He was not so much examined as abused and threatened by Escalus. Lucio asked him to deny, if he dared, that he called the Duke a fool and a coward①, and had had his nose pulled for his impudence.

"To prison with him!" shouted Escalus, but as hands were laid upon him, the Duke pulled off his friar's hood, and was a Duke before them all.

"Now," he said to Angelo, "if you have any impudence that can yet serve you, work it for all it's worth."

"Immediate sentence and death is all I beg," was the reply.

"Were you affianced to Mariana?" asked the Duke.

"I was," said Angelo.

"Then marry her instantly," said his master. "Marry them," he said to Friar Peter, "and return with them here."

"Come hither, Isabel," said the Duke, in tender tones. "Your friar is now your Prince, and grieves he was too late to save your brother;" but well the roguish Duke knew he had saved him.

"O pardon me," she cried, "that I employed my Sovereign in my trouble."

"You are pardoned," he said, gaily.

At that moment Angelo and his wife re-entered. "And now, Angelo," said the Duke, gravely②, "we condemn thee to the block on which Claudio laid his head!"

"O my most gracious lord," cried Mariana, "mock me not!"

---

① coward ['kauəd] n. 懦弱的人
② gravely ['greivli] adv. 严肃地

"You shall buy a better husband," said the Duke.

"O my dear lord," said she,"I crave① no better man."

Isabella nobly added her prayer to Mariana's, but the Duke feigned② inflexibility.

"Provost," he said, "how came it that Claudio as executed at an unusual hour?"

Afraid to confess the lie he had imposed upon Angelo, the Provost said,"I had a private message."

"You are discharged from③ your office," said the Duke. The Provost then departed. Angelo said, "I am sorry to have caused such sorrow. I prefer death to mercy." Soon there was a motion in the crowd. The Provost re-appeared with Claudio. Like a big child the Provost said, "I saved this man; he is like Claudio." The Duke was amused, and said to Isabella,"I pardon him because he is like your brother. He is like my brother, too, if you, dear Isabel, will be mine."

She was his with a smile, and the Duke forgave Angelo, and promoted the Provost.

Lucio he condemned to marry a stout woman with a bitter tongue.

一报还一报

很久很久以前,在维也纳城里实行着一种善柔政策,这是因为当时统治维也纳的公爵维森提奥是一位非常温厚之人,不愿意看到罪犯难过。

结果,当他的辅佐大臣给他看了罪犯名单后,维也纳行为不良者之多让这位好公爵难过地摇头,于是,他决定要让那些做坏事的人受到惩罚。然而,声望对他来说太重要了。他知道,如果从过去的宽容、松弛突然变得严厉起来,也许一向爱戴他的人民就会称他为暴君。因此,他告诉枢密院他有要务要去波兰,并对他们说:"在我离开期间,由安吉洛代我行使职权。"

这个安吉洛表面上看起来品质高尚,但实际上是个很卑鄙的人。他已

---

① crave [kreiv] v. 恳求,渴望
② feigned [feind] adj. 假的,伪装,做作的
③ discharge from 释放,解雇,使免除

经向一位叫玛莉安娜的姑娘许下婚约,然而自从她的嫁妆丢失后,他就认为自己和她毫无关系了。可怜的玛莉安娜虽然过着被人遗弃的生活,却仍然深爱着她那位小气的爱人,每天都渴望能够听到他走近的脚步声。

安吉洛任职以后,公爵就去了一位叫托马斯的修道士那里,并向他要了一身道袍和一本有关布道艺术的册子,因为他并没有打算去波兰而是想留在维也纳看看安吉洛如何执政。

安吉洛上任还不到一天,他就判处了一个名叫克劳迪奥的年轻人死刑,而克劳迪奥自私鲁莽的行为搁在现在充其量也就会被判个严重警告而已。

克劳迪奥有个怪才朋友叫路西奥,他认为如果克劳迪奥美丽的姐姐依莎贝拉去向安吉洛求情的话,他就有获得自由的机会。

依莎贝拉当时住在一个修道院里,还未曾有人获取她的芳心,她觉得她更愿意做一名修女或者尼姑。

同时为克劳迪奥求情的人也不少。

有一位老臣——埃斯卡勒斯——也为他求情。"减轻些惩罚吧,不要杀掉他,"他说,"这位绅士的父亲可是位德高望重的人啊。"

安吉洛不为之所动。"如果有十二个人说我有罪,我就不会请求超出法律的怜悯了。"

安吉洛于是就下令让狱吏于次日上午九点执行死刑。

刚刚下达了命令,就有人来报说,那个罪犯的姐姐想拜见他。

"传她进来。"安吉洛说。

一位美丽的姑娘跟着路西奥进来了,她对安吉洛说:"我就是想要拜见大人您的那个可怜的求情者。"

"哦。"安吉洛说。

听到这个冷冰冰的单音节的词,她的脸红了,不断泛起的红晕为她的脸庞增添了一分美丽。"我弟弟被判处了死刑,"她继续说,"我祈求您饶恕他吧。"

安吉洛说:"犯了罪就要受到惩罚,否则的话,若每一个犯了罪的人都被自由释放,哪有公正可言。"

她正要离开,路西奥低声对她说:"你的态度太冷淡了;即使你想借枚针,说话也要热情诚恳些啊。"

于是依莎贝拉再次向安吉洛求情,甚至听到他说"我不会宽恕他的"她也没有气馁,而当他说"太迟了,他已经被判决了"时她转而开始攻击他。她的斗争是合情合理的,即使那样她也斗不过安吉洛。

她告诉他没有什么能比得上仁慈的力量;她告诉他博爱接受并需要上苍的仁慈,她告诉他拥有强大的力量不错,但要像个巨人一样来使用它;她告诉他闪电劈开橡树却宽恕香桃木。她让他找一下他自己心中的过错,如果能找到,对于他弟弟的性命就没什么好争论的了。

那一刻安吉洛真的在他心中找到了一个过错。他爱上了依莎贝拉的美貌,受到她美丽的诱惑去做那些他不会为别人做的事。

他似乎变得宽容了,因为他对依莎贝拉说:"明天中午之前过来见我。"

无论怎样,她已经成功地把弟弟的生命延长了几个小时。

她离开后,安吉洛的良心谴责他视自己的法律职责为儿戏。

当依莎贝拉第二次拜访他时,他说:"你弟弟活不成了。"

痛苦的依莎贝拉感到震惊,她只说了一句:"即使这样,愿上帝保佑您。"

可正在她要转身离去时,安吉洛感到与失去她相比,他的职责和荣耀不值一提。

"嫁给我,"他说,"克劳迪奥就会被释放。"

"在我嫁给你之前,就算他有二十个脑袋也被砍掉了。"依莎贝拉说。因为那时她感觉出他只是一个假装公正的人。

于是她去牢房探望弟弟,告诉他他必死的消息。起初他夸口说他要拥抱死亡的黑暗,可当他得知如果姐姐嫁给安吉洛就可以保全他的性命时,突然觉得自己的生命要比姐姐的幸福珍贵得多,就哭喊着说:"好姐姐,让我活下去吧。"

"噢,你这个背信弃义的懦夫!噢,你这个虚伪的可怜虫!"她喊道。

正在那时,公爵来了,他自称是罗德维克修士,并以修士的方式对依莎贝拉说了一些话。

公爵告诉她安吉洛已向玛莉安娜许下婚约,并给她讲了他们的爱情故事。然后建议她考虑一下这个计划:让玛莉安娜打扮成依莎贝拉

的样子,戴上面纱接近安吉洛,模仿依莎贝拉的声音告诉他如果他释放了克劳迪奥就嫁给他。并让玛莉安娜取下安吉洛小指上的那枚戒指,以后可以证明见他的那位女子就是玛莉安娜。

依莎贝拉对这个修道士不由得产生了一种敬仰之情,他几乎和真的修

道士一样。因此,她同意了公爵的计划。他们约好在护城河边上的农庄,也就是玛莉安娜的家中见面。

公爵看在街上看见了路西奥,而路西奥看见这个修士打扮的人就大声问:"修士,你有公爵的消息吗?""没有。"公爵说。

路西奥对公爵说了有关安吉洛的事情,然后又跟他说了一件有关公爵的事。公爵反驳了他,路西奥生气了,就称公爵是一个"肤浅、无知的傻子",尽管装作很喜欢他的样子。公爵冷冷地说:"如果我能活着向公爵汇报你的话,他会更好地了解你的。"然后,他又向在街上碰见的埃斯卡勒斯寻问公爵是个怎样的人。埃斯卡勒斯以为自己面对的是一位修士,回答说:"公爵是一位性情温厚的绅士,乐人之所乐。"

于是公爵继续向玛莉安娜的住所走去。

依莎贝拉随后也赶到了,公爵把这两位姑娘相互介绍了一番,她们俩都认为他是个修士。离开公爵,她们进了一个房间来商讨如何救助克劳迪奥。在她们用低沉而真诚的口吻交谈的时候,公爵向窗外望去,看到院子里破败不堪的棚子,长满了黑苔的花坛,由此可以看出玛莉安娜对她的乡下住所心不在焉。有些女人会把她们的花园修整得漂漂亮亮,而她却没有。她是城里人,却忽视了乡间的乐趣,因而他确信安吉洛会使她过得更快乐些。

"我们商讨好了,神父。"和玛莉安娜一起走出来时,依莎贝拉对公爵说。

那天安吉洛就被他遗弃的这位姑娘骗得晕头转向,神魂颠倒,并把戒指取下来给她戴上,这枚戒指上镶着一颗乳白色的宝石,在光下会闪现出一些神秘的颜色。

听到了她大功告成的消息,公爵第二天就前往狱中等候释放克劳迪奥的命令。然而,他还未被释放,公爵却看到有一个字条交到狱吏手中。狱吏大声读出字条上的内容:"无论你听到什么反对的声音,四点之前务必处死克劳迪奥,五点之前把他的脑袋送到我这里来。"公爵听后,感到非常震惊。

可是公爵对狱吏说:"你必须给安吉洛送另外一个脑袋。"然后他拿出一封信和公爵的印章,说:"这是公爵的亲笔信和印章,我告诉你,他马上就要回来了,安吉洛还不知道此事。去交给安吉洛另外一个脑袋。"

这位狱吏想:"这位修士说话语气强硬。我认识公爵的印章也认识他的笔迹。"

最后,他说:"今天早晨狱中死了一个人,是个和克劳迪奥年纪相仿的海盗,胡子的颜色也和他的一样。我把这个脑袋给他送去好了。"

这个海盗的头被按时送到了安吉洛那里,这个与克劳迪奥的很像的脑袋骗过了他的眼睛。

公爵的归来受到热烈的欢迎,老百姓放下铰链打开城门迎接公爵走进维也纳。安吉洛和埃斯卡勒斯如期出面迎接,公爵大力赞扬他们治理有方。

当然,依莎贝拉的到来让安吉洛大为不快,她被安吉洛背信弃义的行为激怒了,于是就跪在公爵面前,恳求公正。

她把事情的经过说完后,公爵大喊:"竟然污蔑我得力的助手,把她押入牢房!等等,是谁指使你过来的?"

"罗德维克修士。"她说。

"有谁认识他?"公爵问。

"我认识,老爷,"路西奥说,"因为他说了对老爷您不恭的话,我就揍了他。"

一个叫彼得的修士却说:"罗德维克修士是一位圣人。"

一位军官把依莎贝拉带走了,玛莉安娜进来了。她拿下她的面纱,对安吉洛说:"这就是你曾经发誓说值得你看一辈子的脸。"

他大胆地看着她,她伸出手来,说:"这只手上戴的戒指就是你想送给另外一个人的。"

"我认识那个女人,"安吉洛说,"我们在谈论婚嫁的时候,我发现她是个轻佻的女人。"

玛莉安娜大声说他们是发过誓言、有过婚约的,而安吉洛却坚持对公爵说这都是那位罗德维克修士编造的。

"他会出现的。"公爵保证说。然后就让埃斯卡勒斯去寻找这个当他在别处时出现、现在又失踪的证人。

不久,在依莎贝拉和狱吏的陪同下,公爵打扮成罗德维克修士的模样再次出现了。他曾经被埃斯卡勒斯检查过、辱骂过、威吓过。路西奥也问他是否敢否认他称公爵是个傻子、懦夫,还因他的厚颜无耻而拉了他的鼻子。

"把他关进大牢!"埃斯卡勒斯叫嚷着,而士兵却抓住了他,公爵拿掉了他的修士帽,站在众人面前的就是公爵本人。

他对安吉洛说:"现在,你若有什么厚颜无耻的话为你自己开脱,尽管说吧。"

"我祈求立即把我判处死刑。"安吉洛回答说。

"你是不是已经向玛莉安娜许下婚约?"公爵问。

"是的。"安吉洛说。

"那就马上娶她为妻。"他的主人说。然后又对彼得修士说:"为他们二人主持完婚礼,再带他们回到这里。"

"依莎贝拉,到这里来,"公爵温柔地说,"你的修士现在变成了你的公爵,令人难过的是他没有来得及救你弟弟的性命。"当然这个智多星的公爵知道自己已经救了她的弟弟。

"噢,请宽恕我,"她哭着说,"我已经麻烦您很多了,老爷。"

"已经宽恕你了。"公爵高兴地说。

这时安吉洛和他的妻子回来了。"现在,安吉洛,"公爵严厉地说,"我们就判你在克劳迪奥被处死的断头台上受刑!"

"噢,仁慈的老爷,"玛莉安娜哭着说,"不要这样捉弄我!"

"你可以找到一个比他更好的丈夫。"公爵说。

"噢,亲爱的老爷,"她说,"我不要更好的丈夫。"

依莎贝拉也大度地替玛莉安娜求情,可是公爵却假装不为之所动。

"狱吏,"他说,"克劳迪奥是怎么在那个不合适的时辰被处死的?"

狱吏害怕坦白他强加于安吉洛身上的谎言,就说:"我有一封密信。"

"你被免职了。"公爵说。狱吏离开了。安吉洛说:"我非常抱歉自己制造了这么多的痛苦,我但求一死而不求饶恕。"不久人群中一阵骚动,原来是狱吏带着克劳迪奥再次出现了。像个大男孩似的狱吏说:"我救了这个人;他特别像克劳迪奥。"公爵被逗乐了,对依莎贝拉说:"我豁免他了,因为他特别像你弟弟。他也像我弟弟,亲爱的依莎贝拉,不知你是否愿意嫁给我。"

她微笑着答应了他,公爵也原谅了安吉洛,狱吏也获得了晋升。

而路西奥则被迫娶了一位身材矮胖、说话刻薄的老婆。

17. Cymbeline

Iachimo and Imogen

Cymbeline① was the King of Britain. He had three children. The two sons were stolen away from him when they were quite little children, and he was left with only one daughter, Imogen②. The King married a second time, and brought up Leonatus③, the son of a dear friend, as Imogen's playfellow; and when Leonatus was old enough, Imogen secretly married him. This made the King and Queen very angry, and the King, to punish Leonatus, banished him from Britain.

Poor Imogen was nearly heart-broken at parting from Leonatus, and he was not less unhappy. For they were not only lovers and husband and wife, but they had been friends and comrades ever since they were quite little children. With many tears and kisses they said "Good-bye." They promised never to forget each other, and that they would never care for

---

① Cymbeline [ˈsimbəli:n] n. 辛白林(男子名)
② Imogen [ˈiməudʒən] n. 依摩琴(女子名)
③ Leonatus [li:ˈəunətəs] n. 里奥那托斯(男子名)

anyone else as long as they lived.

"This diamond was my mother's, love," said Imogen; "take it, my heart, and keep it as long as you love me."

"Sweetest, fairest," answered Leonatus, "wear this bracelet for my sake."

"Ah!" cried Imogen, weeping, "when shall we meet again?"

And while they were still in each other's arms, the King came in, and Leonatus had to leave without more farewell.

When he came to Rome, where he had gone to stay with an old friend of his father's, he spent his days still in thinking of his dear Imogen, and his nights in dreaming of her. One day at a feast some Italian and French noblemen were talking of their sweethearts, and swearing that they were the most faithful and honorable and beautiful ladies in the world. And a Frenchman reminded Leonatus how he had said many times that his wife Imogen was more fair, wise, and constant① than any of the ladies in France.

"I say so still," said Leonatus.

"She is not so good but that she would deceive," said Iachimo②, one of the Italian nobles.

"She never would deceive," said Leonatus.

"I wager," said Iachimo, "that, if I go to Britain, I can persuade your wife to do whatever I wish, even if it should be against your wishes."

"That you will never do," said Leonatus. "I wager this ring upon my finger," which was the very ring Imogen had given him at parting, "that my wife will keep all her vows to me, and that you will never persuade her to do otherwise."

So Iachimo wagered half his estate against the ring on Leonatus's

---

① constant [ˈkɔnstənt] adj. 不变的,持续的,坚决的
② Iachimo [iːˈætʃiməu] n. 依爱奇摩(男子名)

finger, and started forthwith for Britain, with a letter of introduction to Leonatus's wife. When he reached there he was received with all kindness; but he was still determined to win his wager.

He told Imogen that her husband thought no more of her, and went on to tell many cruel lies about him. Imogen listened at first, but presently perceived what a wicked person Iachimo was, and ordered him to leave her. Then he said—

"Pardon me, fair lady, all that I have said is untrue. I only told you this to see whether you would believe me, or whether you were as much to be trusted as your husband thinks. Will you forgive me?"

"I forgive you freely," said Imogen.

"Then," went on Iachimo, "perhaps you will prove it by taking charge of a trunk①, containing a number of jewels which your husband and I and some other gentlemen have bought as a present for the Emperor of Rome."

"I will indeed," said Imogen, "do anything for my husband and a friend of my husband's. Have the jewels sent into my room, and I will take care of them."

"It is only for one night," said Iachimo, "for I leave Britain again tomorrow."

So the trunk was carried into Imogen's room, and that night she went to bed and to sleep. When she was fast asleep, the lid of the trunk opened and a man got out. It was Iachimo. The story about the jewels was as untrue as the rest of the things he had said. He had only wished to get into her room to win his wicked wager. He looked about him and noticed the furniture, and then crept② to the side of the bed where Imogen was asleep and took from her arm the gold bracelet which had

① trunk [trʌŋk] n. 箱子
② creep [kri:p] v. 爬,蹑手蹑脚

been the parting gift of her husband. Then he crept back to the trunk, and next morning sailed for Rome.

When he met Leonatus, he said—

"I have been to Britain and I have won the wager, for your wife no longer thinks about you. She stayed talking with me all one night in her room, which is hung with tapestry① and has a carved chimney-piece, and silver andirons② in the shape of two winking Cupids③."

"I do not believe she has forgotten me; I do not believe she stayed talking with you in her room. You have heard her room described by the servants."

"Ah!" said Iachimo, "but she gave me this bracelet. She took it from her arm. I see her yet. Her pretty action did outsell her gift, and yet enriched it too. She gave it to me, and said she prized it once."

"Take the ring," cried Leonatus, "you have won; and you might have won my life as well, for I care nothing for it now I know my lady has forgotten me."

And mad with anger, he wrote letters to Britain to his old servant, Pisanio, ordering him to take Imogen to Milford Haven, and to murder her, because she had forgotten him and given away his gift. At the same time he wrote to Imogen herself, telling her to go with Pisanio, his old servant, to Milford Haven, and that he, her husband, would be there to meet her.

Now when Pisanio got this letter he was too good to carry out its orders, and too wise to let them alone altogether. So he gave Imogen the letter from her husband, and started with her for Milford Haven. Before he left, the wicked Queen gave him a drink which, she said, would be useful in sickness. She hoped he would give it to Imogen, and that

---

① tapestry [ˈtæpistri] n. 织锦，挂毯
② andiron [ˈændaiən] n. 铁制柴架
③ Cupid [ˈkjuːpid] n. 爱神丘比特

Imogen would die, and the wicked Queen's son could be King. For the Queen thought this drink was a poison, but really and truly it was only a sleeping-draft.

When Pisanio and Imogen came near to Milford Haven, he told her what was really in the letter he had had from her husband.

"I must go on to Rome, and see him myself," said Imogen.

And then Pisanio helped her to dress in boy's clothes, and sent her on her way, and went back to the Court. Before he went he gave her the drink he had had from the Queen.

Imogen went on, getting more and more tired, and at last came to a cave. Someone seemed to live there, but no one was in just then. So she went in, and as she was almost dying of hunger①, she took some food she saw there, and had just done so, when an old man and two boys came into the cave. She was very much frightened when she saw them, for she thought that they would be angry with her for taking their food, though she had meant to leave money for it on the table. But to her surprise they welcomed her kindly. She looked very pretty in her boy's clothes and her face was good, as well as pretty.

"You shall be our brother," said both the boys; and so she stayed with them, and helped to cook the food, and make things comfortable. But one day when the old man, whose name was Bellarius, was out hunting with the two boys, Imogen felt ill, and thought she would try the medicine Pisanio had given her. So she took it, and at once became like a dead creature, so that when Bellarius and the boys came back from hunting, they thought she was dead, and with many tears and funeral songs, they carried her away and laid her in the wood, covered with flowers.

They sang sweet songs to her, and strewed② flowers on her, pale primroses③, and the azure④ harebell, and eglantine, and furred moss, and

---

① dying of hunger 饿得奄奄一息
② strew [struː] v. 撒满,散播
③ primrose ['primrəuz] n. 报春花
④ azure ['æʒə] adj. 蔚蓝的

went away sorrowful. No sooner had they gone than Imogen awoke, and not knowing how she came there, nor where she was, went wandering through the wood.

Now while Imogen had been living in the cave, the Romans had decided to attack Britain, and their army had come over, and with them Leonatus, who had grown sorry for his wickedness against Imogen, so had come back, not to fight with the Romans against Britain, but with the Britons against Rome. So as Imogen wandered alone, she met with Lucius, the Roman General, and took service with him as his page.

When the battle was fought between the Romans and Britons, Bellarius and his two boys fought for their own country, and Leonatus, disguised as a British peasant, fought beside them. The Romans had taken Cymbeline prisoner, and old Bellarius, with his sons and Leonatus, bravely rescued① the King. Then the Britons won the battle, and among the prisoners brought before the King were Lucius, with Imogen, Iachimo, and Leonatus, who had put on the uniform of a Roman soldier. He was tired of his life since he had cruelly ordered his wife to be killed, and he hoped that, as a Roman soldier, he would be put to death.

When they were brought before the King, Lucius spoke out—

"A Roman with a Roman's heart can suffer," he said. "If I must die, so be it. This one thing only will I entreat. My boy, a Briton born, let him be ransomed②. Never master had a page so kind, so duteous③, diligent④, true. He has done no Briton harm, though he has served a Roman. Save him, Sir."

---

① rescue ['reskjuː] v. 援救,营救
② ransom ['rænsəm] v. 敲诈,勒索,赎救
③ duteous ['djuːtjəs] adj. 尽职的,忠贞的
④ diligent ['dilidʒənt] adj. 勤勉的,用功的

Then Cymbeline looked on the page, who was his own daughter, Imogen, in disguise, and though he did not recognize her, he felt such a kindness that he not only spared the boy's life, but he said—

"He shall have any boon he likes to ask of me, even though he ask a prisoner, the noblest taken."

Then Imogen said, "The boon I ask is that this gentleman shall say from whom he got the ring he has on his finger," and she pointed to Iachimo.

"Speak," said Cymbeline, "how did you get that diamond?"

Then Iachimo told the whole truth of his villainy①. At this, Leonatus was unable to contain himself, and casting aside all thought of disguise, he came forward, cursing himself for his folly in having believed Iachimo's lying story, and calling again and again on his wife whom he believed dead.

"Oh, Imogen, my love, my life!" he cried. "Oh, Imogen!"

Then Imogen, forgetting she was disguised, cried out, "Peace, my lord—here, here!"

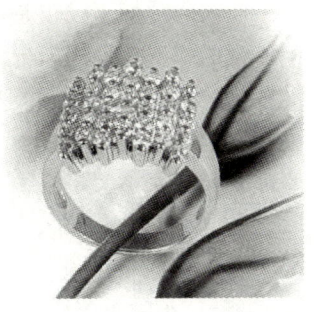

Leonatus turned to strike the forward page who thus interfered in his great trouble, and then he saw that it was his wife, Imogen, and they fell into each other's arms.

The King was so glad to see his dear daughter again, and so grateful to the man who had rescued him (whom he now found to be Leonatus), that he gave his blessing on their marriage, and then he turned to Bellarius, and the two boys. Now Bellarius spoke—

"I am your old servant, Bellarius. You accused me of treason when I had only been loyal to you, and to be doubted, made me disloyal. So I stole your two sons, and see—they are here!" And he brought forward the two boys, who had sworn to be brothers to Imogen when they

---

① villainy ['vɪlənɪ] *n.* 邪恶,坏事,恶行

thought she was a boy like themselves.

The wicked Queen was dead of some of her own poisons, and the King, with his three children about him, lived to a happy old age.

So the wicked were punished, and the good and true lived happy ever after. So may the wicked suffer, and honest folk prosper① till the world's end.

辛　白　林

　　辛白林是不列颠的国王，他有三个孩子。两个儿子在很小的时候就被人偷走了，只有一个女儿依摩琴和他相依为命。国王再婚后，将好友之子里奥那托斯作为依摩琴的玩伴一起抚养。里奥那托斯长大成人后，两人就秘密地结了婚。国王和王后知道此事后勃然大怒，国王为了惩罚里奥那托斯，将他从不列颠流放了出去。

　　可怜的依摩琴同里奥那托斯分别后心都快碎了，里奥那托斯也非常不快乐。因为他们不仅仅是情人、夫妻，更重要的是他们从很小的时候就是志同道合的朋友。他们依依不舍，含泪吻别，并发誓永远不能忘掉彼此，只要健在，此生就不会爱上其他人。

　　"亲爱的，这枚钻戒是我母亲留给我的，"依摩琴说，"拿着它，宝贝，只要你还爱我就不要将它丢弃。"

　　"我的甜心，我的公主，"里奥那托斯回应着，"为了我，你戴上这个手镯吧。"

　　"啊！"依摩琴哭着说，"我们何时才能再见面？"

　　正当他们拥抱在一起时，国王进来了，里奥那托斯没有说一句别离的话就不得不离开了。

　　里奥那托斯到了罗马以后就住在他父亲的一位老朋友那里，对于他心爱的依摩琴，他白天想念，夜里梦见。有一天，在一个宴席上一些意大利和法国的绅士谈论着他们的心上人，并发誓说她们是世界上最忠诚、最高尚、最美丽的女子。一位法国人提到里奥那托斯说了多次的爱妻依摩琴是怎样美丽、聪慧和稳重，她胜过法国的任何一位女子。

　　"我现在还会这么说。"里奥那托斯说。

① prosper ['prɔspə] v. 成功，兴隆，昌盛

"她只是假装那么好的。"一位意大利贵族依爱奇摩说。

"她从来不会欺骗我。"里奥那托斯说。

"我打赌,"依爱奇摩说,"假如我去大不列颠,我能够说服你妻子按照我的想法去做任何事,即使是违背你意愿的事。"

"那么,你永远不会如愿的。"里奥那托斯说。"我以我手指上的这枚戒指打赌,"那是在他们分别时依摩琴送给他的,"我的妻子会遵守她许下的所有诺言,你绝对劝说不了她去做背叛我的事情。"

于是,依爱奇摩拿他一半的财产来和里奥那托斯手指上的那枚戒指打赌,身上带着里奥那托斯写给他妻子的介绍信,前往不列颠。到了之后,他受到了热情的款待,可是他仍想赢取赌注。

他告诉依摩琴她丈夫已经不再想她了,接着又告诉她很多有关里奥那托斯的恶毒的谎话。依摩琴刚开始还听,不久便感觉依爱奇摩是一个很恶毒的人,就命令他离开。于是他说——

"美丽的女士,请原谅我,刚才我说的一切都不是真的。我只是想看看你是否相信我,是否如你丈夫所认为的那样值得信任。你能原谅我吗?"

"当然可以原谅你了。"依摩琴说。

"那么,"依爱奇摩继续说道,"如果你愿意证明你自己,就请保管好这个箱子,这里面装有许多珠宝,是我和你丈夫以及其他绅士们为罗马皇帝买的一份礼物。"

"我当然愿意为我丈夫和他的朋友做任何事情,"依摩琴说,"把这些珠宝送到我的房间,我会保管好的。"

"一个晚上就可以了,"依爱奇摩说,"因为明天我就要离开不列颠了。"

于是这个箱子就被抬进了依摩琴的房间,当晚她就寝入睡了。在她睡得正香时,箱子盖打开了,从里面爬出一个人,那人正是依爱奇摩。原来有关珠宝的故事及他后来说的话都不是真的,他只想进入她的房间用不道德的方式赢取赌注。他环顾四周,仔细观察了家具后,又爬到依摩琴睡觉的床边,把她手腕上的金手镯取了下来,那是她与丈夫分别时丈夫送她的礼物。然后他又爬回箱子里,第二天一早便出发去了罗马。

见到里奥那托斯时,他说——

"我已经去了大不列颠,并且赢取了赌注,因为你妻子再也不会想你了。在她的绣房里我们聊了整整一个晚上,她绣房里有一个挂毯,一个上有雕刻的壁炉架,还有一个白银铸成的柴架,那架子形似两个眉目传情的小爱神。"

"我不相信她已经把我忘记;我不相信你们在她的绣房里聊了整整一个晚上。你肯定是听仆人描述了她的房间。"

"啊!"依爱奇摩说,"可是我亲眼看着她把这个手镯从手腕上取下来给了我。她优美的姿态绝对胜过她的礼物,同时也使这礼物显得更加珍贵。然而她把它给了我,并对我说她曾经珍爱过它。"

"你把戒指拿去吧,"里奥那托斯哭喊着,"你已经赢了;我的命也是你的了,因为现在我知道我的妻子已经将我忘记,生命对我也毫无意义了。"

气得发了疯的里奥那托斯给不列颠的老仆人披萨尼奥写了一封信,命他把依摩琴带到米尔福德港口,并将她杀死,因为她已经将他忘记并把礼物丢弃。同时他又给依摩琴本人写了一封信,要她和他的老仆人披萨尼奥一起去米尔福德港口,他,也就是她的丈夫,会在那里与她会合。

披萨尼奥很善良,他收到这封信后没有执行这个命令,他也很明智,没有将命令置之不理,而是把她丈夫给他的信交给了依摩琴,并和她一起前往米尔福德港口。在他离开之前,邪恶的王后赐了他一杯酒,并对他说这酒对治疗疾病有帮助。她希望他会把酒给依摩琴,依摩琴喝了之后就会死去,这样她的儿子就能继承王位。王后本以为这酒是一种毒药,但事实上,它只是一种催眠剂。

披萨尼奥和依摩琴到了米尔福德港口后,他告诉她她丈夫给他的信的真实内容。

"我必须继续去罗马,我要亲眼看到他。"依摩琴说。

于是披萨尼奥帮她换上男装,将她打扮成男人的模样,送她上路后,自己就回到了王宫。在走之前他把王后赐给他的酒给了依摩琴。

依摩琴继续前行,感到越来越累,最后到了一个山洞。这个山洞有人居住的迹象,那时却空无一人。于是她走了进去,由于当时她已经饿得奄奄一息,看到一些食物放在那里,就把食物吃了。刚刚吃完,就看见一位老人和两个男孩走进了山洞。看到他们进来，依摩琴非常害怕，因为她吃掉了他们的食物，怕他们会生气，尽管她本想留些钱在桌子上。可令她吃惊的是，他们对她非常欢迎。身着男装的依摩琴看起来俊俏伶俐，她的脸蛋也更美丽动人。

"你就做我们的哥哥吧。"两个男孩异口同声地说。于是她留了下来和他们在一起生活，帮助他们做饭，并把一切都安排得妥妥当当、舒舒服服。可是有一天，这位叫培拉律斯的老人和两个男孩出去打猎的时候，依摩琴病倒了，于是她想试着服用披萨尼奥给她的药。服下药后，她立即变得像死了一样。老人和两个男孩打猎回来，以为她已经死了，就含着眼泪，唱着葬歌，把她抬到树林里，用鲜花遮盖了她的身体。

他们为她唱着甜美的歌儿，将花儿洒在她身上，有淡淡的报春花、淡蓝色的蓝铃花、芬芳的野蔷薇花瓣，还有毛茸茸的苍苔，然后悲伤地离开了。他们刚走依摩琴就醒来了，却不知道她怎么到了那里，也不知道自己在哪里，于是就在树林中徘徊。

依摩琴在山洞里住的时候，罗马人已经决定进攻不列颠，他们的军队已经攻了过来。里奥那托斯就在军队里，对于依摩琴，他为自己的行为懊悔不已。于是他回来了，不是替罗马攻打不列颠，而是替不列颠反抗罗马。依摩琴在树林独自徘徊的时候遇见了罗马军队的将军卢休斯，就做了他的一名侍从。

当罗马人和不列颠人激战时，培拉律斯和他的两个孩子也在为国奋战，化装成一名不列颠农民的里奥那托斯也与他们并肩作战。罗马人俘虏了国王辛白林，老培拉律斯带着他的两个儿子还有里奥那托斯，英勇作战，把国王解救了出来。后来，不列颠人大获全胜，被带到国王面前的战俘有卢休斯、依摩琴、依爱奇摩，还有身穿罗马军服的里奥那托斯。自从狠心地下令将爱妻杀死后，里奥那托斯就已厌倦了人生，他假扮成罗马士兵，希望自己能被处死。

他们被带到了国王面前，卢休斯说——

"我是个罗马人，我要用一颗罗马人的心来面对死亡，"他说，"我死不足惜。可是我要向你请求一件事。我的侍从，是土生土长的不列颠人，就宽恕了他吧。当主人的从来没有遇到过这么善良、忠于职守、勤快又可靠的侍从了。虽然他侍候过罗马人，但他从没有做过一

件对不起不列颠人的事。陛下,饶了他吧。"

辛白林看了看眼前的这位小侍从,尽管是自己的女儿依摩琴乔装的,可是还是没有认出来,但国王对他还是有种似曾相识的感觉,不仅饶恕了他的性命,又说道:

"他可以从我这里要求任何恩典,即使要求饶恕哪个身份最高的俘虏的性命我都答应他。"

于是依摩琴指着依爱奇摩说:"我要求的恩典就是,请这位绅士说说他手指上的这枚戒指的来头。"

"说啊,"辛白林说,"你是怎么得到那枚钻戒的。"

依爱奇摩供认了他的全部罪行。听到这些,里奥那托斯再也控制不住自己,抛却了所有伪装自己的想法,径直走上前去,一遍又一遍地诅咒自己愚蠢地相信依爱奇摩的谎言,想到自己残忍地将妻子杀死,他一遍又一遍地狂叫着:

"啊,依摩琴,我的爱人,我的生命!啊,依摩琴!"

看到丈夫如此痛苦,依摩琴忘记了自己的伪装,哭喊道:"好了!我的主啊,我在这里,在这里!"

正处在痛苦中的里奥那托斯正要去揍这个捣乱的侍从,结果发现他就是自己的妻子依摩琴,于是他们拥抱在了一起。

再次看到自己的女儿,国王格外高兴,对救过他性命的里奥那托斯(此时他已认出他了)也心怀感激,于是他由衷地对女儿的婚姻表达祝福,然后又对培拉律斯和他的两个儿子表示感谢。培拉律斯说——

"我是您的老仆人培拉律斯,我对您忠心耿耿却被判了叛国罪,是你的怀疑令我不忠。所以我就把您的两个儿子偷走了,瞧,他们在这里!"他把两个男孩带到国王面前,他们俩曾以为依摩琴像他们一样是男孩,还发誓要成为她的好兄弟。

邪恶的王后最终死于自己的毒酒之下,而国王在他三个孩子的陪伴下颐养天年。

邪恶的人最终得到了惩罚,善良而真诚的人过上了幸福的生活。但愿邪恶永远受苦,真诚与世同在。

18. Pericles

Pericles and Marina

Pericles①, the Prince of Tyre②, was unfortunate enough to make an enemy of Antiochus③, the powerful and wicked King of Antioch④; and so great was the danger in which he stood that, on the advice of his trusty⑤ counselor, Lord Helicanus⑥, he determined to travel about the world for a time. He came to this decision despite the fact that, by the death of his father, he was now King of Tyre. So he set sail for Tarsus⑦, appointing

---

① Pericles [ˈperiˌkliːz] n. 配力克里斯(男子名)
② Tyre [ˈtaiə] n. 泰尔(古代腓基尼的首都, 位于现在的黎巴嫩南部地中海东部)
③ Antiochus [ænˈtaiəkəs] n. 安提奥克斯(男子名)
④ Antioch [ˈæntiɔk] 安提奥克(古叙利亚首都, 现土耳其南部城市)
⑤ trusty [ˈtrʌsti] adj. 可信赖的
⑥ Helicanus [heləˈkænjus] n. 赫力堪纳斯(男子名)
⑦ Tarsus [ˈtɑːsəs] n. 塔尔苏斯(土耳其南部城市)

Helicanus regent① during his absence. That he did wisely in thus leaving his kingdom was soon made clear.

Hardly had he sailed on his voyage, when Lord Thaliard② arrived from Antioch with instructions from his royal master to kill Pericles. The faithful Helicanus soon discovered the deadly purpose of this wicked lord, and at once sent messengers to Tarsus to warn the King of the danger which threatened him.

The people of Tarsus were in such poverty and distress that Pericles, feeling that he could find no safe refuge③ there, put to sea again. But a dreadful storm overtook the ship in which he was, and the good vessel was wrecked, while of all on board only Pericles was saved. Bruised④ and wet and faint, he was flung upon the cruel rocks on the coast of Pentapolis⑤, the country of the good King Simonides⑥. Worn out as he was, he looked for nothing but death, and that speedily. But some fishermen, coming down to the beach, found him there, and gave him clothes and bade him be of good cheer.

"Thou shalt come home with me," said one of them, "and we will have flesh for holidays, fish for fasting days, and moreo'er, puddings and flapjacks⑦, and thou shalt be welcome."

They told him that on the morrow many princes and knights were going to the King's Court, there to joust⑧ and tourney⑨ for the love of his daughter, the beautiful Princess Thaisa⑩.

"Did but my fortunes equal my desires," said Pericles, "I'd wish to

---

① regent ['riːdʒənt] *n.* 摄政者
② Thaliard [θəˈlaiəd] *n.* 泰利阿德(男子名)
③ refuge ['refjuːdʒ] *n.* 庇护, 避难所
④ bruise [bruːz] *v.* 打伤, 撞伤
⑤ Pentapolis [penˈtæpəˌlis] *n.* 潘塔波里斯, 意为"五座城"
⑥ Simonides [saiˈmɔniˌdiːz] *n.* 西蒙尼狄斯(男子名)
⑦ flapjack [ˈflæpdʒæk] *n.* 烙饼, 大薄煎饼
⑧ joust [dʒaust] *n.* 马上枪术比赛
⑨ tourney [ˈtuəni] *n.* 马上比武
⑩ Thaisa [θeisɑ] *n.* 泰莎(女子名)

make one there."

As he spoke, some of the fishermen came by, drawing their net, and it dragged heavily, resisting all their efforts, but at last they hauled① it in, to find that it contained a suit of rusty armor②; and looking at it, he blessed Fortune for her kindness, for he saw that it was his own, which had been given to him by his dead father. He begged the fishermen to let him have it that he might go to Court and take part in the tournament③, promising that if ever his ill fortunes bettered, he would reward them well. The fishermen readily consented, and being thus fully equipped, Pericles set off in his rusty armor to the King's Court.

In the tournament none bore himself so well as Pericles, and he won the wreath of victory, which the fair Princess herself placed on his brows. Then at her father's command she asked him who he was, and whence④ he came; and he answered that he was a knight of Tyre, by name Pericles, but he did not tell her that he was the King of that country, for he knew that if once his whereabouts became known to Antiochus, his life would not be worth a pin's purchase.

Nevertheless Thaisa loved him dearly, and the King was so pleased with his courage and graceful bearing that he gladly permitted his daughter to have her own way, when she told him she would marry the stranger knight or die.

Thus Pericles became the husband of the fair lady for whose sake he had striven with the knights who came in all their bravery to joust and tourney for her love.

Meanwhile the wicked King Antiochus had died, and the people in Tyre, hearing

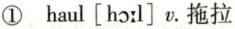

① haul [hɔːl] v. 拖拉
② armor [ˈɑːmə] n. 装甲
③ tournament [ˈtuənəmənt] n. 比赛
④ whence [(h)wens] n. 来处, 根源

no news of their King, urged Lord Helicanus to ascend the vacant throne. But they could only get him to promise that he would become their King, if at the end of a year Pericles did not come back. Moreover, he sent forth messengers far and wide in search of the missing Pericles.

Some of these made their way to Pentapolis, and finding their King there, told him how discontented his people were at his long absence, and that, Antiochus being dead, there was nothing now to hinder him from returning to his kingdom. Then Pericles told his wife and father-in-law who he really was, and they and all the subjects of Simonides greatly rejoiced to know that the gallant① husband of Thaisa was a King in his own right. So Pericles set sail with his dear wife for his native land. But once more the sea was cruel to him, for again a dreadful storm broke out, and while it was at its height, a servant came to tell him that a little daughter was born to him. This news would have made his heart glad indeed, but that the servant went on to add that his wife—his dear, dear Thaisa—was dead.

While he was praying the gods to be good to his little baby girl, the sailors came to him, declaring that the dead Queen must be thrown overboard, for they believed that the storm would never cease so long as a dead body remained in the vessel. So Thaisa was laid in a big chest with spices and jewels, and a scroll on which the sorrowful King wrote these lines:

"Here I give to understand
(If e'er this coffin drive a-land),
I, King Pericles, have lost
This Queen worth all our mundane cost.
Who finds her, give her burying;
She was the daughter of a King;
Besides this treasure for a fee,
The gods requite his charity!"

Then the chest was cast into the sea, and the waves taking it, by and

---

① gallant ['gælənt] *adj.* 英勇的，豪侠的

by washed it ashore at Ephesus, where it was found by the servants of a lord named Cerimon①. He at once ordered it to be opened, and when he saw how lovely Thaisa looked, he doubted if she were dead, and took immediate steps to restore her. Then a great wonder happened, for she, who had been thrown into the sea as dead, came back to life. But feeling sure that she would never see her husband again, Thaisa retired from the world, and became a priestess② of the Goddess Diana.

While these things were happening, Pericles went on to Tarsus with his little daughter, whom he called Marina, because she had been born at sea. Leaving her in the hands of his old friend the Governor of Tarsus, the King sailed for his own dominions③.

Now Dionyza④, the wife of the Governor of Tarsus, was a jealous and wicked woman, and finding that the young Princess grew up a more accomplished⑤ and charming girl than her own daughter, she determined to take Marina's life. So when Marina was fourteen, Dionyza ordered one of her servants to take her away and kill her.

This villain would have done so, but that he was interrupted by some pirates who came in and carried Marina off to sea with them, and took her to Mitylene⑥, where they sold her as a slave. Yet such was her goodness, her grace, and her beauty, that she soon became honored there, and Lysimachus⑦, the young Governor, fell deep in love with her, and would have married her, but that he thought she must be of too humble parentage to become the wife of one in his high position.

① Cerimon [ˈserimən] n. 萨利蒙(男子名)
② priestess [ˈpristis] n. 女祭司
③ dominion [dəˈminjən] n. 主权, 领土
④ Dionyza [ˌdaiəˈnizə] n. 狄奥妮莎(女子名)
⑤ accomplished [əˈkɔmpliʃt] adj. 熟练的, 有才艺的
⑥ Mitylene [ˌmitiˈliːn] n. 密提林
⑦ Lysimachus [laiˈsiməkəs] n. 拉西马卡斯(男子名)

  The wicked Dionyza believed, from her servant's report, that Marina was really dead, and so she put up a monument to her memory, and showed it to King Pericles, when after long years of absence he came to see his much-loved child. When he heard that she was dead, his grief was terrible to see. He set sail once more, and putting on sackcloth①, vowed never to wash his face or cut his hair again. There was a pavilion② erected on deck, and there he lay alone, and for three months he spoke word to none.

  At last it chanced that his ship came into the port of Mitylene, and Lysimachus, the Governor, went on board to enquire whence the vessel came. When he heard the story of Pericles' sorrow and silence, he bethought him of Marina, and believing that she could rouse the King from his stupor③, sent for her and bade her try her utmost to persuade the King to speak, promising whatever reward she would, if she succeeded. Marina gladly obeyed, and sending the rest away, she sat and sang to her poor grief-laden father, yet, sweet as was her voice, he made no sign. So presently she spoke to him, saying that her grief might equal his, for, though she was a slave, she came from ancestors that stood equal to mighty kings.

  Something in her voice and story touched the King's heart, and he looked up at her, and as he looked, he saw with wonder how like she was to his lost wife, so with a great hope springing up in his heart, he bade her tell her story.

  Then, with many interruptions from the King, she told him who she was and how she had escaped from the cruel Dionyza. So Pericles knew that this was indeed his daughter, and he kissed her again and again, crying that his great seas of joy drowned him with their sweetness. "Give me my robes," he said, "O Heaven, bless my girl!"

  Then there came to him, though none else could hear it, the sound of

---

① sackcloth ['sækklɔθ] n. 麻袋布
② pavilion [pə'viljən] n. 大帐篷,亭,阁
③ stupor ['stjuːpə] n. 昏迷

heavenly music, and falling asleep, he beheld① the goddess Diana, in a vision.

"Go," she said to him, "to my temple at Ephesus, and when my maiden priests are met together, reveal how thou at sea didst lose thy wife."

Pericles obeyed the goddess and told his tale before her altar. Hardly had he made an end, when the chief priestess, crying out, "You are—you are—O royal Pericles!" fell fainting to the ground, and presently recovering, she spoke again to him, "O my lord, are you not Pericles?" "The voice of dead Thaisa!" exclaimed the King in wonder. "That Thaisa am I," she said, and looking at her he saw that she spoke the very truth.

Thus Pericles and Thaisa, after long and bitter suffering, found happiness once more, and in the joy of their meeting they forgot the pain of the past. To Marina great happiness was given, and not only in being restored to her dear parents; for she married Lysimachus, and became a princess in the land where she had been sold as a slave.

泰尔亲王配力克里斯

泰尔亲王配力克里斯不幸得罪了安提奥克斯,强大而又邪恶的安提奥克国王。配力克里斯面临着极大的危险,在他忠心耿耿的参事赫力堪纳斯勋爵的建议下,他决定周游世界一段时间。尽管实际上在他父亲死后他已是泰尔的国王,他还是作出了这个决定。于是他乘船向塔尔苏斯进发,在他离开期间把国事交给赫力堪纳斯掌管。不久,事实便证明了他的离开绝对是明智之举。

他刚刚起航,安提奥克的大臣泰利阿德就带着他主子要他杀死配力克里斯的使命到达了。忠心耿耿的赫力堪纳斯很就发现了这个邪恶大臣的索命企图,并立刻派信使去塔尔苏斯,提醒国王面临的危险。

塔尔苏斯人民非常贫困,生活很艰难,配力克里斯发现那里没有安全的藏身之地,于是又起航出发了。然而一场可怕的风暴袭击了他所乘的船,好好的一艘船被毁了,船上所有人中只有配力克里斯幸免于难。伤痕累累、浑

---

① behold [bi'həuld] v. 把……视为

  身湿透又无力的他被海浪冲到潘塔波里斯海岸冰冷的岩石上。这个国家有个善良的国王叫西蒙尼狄斯。筋疲力尽的他感觉自己只是更快地寻死来了。然而,有几个来到海滩上的渔民发现了他,给他衣服穿,并让他快乐起来。

  "你跟我回家吧,"其中一个渔民说,"我们节日有肉吃,禁斋日有鱼吃,还有布丁和烙饼,你会受到欢迎的。"

  他们还告诉他第二天就会有许多王子和骑士到国王的宫廷参加比武盛会,来博取国王美丽的女儿泰莎公主的爱。

  "可是我的命运不济,"配力克里斯说,"我也希望自己能在那里比武。"

  正说着,一些渔民从旁边经过,他们正在拉渔网,特别沉,他们奋力往上拉,结果拉上来了一套锈迹斑斑的甲胄,配力克里斯上前一看,开始感谢命运的垂怜,因为这就是他丢的那套甲胄,是亡父留给他的。于是他就祈求渔夫们让他穿上它去宫廷参加比武,并保证如果时来运转的话,他会好好报答他们。这些渔夫们欣然同意,装备好后,配力克里斯就穿上他那套锈迹斑斑的甲胄前往王宫。

  比武盛会上,配力克里斯从众人中脱颖而出并取得了胜利,于是美丽的公主亲自给他戴上了花环。按照父王的吩咐,她询问了他的身份及来历;他回答说他是泰尔的一名骑士,叫配力克里斯,却没有告诉她他就是那个国家的国王,因为他知道他的下落一旦被安提奥克斯知道,他的生命就变得一文不值。

  不过,泰莎公主非常爱他,并告诉国王说非这个骑士不嫁,国王也对他的勇气和优雅的谈吐非常满意,欣然同意一切按照女儿的意愿行事。

  于是配力克里斯就成为这位美丽女子的丈夫,为了她从从容容地把那些凭武艺跟他争夺泰莎的爱的勇敢的武士们全打败了。

  与此同时,邪恶的国王安提奥克斯死了,而泰尔的老百姓听不到他们国王的消息,就力劝赫力堪纳斯勋爵来接替他空缺的王位。可赫力堪纳斯向他们保证说,如果配力克里斯年底还不回来他就登基。而且,他已经派信使到处寻找失踪的配力克里斯。

  有些信使到了潘塔波里斯,发现他们的国王在那里,就告诉他说他离开泰尔的日子太久,老百姓对此不满,何况安提奥克斯已死,再也没有什么能阻止他回国了。于是配力克里斯把他的真实身份告诉了他的妻子和岳父,他们父女二人和西蒙尼狄斯的所有朝臣得知泰莎勇敢的丈夫原来也是一位国王以后,真是又惊又喜。不久,配力克里斯就带着爱妻踏上了回国的旅途。配力克里斯和大海就是冤家对头,他又遭遇了一场可怕的风暴,在风暴最强烈的时候,一位仆人过来告诉他说他的一个小女儿出生了。这个消息让他心中充满了喜悦,可是仆人继续说,他的妻子——他心爱的泰莎——死了。

当他祈祷老天保佑他的小女儿平平安安时,船员过来告诉他说必须把死去的王后扔出船去,因为他们认为,如果尸体放在船上的话风暴是不会停止的。于是泰莎被装进了一个大箱子,里面放着香料和珠宝,还有一个纸卷,悲伤的国王在上面写着:

"泰尔国王明四方
（如若此棺冲上岸）,
余今悲恸失王后,
其贤令世抬头望。
寻此棺者请安葬,
她本王女宫中养。
随棺珠宝为酬劳,
此善必为上天眷！"

于是箱子被扔进了大海,海浪将其吞没,并慢慢地把它冲到了以弗所的岸边,萨利蒙大人的仆人发现了它。萨利蒙立即下令把箱子打开,却看见泰莎美丽的脸庞,怀疑她是否真的死去,于是立即进行抢救。奇迹出现了,被当作死人而扔入大海的泰莎复活了。但是想到再也见不到丈夫,泰莎就到狄安娜神庙出家做了一个修女。

与此同时,配力克里斯带着小女儿继续向塔尔苏斯行进,因为她是在海上出生的,他就给她取名为玛丽娜。把女儿托付给他的老朋友塔尔苏斯的总督照顾后,国王又向自己的领地出发了。

而塔尔苏斯总督的妻子狄奥妮莎是一个妒忌狠心又阴险毒辣的女人,她发现这个年幼的公主长大后比自己的女儿更聪明更迷人,就决定要杀死玛丽娜。玛丽娜十四岁时,狄奥妮莎命她的一位仆人将玛丽娜带走并杀掉她。当这个邪恶的人正要动手时,一群海盗过来把玛丽娜抢走并带到海上去了,然后又把她卖到密提林做了奴隶。然而她善良、优雅和美丽的好名声很快就在当地传开了,密提林年轻的总督拉西马卡斯深深地爱上了她并想娶她为妻,可是又认为她的出身可能很低贱而不配做他这种有高贵身份的

人的妻子。

邪恶的狄奥妮莎从她仆人那里得知玛丽娜真的死了,为此还为她立了一个墓碑以表纪念;当多年没有见过爱女的国王配力克里斯来看望女儿时,狄奥妮莎却将墓碑指给他看。听到女儿已不在人世的消息,他悲伤至极。他身披麻衣再次起航,发誓永不洗脸,永不理发。他在甲板上搭了一个棚子,自己躺在那里,三个月来一句话也没说。

最后,一个偶然的机会,他的船到了密提林的港口,总督拉西马卡斯上船询问船的来处。听说了配力克里斯的悲伤沉默的故事,他想到了玛丽娜,并相信她能够把国王从恍惚中唤醒。于是派人把玛丽娜找来,让她尽力使国王开口说话,并保证说如果成功,他就会答应她的任何请求。玛丽娜欣然同意,她把其他人都打发走,坐在那里为这位可怜忧伤的父亲唱歌,然而,国王对她甜美的嗓音无动于衷。过了一会儿,她就对他说,他们两人的忧伤不相上下,因为,尽管她是个奴隶,她的祖先却世世代代是君王。

她的声音和她的故事触动了国王的心弦,于是他抬头看了看她,看着看着,他惊喜地发现她和他已故的爱妻长得多像啊,他心中不由得升起了无限希望,并让她讲述她的经历。

于是,玛丽娜跟他讲了自己的身世以及她怎样从残忍的狄奥妮莎手中逃脱,其间国王多次问话打断她的故事。配力克里斯惊喜地发现眼前的这个女孩儿正是他的女儿,他哭着一遍又一遍地亲吻她,喜悦的泪水将他和他的宝贝女儿淹没。"把袍子给我拿来,"他说,"噢,苍天啊,保佑我的女儿吧!"

此时,他耳边响起了天堂里的音乐,尽管只有他一个人能够听见,缓缓入睡后,在梦中他看见了女神狄安娜。

"去,"狄安娜对他说,"到我以弗所的神庙见见我纯洁的修女,告诉她你怎样在大海中失去了你的爱妻。"

配力克里斯照着狄安娜说的去做,在她的祭坛前讲述了自己的经历。他还没有说完,修女就哭出声来:"你是——你是——噢,尊贵的配力克里斯!"说完就昏倒在地。不久她苏醒过来,又对他说:"噢,我的主啊,难道你不是配力克里斯吗?""已经死去的泰莎的声音!"配力克里斯惊呼道。"我就是泰莎。"她说。仔细看了看她,他发现她说的确实是真的。

经历了长久磨难的配力克里斯和泰莎再次找到了幸福,沉浸在重逢的喜悦中的他们忘却了过去的痛苦。更幸福的人儿非玛丽娜莫属,她不但与双亲团圆,而且又嫁给了拉西马卡斯,并在这个被贩卖为奴的地方做了王妃。

19. The Tempest

Prince Ferdinand in the Sea

Prospero①, the Duke of Milan, was a learned and studious② man, who lived among his books, leaving the management of his dukedom to his brother Antonio, in whom indeed he had complete trust. But that trust was ill-rewarded, for Antonio wanted to wear the duke's crown himself, and, to gain his ends, would have killed his brother but for the love the people bore him. However, with the help of Prospero's great enemy, Alonso, King of Naples, he managed to get into his hands the dukedom③ with all its honor, power, and riches. For they took Prospero to sea, and when they were far away from land, forced him into a little boat with no tackle, mast, or sail. In their cruelty and hatred they put his little

---

① Prospero [ˈprɔspərəu] n. 普洛斯彼罗(男子名)
② studious [ˈstjuːdjəs] adj. 勤学的，认真的
③ dukedom [djuːkdəm] n. 公爵领地，公爵爵位

daughter, Miranda① (not yet three years old), into the boat with him, and sailed away, leaving them to their fate②.

But one among the courtiers with Antonio was true to his rightful master, Prospero. To save the duke from his enemies was impossible, but much could be done to remind him of a subject's③ love. So this worthy lord, whose name was Gonzalo④, secretly placed in the boat some fresh water, provisions, and clothes, and what Prospero valued most of all, some of his precious books.

The boat was cast on an island, and Prospero and his little one landed in safety. Now this island was enchanted, and for years had lain under the spell of a fell witch, Sycorax⑤, who had imprisoned in the trunks of trees all the good spirits she found there. She died shortly before Prospero was cast on those shores, but the spirits, of whom Ariel was the chief, still remained in their prisons.

Prospero was a great magician, for he had devoted himself almost entirely to the study of magic during the years in which he allowed his brother to manage the affairs of Milan. By his art he set free the imprisoned spirits, yet kept them obedient⑥ to his will, and they were more truly his subjects than his people in Milan had been. For he treated them kindly as long as they did his bidding, and he exercised his power over⑦ them wisely and well. One creature alone he found it necessary to treat with harshness⑧: this was Caliban, the son of

---

① Miranda [mi'rænda] n. 米兰达(女子名)
② leaving them to their fate 让他们听凭命运的摆布
③ subject ['sʌbdʒikt] n. 题目；臣民
④ Gonzalo [gɔn'zɑːləu] n. 贡柴罗(男子名)
⑤ Sycorax ['sikəræks] n. 西考拉克斯(女子名)
⑥ obedient [ə'biːdjənt] adj. 服从的，孝顺的
⑦ be exercised over 对……施加影响
⑧ harshness ['hɑːʃnis] n. 严厉

the wicked old witch, a hideous①, deformed monster, horrible to look on, and vicious② and brutal in all his habits.

When Miranda was grown up into a maiden, sweet and fair to see, it chanced that Antonio and Alonso, with Sebastian, his brother, and Ferdinand, his son, were at sea together with old Gonzalo, and their ship came near Prospero's island. Prospero, knowing they were there, raised by his art a great storm, so that even the sailors on board gave themselves up for lost; and first among them all Prince Ferdinand leaped into the sea, and, as his father thought in his grief, was drowned. But Ariel brought him safe ashore; and all the rest of the crew, although they were washed overboard, were landed unhurt in different parts of the island, and the good ship herself, which

they all thought had been wrecked, lay at anchor in the harbor whither Ariel had brought her. Such wonders could Prospero and his spirits perform.

While yet the tempest was raging, Prospero showed his daughter the brave ship laboring in the trough of the sea, and told her that it was filled with living human beings like themselves. She, in pity of their lives, prayed him who had raised this storm to quell③ it. Then her father bade her to have no fear, for he intended to save every one of them.

Then, for the first time, he told her the story of his life and hers, and that he had caused this storm to rise in order that his enemies, Antonio and Alonso, who were on board, might be delivered into his hands.

---

① hideous [ˈhidiəs] *adj.* 骇人听闻的,可怕的
② vicious [ˈviʃəs] *adj.* 恶的,不道德的,恶意的
③ quell [kwel] *v.* 镇压

When he had made an end of his story he charmed her into sleep, for Ariel was at hand, and he had work for him to do. Ariel, who longed for his complete freedom, grumbled to be kept in drudgery, but on being threateningly reminded of① all the sufferings he had undergone when Sycorax ruled in the land, and of the debt of gratitude he owed to the master who had made those sufferings to end, he ceased to complain, and promised faithfully to do whatever Prospero might command.

"Do so," said Prospero, "and in two days I will discharge② thee."

Then he bade Ariel take the form of a water nymph and sent him in search of the young prince. And Ariel, invisible to Ferdinand, hovered near him, singing the while—

"Come unto these yellow sands

And then take hands:

Court'sied when you have, and kiss'd

(The wild waves whist),

Foot it featly here and there;

And, sweet sprites, the burden bear!"

And Ferdinand followed the magic singing, as the song changed to a solemn③, and the words brought grief to his heart, and tears to his eyes, for thus they ran—

"Full fathom five thy father lies;

Of his bones are coral made.

Those are pearls that were his eyes,

Nothing of him that doth fade,

But doth suffer a sea-change

Into something rich and strange.

Sea-nymphs④ hourly ring his knell.

Hark! now I hear them,—ding dong bell!"

---

① remind of 提醒, 使记起
② discharge [dis'tʃɑːdʒ] v. 卸下, 放出
③ solemn air ['sɔləm] adj. 庄严的
④ sea-nymph n. 海仙女

And so singing, Ariel led the spell-bound prince into the presence of Prospero and Miranda. Then, behold! all happened as Prospero desired. For Miranda, who had never, since she could first remember, seen any human being save her father, looked on the youthful prince with reverence in her eyes, and love in her secret heart.

"I might call him," she said, "a thing divine, for nothing natural I ever saw so noble!"

And Ferdinand, beholding her beauty with wonder and delight, exclaimed, "Most sure the goddess on whom these airs attend!"

Nor did he attempt to hide the passion which she inspired in him, for scarcely had they exchanged half a dozen sentences, before he vowed to make her his queen if she were willing. But Prospero, though secretly delighted, pretended wrath①.

"You come here as a spy," he said to Ferdinand. "I will manacle② your neck and feet together, and you shall feed on fresh water mussels, withered roots and husk, and have sea-water to drink. Follow."

"No," said Ferdinand, and drew his sword. But on the instant Prospero charmed him so that he stood there like a statue, still as stone; and Miranda in terror prayed her father to have mercy on her lover. But he harshly refused her, and made Ferdinand follow him to his cell. There he set the Prince to work, making him remove thousands of heavy logs of timber and pile them up; and Ferdinand patiently obeyed, and thought his toil③ all too well repaid by the sympathy of the sweet Miranda.

She in very pity would have helped him in his hard work, but he would not let her, yet he could not keep from her the secret of his love, and she, hearing it, rejoiced and promised to be his wife.

Then Prospero released him from his servitude④, and glad at heart, he gave his consent to their marriage.

---

① wrath [rɔːθ] *n.* 愤怒
② manacle ['mænəkl] *n.* 手铐
③ toil [tɔil] *n.* 辛苦
④ servitude ['səːvitjuːd] *n.* 奴隶状态,惩役

"Take her," he said, "she is thine own."

In the meantime, Antonio and Sebastian in another part of the island were plotting the murder of Alonso, the King of Naples, for Ferdinand being dead, as they thought, Sebastian would succeed to the throne on Alonso's death. And they would have carried out their wicked purpose while their victim was asleep, but that Ariel woke him in good time.

Many tricks did Ariel play them. Once he set a banquet① before them, and just as they were going to fall to, he appeared to them amid thunder and lightning in the form of a harpy②, and immediately the banquet disappeared. Then Ariel upbraided③ them with their sins and vanished too.

Prospero by his enchantments drew them all to the grove without his cell, where they waited, trembling and afraid, and now at last bitterly repenting them of their sins.

Prospero determined to make one last use of his magic power, "And then," said he, "I'll break my staff and deeper than did ever plummet④ sound I'll drown my book."

So he made heavenly music to sound in the air, and appeared to them in his proper shape as the Duke of Milan. Because they repented, he forgave them and told them the story of his life since they had cruelly committed him and his baby daughter to the mercy of wind and waves. Alonso, who seemed sorriest of them all for his past crimes, lamented⑤ the loss of his heir. But Prospero drew back a curtain and showed them Ferdinand and Miranda playing at chess. Great was Alonso's joy to greet his loved son again, and when he heard that

① banquet ['bæŋkwit] n. 宴会,宴席
② harpy ['hɑːpi] n. 残酷贪婪的人,鹰身女妖
③ upbraid [ʌp'breid] v. 责备
④ plummet ['plʌmit] n. 铅锤
⑤ lament [lə'ment] v. 哀悼

the fair maid with whom Ferdinand was playing was Prospero's daughter, and that the young folks had plighted① their troth②, he said—

"Give me your hands, let grief and sorrow still embrace his heart that doth not wish you joy."

So all ended happily. The ship was safe in the harbor, and the next day they all set sail for Naples, where Ferdinand and Miranda were to be married. Ariel gave them calm seas and auspicious③ gales; and many were the rejoicings at the wedding.

Then Prospero, after many years of absence, went back to his own dukedom, where he was welcomed with great joy by his faithful subjects. He practiced the arts of magic no more, but his life was happy, and not only because he had found his own again, but chiefly④ because, when his bitterest foes who had done him deadly wrong lay at his mercy, he took no vengeance⑤ on them, but nobly forgave them.

As for Ariel, Prospero made him free as air, so that he could wander where he would, and sing with a light heart his sweet song—

"Where the bee sucks, there suck I:

In a cowslip's bell I lie;

There I couch when owls do cry.

On the bat's back I do fly

After summer, merrily:

Merrily, merrily, shall I live now,

Under the blossom that hangs on the bough."

暴 风 雨

米兰公爵普洛斯彼罗是一个博学而又勤奋的人,他生活在书堆里,把他

---

① plight [plait] *v.* 保证,约定
② troth [trəuθ] *n.* 誓言
③ auspicious [ɔːsˈpiʃəs] *n.* 吉兆的,幸运的
④ chiefly [ˈtʃiːfli] *adv.* 首要,主要地
⑤ vengeance [ˈvendʒəns] *n.* 复仇,报仇

的政务委托给了他真正完全信任的弟弟安东尼奥。可这种信任却得到了恶报,因为安东尼奥想自己戴上公爵的冠冕。为达此目的,他本想杀死自己的哥哥,可人民对公爵的拥戴使他没能得手。然而,在普洛斯彼罗的大仇家——那不勒斯的国王阿隆索——的帮助下,安东尼奥夺取了公国,他拥有了荣耀、权利和财富。他们把普洛斯彼罗带往大海,在一个远离陆地的地方,逼迫他上了一条没有绳索、没有桅杆、没有帆的小船。更为残忍的是他们把他未满三岁的小女儿米兰达也带上了小船,然后扬帆而去,留他们听凭命运的摆布。

可是在安东尼奥的朝臣里面,有一位大臣对他真正的主人普洛斯彼罗忠心耿耿。他不能把公爵从敌人手中解救出来,他所能做的就是让公爵感受到一位臣子的爱戴。于是这位好心的大臣——贡柴罗——偷偷地在船里放了一些淡水、干粮、衣裳,还有对普洛斯彼罗来说最有价值的东西,一些他珍爱的书籍。

小船漂流到一个小岛,普洛斯彼罗和他的小女儿在那里安全登陆。当时这个小岛被施了巫术,多年来受制于一个名叫西考拉克斯的可怕的女巫,她把所有善良的精灵都囚禁在了大树干里。在普洛斯彼罗漂流到这个小岛后不久西考拉克斯就死了,可这些小精灵仍被困在囚牢里,它们的头目是爱丽儿。

普洛斯彼罗是位了不起的巫师,在他委托弟弟替他掌管米兰朝政的这些年里,他已经在潜心研究巫术了。凭借自己的魔法他把被囚的精灵释放了出来,并让它们听从他的意愿,它们比米兰的臣民们还要忠诚。因为只要听从命令,它们就会受到款待,况且他知道怎样巧妙地指挥它们。他发现有必要好好教训一个家伙:邪恶的老巫婆之子——卡利班,一个可怕、相貌丑陋的怪物,他性情残暴,行为乖张。

米兰达长大以后出落成了一位美丽、恬静的少女。一天,安东尼奥和阿隆索,及其弟西巴斯辛、其子腓迪南,还有老臣贡柴罗在海上航行,他们的船靠近了普洛斯彼罗的小岛。知道他们在附近,普洛斯彼罗就施魔法产生了一阵暴风雨,连船员也因迷路而放弃了航行;所有人中,腓迪南王子率先跳进了海中,他的父亲以为他被淹死了,十分悲伤。爱丽儿把他安全地带到岸边;船上的其他人尽管被冲出甲板,也都安全地在海岛的不同地点登上了岸。他们都以为船被摧毁了,可它却完好无损地在港口抛锚,原来这都是爱丽儿的功劳。这样的奇迹也只有普洛斯彼罗和他的精灵们能够创造。

尽管暴风雨还在肆虐,普洛斯彼罗让女儿观看船在汹涌的海里勇敢地挣扎,并告诉她船上挤满了像他们一样的人。米兰达非常同情这些生命,就祈求父亲将暴风雨平息下去。于是父亲告诉她不要害怕,因为他会救助每一个人。

于是,他第一次给女儿讲述了他们俩的故事,还有他制造这场暴风雨是为了让他的敌人——船上的安东尼奥和阿隆索落入他的手中。

他把故事讲完后便哄女儿入睡,因为他还要吩咐爱丽儿为他办些事。渴望自由的爱丽儿,抱怨困住自己的苦差使,但每每想到西考拉克斯控制这个岛屿时他所遭受的种种苦难,还有结束了那些苦难、使他心存感激的主人时,他就停止了抱怨,并发誓无论主人要求他做什么他都会尽心尽力地去做。

"就这样吧,"普洛斯彼罗对他说,"两天后我就给你自由。"

于是他让爱丽儿变成一个仙女去寻找年轻的王子。腓迪南看不见爱丽儿,爱丽儿则在他旁边边盘旋边哼唱着——

"登上金色沙滩
来把手儿相牵:
求爱亲吻之后
(狂浪悄声不见),
到处足迹齐整,
精灵重担在肩!"

腓迪南跟随着这魔幻般的歌声前行,这首歌让气氛变得肃穆,歌词触动了他的心弦,泪水也弥漫了他的双眼,于是他们奔跑起来——

"你的父亲睡于深渊,
他的骨骸变成珊瑚,
珍珠就是他的双眼,
通身没有一点腐烂,
只是随着海水变换,
变得富丽而又奇幻。
海上仙女敲钟鸣丧,
我听到了叮叮当当。"

爱丽儿边唱着歌,边把受魔咒控制的王子带到了普洛斯彼罗和米兰达

的面前。瞧！一切都按照普洛斯彼罗期望的发生了。对于米兰达来说，打记事起，除了父亲之外，她从未见过其他人，看着眼前这位年轻的王子，米兰达双眼充满了崇敬，心底悄悄地滋生了爱慕之情。

"我可以称他精灵吧，"她说，"因为我从未见过如此神圣如此高贵的人啊！"

而腓迪南则注视着眼前的这位美人，满心欢喜地惊呼："一定是仙女下凡啊！"

他根本无法掩藏自己对米兰达的激情，一句话还没有跟米兰达说，就发誓如果米兰达愿意他就让她做自己的王后。而普洛斯彼罗虽然暗地里欢喜，他还是佯装生气。

"你是来这里当间谍的吧？"他对腓迪南说，"我要把你的脖子和脚捆在一起，叫你吃淡水贝蛤、枯树根和果壳，喝海水。来吧！"

"不成，"腓迪南说着便拔出剑来。可是普洛斯彼罗立即用咒语把腓迪南定在原地，就像石头雕塑一般，一动不动。米兰达满怀恐惧，祈求父亲善待她的爱人，可是普洛斯彼罗粗暴地拒绝了女儿，并把腓迪南关进了囚牢。他让王子在那里干活，让他把成千上万根木头挪开再堆起来。腓迪南耐心地顺从了，他认为假若做这种苦力能博取美丽的米兰达的同情也是值得的。

米兰达满怀着同情要帮腓迪南干活，可是他不让，他掩饰不住内心对她的爱慕，而米兰达听到了他的心声后欣喜若狂，并答应做他的妻子。

于是，普洛斯彼罗把他从奴役中释放出来，满怀喜悦地同意了他们的婚事。

"带着她，"他说，"她是你的了。"

与此同时，安东尼奥和西巴斯辛在岛的另一个地方正阴谋着要谋杀阿隆索，那不勒斯的国王。他们认为腓迪南已经死了，阿隆索死后西巴斯辛就可以登上国王的宝座。他们本想趁他睡觉时实施他们邪恶的计划，但爱丽儿及时将其叫醒了，他们才没能得逞。

爱丽儿想了种种诡计捉弄他们。有一次，他设了一桌美味的宴席，他们刚要吃的时候，突然电闪雷鸣，爱丽儿变成鹰身女怪的模样出现在他们眼前，即刻间，那桌宴席不见了。爱丽儿斥责了他们的罪行后也消失了。

普洛斯彼罗施魔法把他们引到他的小屋外面的小树林里,他们一伙人又惊又怕,瑟瑟发抖地站在那里一边等待,一边深深地忏悔自己的恶行。

普洛斯彼罗决定最后一次使用魔法。"从此以后,"他说,"我要把我的精灵遣散,并将我的魔法书深深地沉入海底。"

于是他在天空奏响了天籁之声,然后以米兰公爵的形象出现在他们面前。由于他们已经忏悔,他决定原谅他们,并对他们讲述了他惨遭迫害,和小女儿听凭风浪摆布的经历。对于过去的罪行,阿隆索是最后悔的一个,更因失去子嗣而悲恸。普洛斯彼罗拉开了门帘,他们看到腓迪南正在和米兰达下棋。再次看到爱子,阿隆索喜出望外,当他听说这位正和腓迪南下棋的美丽女子就是普洛斯彼罗的爱女,并且这对年轻人已经许下婚约时,他激动地说道——

"把你的手给我,让痛苦和悲伤紧紧拥抱那些不希望你快乐的人的心房。"

一切以欢快而结束。船安全地停泊在港口,第二天他们一起前往那不勒斯,腓迪南和米兰达要在那里举行婚礼。爱丽儿带给了他们平静的大海和吉祥的海风。婚礼上,所有人都喜气洋洋。

离开多年,普洛斯彼罗又回到了自己的公国,他忠诚的臣民们欢天喜地地迎接他的归来。他不再使用魔法了,他的生活依然幸福。不仅仅是因为他又找到了自我,更重要的是尽管曾经迫害他的凶手落在他的手中,他非但没有复仇,反而大度地宽恕了他们。

至于爱丽儿,普洛斯彼罗让他如空气般自由,于是他能够欢快地唱着甜美的歌儿四处畅翔:

"我在蜜蜂吮吸之处吮吸:
在莲香花的花冠里休憩;
直睡到猫头鹰啼叫时分。
我坐在蝙蝠的背上飞行,
快乐地追赶着炎炎夏季:
现在我要快乐地快乐地,
在挂满枝头的花下生息。"

20. Winter's Tale

Hermione

Leontes① was the King of Sicily, and his dearest friend was Polixenes②, King of Bohemia③. They had been brought up together, and only separated when they reached man's estate and each had to go and rule over his kingdom. After many years, when each was married and had a son, Polixenes came to stay with Leontes in Sicily.

---

① Leontes [liːˈɔntiːz] n. 里昂提斯(男子名)
② Polixenes [pəˈliksəniːz] n. 波力克希尼斯(男子名)
③ Bohemia [bəuˈhiːmjə] n. 波希米亚(以前为中欧的一个国家,现为捷克一部分)

Leontes was a violent-tempered① man and rather silly, and he took it into his stupid head that his wife, Hermione②, liked Polixenes better than she did him, her own husband. When once he had got this into his head, nothing could put it out; and he ordered one of his lords, Camillo③, to put a poison in Polixenes' wine. Camillo tried to dissuade④ him from this wicked action, but finding he was not to be moved, pretended to consent. He then told Polixenes what was proposed against him, and they fled from the Court of Sicily that night, and returned to Bohemia, where Camillo lived on as Polixenes' friend and counselor⑤.

Leontes threw the Queen into prison; and her son, the heir to the throne, died of sorrow to see his mother so unjustly and cruelly treated.

While the Queen was in prison she had a little baby, and a friend of hers, named Paulina, had the baby dressed in its best, and took it to show the King, thinking that the sight of his helpless little daughter would soften his heart towards his dear Queen, who had never done him any wrong, and who loved him a great deal more than he deserved; but the King would not look at the baby, and ordered Paulina's husband to take it away in a ship, and leave it in the most desert and dreadful⑥ place he could find, which Paulina's husband, very much against his will, was obliged to do.

Then the poor Queen was brought up⑦ to be tried for treason in preferring Polixenes to her King; but really she had never thought of anyone except Leontes, her husband. Leontes had sent some messengers to ask the god, Apollo, whether he was not right in his cruel thoughts of the Queen. But he had not patience to wait till they came back, and so it

① violent-tempered 坏脾气的
② Hermione [hə:'maiəni] n. 赫米迈厄妮（女子名）
③ Camillo [kə'mi:ləu] n. 卡米罗（男子名）
④ dissuade [di'sweid] v. 劝阻
⑤ counselor ['kaunsələ] n. 顾问，法律顾问
⑥ dreadful ['dredful] adj. 可怕的
⑦ bring up 教育，培养；带上法庭

happened that they arrived in the middle of the trial. The Oracle① said—

"Hermione is innocent, Polixenes blameless, Camillo a true subject, Leontes a jealous tyrant, and the King shall live without an heir, if that which is lost be not found."

Then a man came and told them that the little Prince was dead. The poor Queen, hearing this, fell down in a fit; and then the King saw how wicked and wrong he had been. He ordered Paulina and the ladies who were with the Queen to take her away, and try to restore her. But Paulina came back in a few moments, and told the King that Hermione was dead.

Now Leontes' eyes were at last opened to his folly. His Queen was dead, and the little daughter who might have been a comfort to him he had sent away to be the prey of wolves and kites. Life had nothing left for him now. He gave himself up to his grief, and passed in any sad years in prayer and remorse②.

The baby Princess was left on the seacoast of Bohemia, the very kingdom where Polixenes reigned. Paulina's husband never went home to tell Leontes where he had left the baby; for as he was going back to the ship, he met a bear and was torn to pieces. So there was an end of him.

But the poor deserted little baby was found by a shepherd. She was richly dressed, and had with her some jewels, and a paper was pinned to her cloak, saying that her name was Perdita③, and that she came of noble parents.

The shepherd, being a kind-hearted man, took home the little baby to his wife, and they brought it up as their own child. She had no more teaching than a shepherd's child generally has, but she inherited④ from her royal mother many graces and charms, so that she was quite different from the other maidens in the village where she lived.

① oracle [ˈɔrəkl] *n.* 神谕, 预言
② remorse [riˈmɔːs] *n.* 懊悔, 怜悯
③ Perdita [ˈpəːditə] *n.* 潘迪塔 (女子名)
④ inherit [inˈherit] *n.* 继承

One day Prince Florizel①, the son of the good King of Bohemia, was hunting near the shepherd's house and saw Perdita, now grown up to a charming woman. He made friends with the shepherd, not telling him that he was the Prince, but saying that his name was Doricles②, and that he was a private gentleman; and then, being deeply in love with the pretty Perdita, he came almost daily to see her.

The King could not understand what it was that took his son nearly every day from home; so he set people to watch him, and then found out that the heir of the King of Bohemia was in love with Perdita, the pretty shepherd girl. Polixenes, wishing to see whether this was true, disguised himself, and went with the faithful Camillo, in disguise too, to the old shepherd's house. They arrived at the feast of sheep-shearing③, and, though strangers, they were made very welcome. There was dancing going on, and a peddler was selling ribbons and laces and gloves, which the young men bought for their sweethearts.

Florizel and Perdita, however, were taking no part in this gay scene, but sat quietly together talking. The King noticed the charming manners and great beauty of Perdita, never guessing that she was the daughter of his old friend, Leontes. He said to Camillo—

"This is the prettiest low-born lass that ever ran on the green sward④. Nothing she does or seems but smacks of⑤ something greater than herself—too noble for this place."

And Camillo answered, "In truth she is the Queen of curds and cream⑥."

But when Florizel, who did not recognize his father, called upon the strangers to witness his betrothal⑦ with the pretty shepherdess, the King

① Florizel [ˈflɔrizel] n. 弗罗利泽(男子名)
② Doricles [ˈdɔrikliːz] n. 多利克思(男子名)
③ sheep-shearing 剪羊毛
④ sward [swɔːd] n. 草地,草皮
⑤ smack of 有点像;带有……味道
⑥ curds and cream 凝乳和乳酪,这里指"牧羊人"
⑦ betrothal [biˈtrəuðəl] n. 婚约

made himself known and forbade the marriage, adding that if ever she saw Florizel again, he would kill her and her old father, the shepherd; and with that he left them. But Camillo remained behind, for he was charmed with Perdita, and wished to befriend her.

Camillo had long known how sorry Leontes was for that foolish madness of his, and he longed to go back to Sicily to see his old master. He now proposed that the young people should go there and claim the protection of Leontes. So they went, and the shepherd went with them, taking Perdita's jewels, her baby clothes, and the paper he had found pinned to her cloak.

Leontes received them with great kindness. He was very polite to Prince Florizel, but all his looks were for Perdita. He saw how much she was like the Queen Hermione, and said again and again: "Such a sweet creature my daughter might have been, if I had not cruelly sent her from me."

When the old shepherd heard that the King had lost a baby daughter, who had been left upon the coast of Bohemia, he felt sure that Perdita, the child he had reared, must be the King's daughter, and when he told his tale and showed the jewels and the paper, the King perceived① that Perdita was indeed his long-lost child. He welcomed her with joy, and rewarded the good shepherd.

Polixenes had hastened after his son to prevent his marriage with Perdita, but when he found that she was the daughter of his old friend, he was only too glad to give his consent.

Yet Leontes could not be happy. He remembered how his fair Queen, who should have been at his side to share his joy in his daughter's happiness, was dead through his unkindness, and he could say nothing for a long time but, "Oh, thy mother! thy mother!" and ask forgiveness of the King of Bohemia, and then kiss his daughter again, and then the Prince Florizel, and then thank the old shepherd for all his goodness.

Then Paulina, who had been high all these years in the King's favor,

---

① perceive [pə'si:v] v. 察觉

because of her kindness to the dead Queen Hermione, said: "I have a statue made in the likeness of the dead Queen, a piece many years in doing, and performed by the rare Italian master, Giulio Romano. I keep it in a private house apart, and there, ever since you lost your Queen, I have gone twice or thrice a day. Will it please your Majesty to go and see the statue?"

So Leontes and Polixenes, and Florizel and Perdita, with Camillo and their attendants, went to Paulina's house where there was a heavy purple curtain screening off an alcove①; and Paulina, with her hand on the curtain, said: "She was peerless② when she was alive, and I do believe that her dead likeness excels whatever yet you have looked upon, or that the hand of man hath done. Therefore I keep it lonely, apart. But here it is—behold, and say, 'tis well."

And with that she drew back the curtain and showed them the statue. The King gazed and gazed on the beautiful statue of his dead wife, but said nothing.

"I like your silence," said Paulina; "it the more shows off your wonder. But speak, is it not like her?"

"It is almost herself," said the King, "and yet, Paulina, Hermione was not so much wrinkled, nothing so old as this seems."

"Oh, not by much," said Polixenes.

"Al," said Paulina, "that is the cleverness of the carver, who shows her to us as she would have been had she lived till now."

And still Leontes looked at the statue and could not take his eyes away.

"If I had known," said Paulina, "that this poor image would so have stirred your grief, and love, I would not have shown it to you."

---

① alcove [ˈælkəuv] n. 凹室,壁橱
② peerless [ˈpiəlis] adj. 出类拔萃的,无与匹敌的

But he only answered,"Do not draw the curtain."

"No, you must not look any longer," said Paulina, "or you will think it moves."

"Let be! let be!" said the King. "Would you not think it breathed?"

"I will draw the curtain," said Paulina; "you will think it lives presently."

"Ah, sweet Paulina," said Leontes, "make me to think so twenty years together."

"If you can bear it," said Paulina, "I can make the statue move, make it come down and take you by the hand. Only you would think it was by wicked magic."

"Whatever you can make her do, I am content to look on," said the King.

And then, all folks there admiring and beholding, the statue moved from its pedestal①, and came down the steps and put its arms round the King's neck, and he held her face and kissed her many times, for this was no statue, but the real living Queen Hermione herself. She had lived hidden, by Paulina's kindness, all these years, and would not discover herself to her husband, though she knew he had repented, because she could not quite forgive him till she knew what had become of her little baby.

Now that Perdita was found, she forgave her husband everything, and it was like a new and beautiful marriage to them, to be together once more.

Florizel and Perdita were married and lived long and happily.

To Leontes his many years of suffering were well paid for in the moment when, after long grief and pain, he felt the arms of his true love around him once again.

---

① pedestal ['pedistl] *n.* 基架,底座

冬天的故事

西西里岛的国王里昂提斯和波希米亚的国王波力克希尼斯是最要好的朋友。两人曾一起长大,长大成人后因要统治各自的国家才不得不分开。多年以后,两人都结了婚,并各育一子,波力克希尼斯来到西西里岛看望里昂提斯。

里昂提斯性情暴戾并愚蠢至极,他的傻脑袋竟然认为他妻子赫米迈厄妮爱波力克希尼斯胜于爱他。这种想法一旦进入了他的脑子,就怎么也出不来。于是他命令他的一位臣子卡米罗用毒酒将波力克希尼斯毒死。卡米罗极力劝他不要实施这个邪恶的计划,却发现他根本无法劝阻国王,于是就假装答应下来,然后他把国王的计划告诉了波力克希尼斯,当夜他们就一起从西西里岛的皇宫逃到了波希米亚。从此,卡米罗就在波希米亚住了下来,并成为国王的知己和参士。

里昂提斯把王后关进了牢房;她的儿子,也就是王位的继承人,看到母亲受到如此不公平的虐待,伤心过度而死。

王后在狱中生下了一个孩子,她的朋友宝丽娜带着穿戴好的婴儿去给国王看,希望国王看到无助的小女儿后会对王后心软起来。实际上,王后并没有做什么对不起国王的事,并深深地爱着他,尽管他并不值得她这样爱;然而,国王没有看婴儿一眼,就让宝丽娜的丈夫用船将婴儿带走,将其扔到最荒凉最恐怖的地方。虽然很不情愿,但是宝丽娜的丈夫不得不执行国王的命令。

可怜的王后因为更喜欢波力克希尼斯而被判叛国罪,可是除了丈夫里昂提斯外,她真的从没有想过其他人。里昂提斯已经派信使去阿波罗神庙问神谕他是否冤枉了王后,然而,他已没有耐心等他们回来。正当不幸的王后在受审的时候,信使们回来了。神谕说——

"赫米迈厄妮是无辜的,波力克希尼斯无可责备,卡米罗是个忠实的臣子,里昂提斯是个多疑的暴君,如果那失去的找不回来,国王将不会有继承人。"

正在那时,一个人来禀报说小王子死了。听到这个消息,可怜的王后昏厥了过去;这时国王才恍然明白他所做的一切是多么恶毒,多么令人不齿啊!于是他命令宝丽娜和其他婢女把王后带走,想法把她救醒。过了一会儿,宝丽娜回来告诉国王说,赫米迈厄妮去世了。

此刻,里昂提斯终于意识到他的行为是多么愚蠢。王后死了,唯一能给他安慰的女儿也被他送走,成为野狼和鸢的猎物。现在,生命没有给他留下任何东西,他悔恨交加,在祈祷和悔恨中度过了许多年。

小公主被丢弃在波希米亚的海岸上,这里正是波力克希尼斯统治的王国。宝丽娜的丈夫没有回去向里昂提斯报告把孩子丢在了什么地方,因为他刚要回到船上的时候,一只熊跳了出来把他撕成了碎片。他就这样死了。

一个牧羊人发现了这个可怜的弃婴。孩子穿着华丽的衣裳,戴着珠宝,斗篷上还别着一张纸条,上面写着她的名字潘迪塔,并说她出身高贵。

这个好心的牧羊人把婴儿带回了家,交给了他的妻子。他们把她当作自己的孩子抚养长大。虽然她受的教育不过是一个牧羊人的女儿所能得到的,可是她从母后那里继承了美丽和优雅,所以,她与村里的其他女孩很不一样。

有一天,波希米亚善良的国王的儿子弗罗利泽在牧羊人家附近打猎时看到了潘迪塔,现在她已经出落成一个迷人的姑娘了。弗罗利泽就和牧羊人交了朋友,他没有告诉牧羊人他是个王子,而说他的名字叫多利克思,是个平民。他深深地爱上了美丽的潘迪塔,几乎天天来看她。

国王不明白为什么儿子几乎天天都要出门,就派人监视他,他们发现波希米亚的王位继承人爱上了美丽的牧羊女潘迪塔。波力克希尼斯想看看这是否是真的,于是就和他忠实的卡米罗化了装一起去了老牧羊人的家。那时候牧人们正在为庆祝剪羊毛的节日举行盛会。虽说是陌生人,他们也受到了热情的欢迎。舞会在进行中,一个货郎正在卖丝带、饰带和手套,年轻小伙子们挣着去买给他们的心上人。

然而弗罗利泽和潘迪塔,没有参加这一欢乐的盛会,而是安安静静地坐在一起谈心。国王看到了举止优雅、美丽动人的潘迪塔,却猜不出她正是老友里昂提斯的女儿。他对卡米罗说——

"这是一个在绿草地上奔跑的出身低微又最美丽的姑娘。她的一言一行都好像比她自己的身份高一些,她高贵得跟这个地方一点儿也不相称。"

卡米罗回答说:"真的呢,在这些牧羊人中间她可称得上是女王了。"

可是弗罗利泽并没有认出父亲来,并让这些陌生人做他和美丽的牧羊女的证婚人。国王现出身来,反对这门婚事,并对潘迪塔说如果她再与弗罗利泽见面,他就会将她和她的老父亲处死,说完便拂袖而去。由于被潘迪塔迷住了,卡米罗留了下来,希望能帮助她。

卡米罗早就知道里昂提斯已经对自己愚蠢又疯狂的行为感到后悔了,

他也很想回西西里岛看望他的老主人。于是他就建议这对情侣去西西里岛寻求里昂提斯的庇护。于是他们就带上了牧羊人一起去了西西里岛,牧羊人把潘迪塔的珠宝、她婴孩时候穿的衣裳和那张他发现别在她斗篷上的字条都随身带了去。

里昂提斯热情地接待了他们。他对弗罗利泽王子以礼相待,可是他的注意力全集中在潘迪塔身上,因为她长得太像赫米迈厄妮王后了,于是他一遍又一遍地说:"要是我没有残忍地把女儿送走,她也会长成这么一个可爱的姑娘了。"

当老牧羊人得知国王丢了一个女儿,而那女儿又被遗弃在波希米亚的海岸上时,他确信他收养的孩子潘迪塔就是国王的女儿。他告诉了大家他的经历,并把珠宝和那张纸交给国王看。国王明白了潘迪塔就是他丢散多年的孩子。他激动地欢迎女儿的归来,并赏赐了善良的牧羊人。

波力克希尼斯拼命追赶儿子,并阻止他和潘迪塔的婚姻,但当他发现她竟然是老朋友的女儿,他非常高兴了,并欣然同意了这门婚事。

然而,里昂提斯却高兴不起来。他想起了美丽的王后,她本应该在他身边分享女儿的幸福,却死于自己的残忍。他许久说不出话来,除了"唉,你的母亲!你的母亲!"他请求波希米亚国王的宽恕,然后再次吻了女儿,还有弗罗利泽王子,并感谢了这位老牧羊人的恩德。

由于对已去世的王后忠心耿耿,宝丽娜这些年来深受国王的喜爱。她说:"我有一尊雕像,是杰出的意大利大师裘里奥·罗曼诺经多年雕刻而成,这尊雕像跟王后一模一样。我将它单独放在私人的房子里,自从王后去世后,我每天都去看上两三次。陛下想不想去看看?"

于是里昂提斯、波力克希尼斯、弗罗利泽、潘迪塔,还有卡米罗和随从们一同去了宝丽娜的房子,凹室一处被厚厚的紫色帘子隔开,宝丽娜将手放在帘子上,说:"她活着的时候,她的美无人能及,我相信她的雕像美得超过你见过的模样,因为是出自大师之手,因此我将其单独存放。瞧,就是这个,不错吧。"

说着,她将帘子拉开,雕像出现在大家面前。国王看了又看亡妻美丽的雕像,一句话也说不出来。

"我喜欢您的沉默,"宝丽娜说,"这更能表示您的惊奇。这尊雕像不是很像您的王后吗?"

"这几乎就是她本人,"国王说,"可是,宝丽娜,赫米迈厄妮没有这么多皱纹,也没有这个雕像看起来这么老。"

"噢,是没那么多。"波力克希尼斯说。

"啊,"宝丽娜回答,"这就是雕刻家的高明之处,他将今天的赫米迈厄妮展示给我们,好像她一直活到了现在。"

里昂尼斯仍一直盯着雕塑看,眼睛舍不得离开。

"如果我知道,"宝丽娜说,"这尊可怜的雕像会激起您的悲伤和爱,我就不会让您看了。"

可他只回答说:"别拉下帘子。"

"不行,您不能再看了,"宝丽娜说,"你快要把她当活人了。"

"快看,快看!"国王说,"你不觉得她在呼吸吗?"

"我要把帘子拉上了,"宝丽娜说,"您现在就把她当做活人了。"

"啊,可爱的宝丽娜,"里昂提斯说,"让我足足思念了二十年。"

"如果你可以忍受的话,"宝丽娜说,"我能让雕像移动,并让她下来牵住你的手。只是你会认为这是什么妖术而已。"

"无论你叫她做什么,我都愿意瞧。"国王说。

于是,所有的人都充满期待地看着,雕像从石座上走了下来,用胳膊搂住了国王的脖子,他捧着她的脸吻了许久,因为这并非雕像而是活生生的王后赫米迈厄妮本人。这些年来,赫米迈厄妮一直和善良的宝丽娜秘密地生活在一起,不愿意让丈夫找到自己。尽管她知道他一直在忏悔,但想到他对小女儿的残酷行为,就无法原谅他,直到她得知小女儿长成了什么样子。

现在潘迪塔被找到了,她就原谅了丈夫的所作所为。对他们来说,再次相聚就如新婚一样甜蜜。

弗罗利泽和潘迪塔结了婚并幸福地生活在一起。

对里昂提斯而言,诸多年来的苦难在瞬间得到了补偿。在长久的悲恸之后,他感觉到了真爱的臂膀再次将他拥抱。

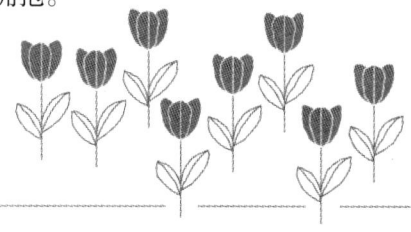